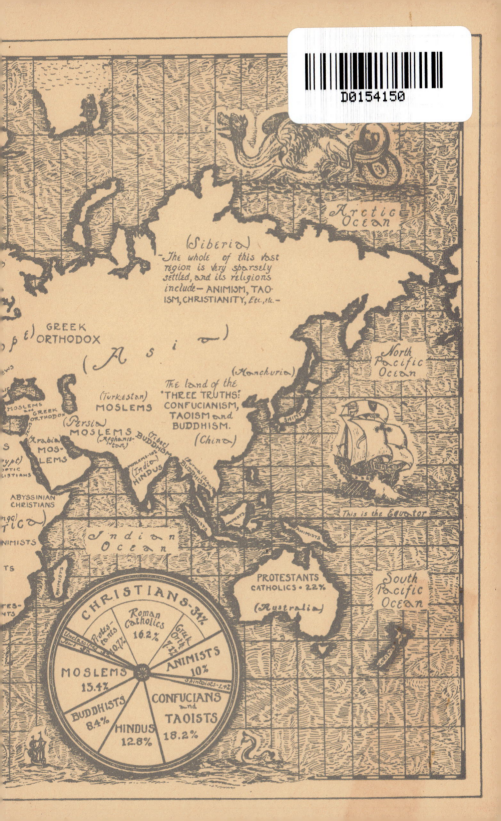

THIS
BELIEVING WORLD

A Simple Account of the
Great Religions of Mankind

BY

LEWIS BROWNE

Author of
"STRANGER THAN FICTION: A SHORT HISTORY
OF THE JEWS"

WITH MORE THAN SEVENTY
ILLUSTRATIONS AND ANIMATED
MAPS DRAWN BY THE AUTHOR

New York
THE MACMILLAN COMPANY
1926

Printed in the United States of America by
THE FERRIS PRINTING COMPANY, NEW YORK

To

H. G. WELLS

ACKNOWLEDGMENTS

The author's gratitude is due to the below-mentioned scholars for their painstaking examination and criticism of the various chapters of this book dealing with their own fields of specialized research:

Professor F. J. Foakes Jackson, author of *A History of the Christian Church, Introduction to Church History,* etc.

Professor Robert Ernest Hume, author of *The Thirteen Principal Upanishads, The World's Living Religions,* etc.

Professor Charles P. Fagnani, author of *A Primer of Hebrew, The Beginnings of History According to the Jews,* etc.

Professor Joshua Bloch, Chief of the Semitics Division, New York Public Library.

The author is indebted also to Dr. Leo Mayer of the Palestine Department of Antiquities, to Dr. W. F. Albright, Director of the American School of Oriental Research, and to Dr. Herbert Danby, Canon of St. George's Cathedral Church in Jerusalem, for much kindly assistance in the gathering of material on the history of the three religions which have shrines in Jerusalem; to Anna W. Anspach,

ACKNOWLEDGMENTS

of South Orange, for her careful reading of the proofs and preparation of the index; and especially to the Rev. W. H. Murray, *of New York, whose unflagging interest in this book from its inception has been a source of vast encouragement and help.*

L. B.

CONTENTS

PAGE

PROLOGUE 19

BOOK ONE

HOW IT ALL BEGAN

I. MAGIC 27

1: How the savage tried to explain the evils that befell him—he imagined all objects were animate—self-preservation and magic. 2: Religion and faith defined—the technique of magic—the dawn of the idea of the "spirit"—animism. 3: Man begins to think he can exploit the spirits—shamanism—the charlatan in the early advance of religion. 4: Fetishism. 5: Idolatry—the beginning of sacrifice—of prayer—of the church. 6: Taboo.

II. RELIGION 42

1: The attempt to coerce the spirits gives way to the attempt to cajole them—but magic does not disappear—sacrifices. 2: The seasonal festivals—sex rites—the sacraments. 3: How the great gods were created. 4: How the ideas of sin, conscience, and future retribution arose—religion saves morality for a high price—prophet vs. priest. 5: How religion made society possible—and desirable—how it gave rise to art—the significance of Primitive Religion.

BOOK TWO

HOW RELIGION DEVELOPED IN THE ANCIENT WORLD

I. THE CELTS 60

1: The primitive gods—Druids—the mistletoe cult. 2: The festivals—the great holocausts—Beltane—Lugnasad—Samhain—ghost-worship.

II. THE BABYLONIANS 65

1: The Semitic goddesses—how the Babylonian gods arose—trinities. 2: Ishtar and the sex rites—holy prostitution—astrology. 3: The priesthood—its vices—and virtues. 4: The defects of the religion—polydemonism—a ritualized morality—Shabatum and mythology—contrast with Hebrew versions of same—fear.

9

CONTENTS

PAGE

III. THE EGYPTIANS 75
1: Original animal-worship—the growth of the gods—the priests. 2: The idea of monotheism emerges. 3: The reformation under Ikhnaton—reaction. 4: The religion of the masses—Osiris—the future life—why the pyramids were built. 5: The dead—the Judgment Day—the resort to magic.

IV. THE GREEKS 89
1: The Minoan religion—how the Greek gods arose—the Olympian cult. 2: The Olympian cult fails—the learned take to philosophy. 3: The masses take to magic—and the "mysteries"—the savior-god idea—how men tried to become divine. 4: The desire for a future life—and how the mysteries satisfied it.

V. THE ROMANS 100
1: Original worship of household spirits—the state religion arises—and is intensified. 2: Why the state religion failed—the coming of the mysteries—Cybele—Attis—the other foreign cults. 3: Augustus restores the state religion—the god-emperor—the reaction—the Cynics. 4: Why decadent Rome took to the mysteries —Mithras—its significance. 5: Conclusion—Why these ancient cults cannot be called "dead"—the significance of their other-worldly appeal.

BOOK THREE

WHAT HAPPENED IN INDIA

I. BRAHMANISM 119
1: The primitive Aryan gods—the Vedas. 2: The Aryans move to the Ganges—caste—the brahmins. 3: The Upanishads—the Over-Soul—transmigration—Nirvana —the growth of asceticism.

II. JAINISM 129
1: Mahavira—his gospel. 2: How the gospel of Mahavira was corrupted—Jainism today.

III. BUDDHISM 134
1: The story of Gautama. 2: His gospel—its implications—the Law of Karma. 3: How Gautama spread his gospel. 4: Early history of Buddhism—deification of Buddha—Asoka—the new Buddhism in China—Tibet—Japan—India—Ceylon.

10

CONTENTS

PAGE

IV. HINDUISM 150

1: The dominant religion in India today—caste—the trinity—the divisiveness in Hinduism. 2: Vishnu—the avatars—the Bhagavad-Gita—Krishna—theology in Vishnuism. 3: Shiva—his popularity—the Tantra—sex in religion. 4: Hindu philosophy—yoga—the mystic ecstasy. 5: The religion of the lower classes.

BOOK FOUR
WHAT HAPPENED IN CHINA

I. CONFUCIANISM 169

1: The primitive religion of China—ancestor-worship—the state cult—the popular religion—burial customs—family festivals—why did China advance so early? 2: The story of Confucius. 3: The work of Confucius—his gospel—his place in history. 4: The deification of Confucius.

II. TAOISM 183

1: The life of Lao-Tze—the Tao-Teh-king—the gospel—was Lao-Tze a religious teacher? 2: The degeneration of Taoism—alchemy—gods and priests—the deification of Lao-Tze.

III. BUDDHISM 191

1: How it entered China—why it succeeded there—its rise and fall. 2: The Land of the "Three Truths"—popular worship.

BOOK FIVE
WHAT HAPPENED IN PERSIA

I. ZOROASTRIANISM 199

1: The animism of early Iran—did Zoroaster ever live?—the legends concerning his life. 2: The gospel of Zoroaster—Good vs. Evil—the fire-altars—the future life. 3: The ordeal of Zoroaster—his first converts—death. 4: The corruption of the gospel—ritual—burial customs—"defilement"—the priesthood—Mithraism. 5: The influence of Zoroastrianism on Judiasm—on Christianity—on Islam—the Parsees.

CONTENTS

BOOK SIX

WHAT HAPPENED IN ISRAEL

PAGE

I. JUDAISM 223

1: The cradle of the Hebrew people—the lure of the Fertile Crescent—Egypt and the Exodus. 2: Moses—the covenant with Yahveh. 3: How the nature of Yahveh changed in Canaan. 4: The political history of the Hebrews. 5: The work of the prophets. 6: Amos—Hosea—Isaiah—Micah—Jeremiah—Yahveh becomes God. 7: The spiritual exaltation of Israel—the Messianic Promise—its influence during the Babylonian Exile—Deutero-Isaiah. 8: The rise of the priests—their influence—the new prophets—the Destruction of Jerusalem—the Messianic Dream again. 9: The rise of the rabbis—the Wall of Law—Judaism today—Zionism—the goy-fearing people—Messianism, the heart of Judaism.

BOOK SEVEN

WHAT HAPPENED IN EUROPE

I. JESUS 257

1: Palestine in the first century—the Zealots and saints. 2: The childhood of Jesus—youth. 3: John the Baptist—Jesus begins to preach. 4: His heresies—his tone of authority—did Jesus think himself the Messiah? 5: Jesus goes to Jerusalem—falls out of favor—is arrested, tried, and crucified. 6: The "resurrection"—the disciples begin to preach. 7: The religion of the Nazarenes—the growing saga about Jesus.

II. CHRIST 276

1: The mysteries in the Roman Empire—the philosophies. 2: The story of Saul of Tarsus. 3: The work of Paul. 4: Jesus becomes the Christ—the compromises with paganism—the superiority of Christianity—the writing of the Gospels—persecution by Rome. 5: Constantine and the triumph of Christianity. 6: The cost of success—the schisms. 7: The spread of Christianity—the ethical element in Christianity—how it sobered Europe. 8: The development of the Church—Protestantism—why Christianity has succeeded.

CONTENTS

BOOK EIGHT

WHAT HAPPENED IN ARABIA

PAGE

I. MOHAMMEDANISM 305

    1: The idolatrous religion of primitive Arabia—Mecca and the Kaaba. 2: The story of Mohammed—his gospel. 3: The preaching of the gospel to the Meccans. 4: The preaching to the pilgrims. 5: The flight to Medina. 6: The Jews refuse to be converted—conflict with Mecca. 7: The military character of Islam—the Holy War. 8: The character of Mohammed—his compromises—the pagan elements in Islam. 9: The qualities in the religion.

BIBLIOGRAPHY 335

INDEX 341

13

LIST OF ILLUSTRATIONS

	PAGE
JERUSALEM SLEEPS	17
MOUNTAINS THAT ROARED AND BELCHED LAVA	31
WITH THOSE AMULETS THE SAVAGE WAS NOT AFRAID	37
THIS WAS THE FIRST CHURCH BUILT	39
DEAD BODIES WERE TABOO	41
AGRICULTURE WAS A MATTER OF RELIGION	46
THE IDOL	48
THE GOD IN THE SKY SAW ALL	52
STONEHENGE	62
BABYLONIA	66
THE GREAT MOTHER GODDESSES	69
ANCIENT EGYPT	80
PYRAMIDS BY THE NILE	84
ANCIENT GREECE	90
MEN FLED TO THE JUNGLES	128
WHAT HAPPENED IN INDIA	135
BUDDAH WAS SEATED BENEATH A BANYAN TREE	138
HOW BUDDHISM SPREAD	149
SHIVA	157
IDOLS GROTESQUE BEYOND WORDS	164
KING-FU-TZE	177
A CONFUCIAN TEMPLE	182
A "PROFESSOR OF TAOISM"	190
A CHINESE BUDDHA	192
A CHINESE ALTAR	193
ZOROASTER SEEKS SALVATION	202
THE WANDERINGS OF ZOROASTER	207

PAGE

THE TURANIANS WERE BEDOUIN RAIDERS . . . 209
THE PROPHET OF IRAN 211
THE AHRIMAN DRAGON 214
HERE GO THE HEBREWS 225
THE EXODUS 227
WHAT THE HEBREWS BUILT IN EGYPT 228
IN THE WILDERNESS 230
THE BRIDGE BETWEEN THE EMPIRES 234
THE DIVIDED KINGDOM 237
JEREMIAH 241
BY THE WATERS OF BABYLON 243
THE MAN FROM GALILEE 260
THE PATH OF JESUS 269
THE SAVIOR-GODS 278
SAUL OF TARSUS 280
THE WANDERINGS OF PAUL 282
CHRISTIANITY IN 110 A. D. 287
CHRISTIANITY AFTER CONSTANTINE 290
A PRIESTESS OF BRIDGET 295
MOHAMMED WAS A LOWLY CAMEL BOY . . . 308
THE DESERT 311
MOHAMMED SAT IN THE BAZAARS AND PREACHED . 316
MOHAMMED RETURNS TO MECCA 324
ON THE WAY TO MECCA 329
THE SHRINE OF A DESERT SAINT 331

PROLOGUE—JERUSALEM SLEEPS. . . .

17

PROLOGUE

FROM afar, from over the hills —from another world it would seem—one hears the tinkling of camel bells. Faintly one hears the sound, very faintly: a cold, hesitant drip-drip of music falling in the night. . . . Save for that there is silence, vast silence that fills each alley in the ancient town, that sinks deep into each hole and cranny, that rises high over the very top of the city wall. For Jerusalem sleeps. . . . The night is almost spent, and in the east the blue of the heavens has turned to that vivid gray-green presaging the dawn. But still Jerusalem sleeps . . . and there is silence . . . save for that low drip-drip of music from distant camel-bells. . . .

And then of a sudden there is a cry—a strained, eerie, Arab cry. Like a hard-flung dirk its first note comes hurtling through the air, piercing one's ear-drum and quivering there. From somewhere up above the flat-roofed houses, from the minaret high over some unseen mosque, it comes: a long, dragging, intermittent call let loose from lungs strained to bursting:

19

Allahu Akbar! Allahu Akbar!

So it comes, swooping through the heavens:

"Allah is greatest!   Allah is greatest!
I testify there is no God but Allah!
I testify that Mohammed is the prophet of Allah!
Come to prayer!   Come to salvation!
Prayer is better than sleep!   Prayer is better than sleep!
Allahu Akbar!   Allahu Akbar!
Allah is greatest!   Allah is greatest!
There is no God but Allah!"

And then it is no more.   As suddenly as the cry began it ceases! . . . But Jerusalem sleeps no longer.   The first angry orange streak of day has just spilled over the crest of the Jordan hills; and in the town there begins a gathering confusion.   Out of holes in the walls, out of the narrow doors of hovels, black and cold as caves, crawl phantom-like men and boys.   Disheveled, they emerge from crevices in dark archways, from hidden stairways, from what look like catacombs.   And slip-slop, slip-slop, their ill-shod feet go shuffling down the cobbled streets. . . . Here goes a man, lean and swart, in tasseled black head-shawl, brown Arab cloak, and sandals of worn camel-hide.   There goes one, bearded, pale, and bent, in a broad fur *shtreimel,* plum velvet *kaftan,* and boots made for Russian snows.   Over there goes a third, fat and crafty-eyed, in a rakish red fez, European suit, and American shoes that are new and squeaky. . . . Here comes a Carmelite monk, all brown and ursine, with a little brown cap over his tonsure; there goes a Greek priest, all black and bovine, his oiled locks tight in a top-knot.   A little Anglican missionary,

his back-buttoned collar large enough to swallow his
head, stumbles hurriedly down the steps of some hospice.
A Yemenite Jew, shrunken, yellow, and still wet from
"nail water," sidles along as though fleeing a ghost. A
filthy Arab beggar, his sore eyes already thick with flies,
beats with his cane as he drags his naked feet over the
stones. . . . And so they go, slip-slop, slip-slop . . .
more and more of them . . . slip-slop, slip-slop . . .
a mad procession of hurrying phantoms in the half-
light of the dawn. . . .

To that muezzin who utters the call to prayer from
the high minaret, they would seem like ants—if he
could but see them. Like multi-colored ants they would
seem as they swarm out of holes and from under archways. But he cannot see them, for he is blind—as becomes a muezzin. (A seeing man, if he were made
muezzin, might see far too much from his lofty minaret:
for instance, women in the privacy of their courtyards
with their faces unveiled!) Could he but see them from
his height, those men would look like so many insects
scurrying about amid debris. . . .

But one who looks from no such tower, one who
walks the earth to regard these creatures, can see that
they are not at all insects. For there are lights in their
eyes, darting gleams, whereof no insects in all creation
could boast. There are lights of hatred in those eyes,
lights of hatred or dread or suspicion. It would seem
that they feel as enemies to each other, these hundreds
of creatures swarming in this ancient town. (Could
mere ants feel as much?) . . . That Arab in his robe
looks with loathing on the Armenian in his sack suit;
and both look with disdain on the Jew in *shtreimel* and

kaftan. The Carmelite monk looks with anger at the Anglican missionary; and both look with contempt on the Greek priest. Hatred seems to be all around one: almost a noxious vapor that one can see, a veritable reek that one can smell. These creatures seem unable to bear the very sight of each other. They actually seem ready to kill!

They *have* killed in this ancient town, killed until every alley was flooded with blood. Not a wall in all this maze of walls but has rung with the groans of the dying. Skulls beyond counting have been cracked on these flags; throats unnumbered have been slit in these dark doorways. They've murdered and pillaged and raped in this old holy town till now it is all but one Golgotha, one bloody Hill of Skulls. . . . And if you would know why, you need only look into the eyes of those hurrying phantoms. Readily they will tell you; explicitly. Men have slaughtered and ravished in Jerusalem because they had—religion. Men have gouged eyes and ripped bellies because they—believed! . . . Believed in what? In God? . . . Hardly. . . . No, they have believed only in mere vocables—Yahveh, Christ, or Allah: those vocables that are the fingers wherewith men try to point to God.

Strange potency, this thing we call Religion! It has made men do barbarities quite beyond the reaches of credence. For it men have done foulnesses below the foulness done even by beasts. Yet for it also men have done benevolences such as transcend the benevolences of angels. If men have killed and died for religion, men have also lived for it. Not merely lived *for* it, but *by* it. . . . That cowering Yemenite Jew slinking in the shadow of the archways sloughs off his terror and becomes a king when he enters his synagogue. His bent shoulders straighten, his sagging knees become firm, and the blessedness of peace lightens his eyes. . . . That blind Arab beggar, a mere frame of bones hung over with smelling rags, becomes a sultan when he stands at prayer in his mosque. He stands healed there of his ailments; he becomes a changed man with a vision reaching through his world to Paradise. . . . That dark-eyed Syrian girl, poor trull whose lips have caressed the flesh of twenty races, becomes clean once more when she kneels at the feet of the virgin. Strength floods into her tortured bones, healing comes to her flesh. Life, so long a hell of lust and lechery, becomes now wondrously clean and worthy. She feels saved—*saved!*

Strange potency, this thing we call Religion! It came into man's world untold centuries ago, and it is still in man's world today. It is still there, deep and tremendous: a mighty draught for a mightier thirst, a vast richness to fill a vaster need. No matter where one turns in time or space, there it is inescapably. Wherever there is a man, there there seems to be also a spirit or a god; wherever there is human life, there there is also faith. . . .

One wonders about it. What is it, this thing we call Religion? Whence did it come? And why? And how? . . . What was it yesterday? What is it today?—And what will it become tomorrow? . . .

M'LON LAZARUS, JERUSALEM
   LAND OF ISRAEL
     July 2, 1925

BOOK ONE

HOW IT ALL BEGAN

I. MAGIC

1: How the savage tried to explain the evils that befell him—he imagined all objects were animate—self-preservation and magic. 2: Religion and faith defined—the technique of magic—the dawn of the idea of the "spirit"—animism. 3: Man begins to think he can exploit the spirits—shamanism—the charlatan in the early advance of religion. 4: Fetishism. 5: Idolatry—the beginning of sacrifice—of prayer—of the church. 6: Taboo.

II. RELIGION

1: The attempt to coerce the spirits gives way to the attempt to cajole them—but magic does not disappear—sacrifices. 2: The seasonal festivals—sex rites—the sacraments. 3: How the great gods were created. 4: How the ideas of sin, conscience, and future retribution arose—religion saves morality for a high price—prophet vs. priest. 5: How religion made society possible—and desirable—how it gave rise to art—the significance of Primitive Religon.

26

BOOK ONE:

HOW IT ALL BEGAN

I. MAGIC

IN the beginning there was fear; and fear was in the heart of man; and fear controlled man. At every turn it whelmed over him, leaving him no moment of ease. With the wild soughing of the wind it swept through him; with the crashing of the thunder and the growling of lurking beasts. All the days of man were gray with fear, because all his universe seemed charged with danger. Earth and sea and sky were set against him; with relentless enmity, with inexplicable hate, they were bent on his destruction. At least, so primitive man concluded. . . . It was an inevitable conclusion under the circumstances, for all things seemed to be forever going against man. Boulders toppled and broke his bones; diseases ate his flesh; death seemed ever ready to lay him low. And he, poor gibbering half-ape nursing his wound in some draughty cave, could only tremble with fear. He could not give himself stoical courage with the thought that much of the evil that occurred might be accidental. He could not so much as conceive

27

of the accidental. No, so far as his poor dull pate could read the riddle, all things that occurred were full of meaning, were *intentional*. The boulder that fell and crushed his shoulder had *wanted* to fall and crush it. Of course! . . . The spear of heaven-fire that had turned his squaw to cinders had consciously *tried* to do that very thing. Obviously! . . .

To the savage there was nothing absurd in the idea that everything around him bore him malice, for he had not yet discovered that some things were inanimate. In the world he saw about him, *all* objects were animate: sticks, stones, storms, and all else. He shied at each of them suspiciously, much as a horse shies suspiciously at bits of white paper by the roadside. And not merely were all things animate to the savage, but they were seething with emotions, too. Things could be angry, and they could feel pleased; they could destroy him if they so willed, or they could let him alone.

Perhaps, as Professor George Foot Moore slyly reminds us, even civilized folk instinctively cling to that primitive notion. Children angrily kick the tables against which they bump their heads, as though those tables were human. Grown men mutter oaths at the rugs over which they stumble, for all the world as though those rugs had intentionally tried to trip them. And it may be that young and old still do such irrational things only because even today there still lingers in the mind of man the savage notion that all objects are animate. When caught off his guard, man still is betrayed into trying to punish, either with a blow or with consignment to hell-fire, the inanimate objects that happen to cause him pain.

After all, civilized people at bottom are perilously close to the savage. Instinctively he too wanted to thrash whatever seemed to bring him evil. Only he was afraid. From experience he knew that fighting was useless, that the enemy-objects, the falling boulders that maimed him, and the flooding streams that wrecked his hut, were in some uncanny way proof against his spears and arrows. That was why he was finally forced to resort to more subtle methods of attack. Since blows could not subdue the hostile rocks or streams, our ancestor tried to subdue them with magic. He thought words might avail: strange syllables uttered in groans, or meaningless shouts accompanied by beating tom-toms. Or he tried wild dances. Or luck charms. If these spells failed, then he invented others; if those in turn failed, then he invented still others. Of one thing he seemed most stubbornly convinced: that *some* spell would work. Somehow the hostile things around him *could* be appeased or controlled, he believed; somehow death *could* be averted. Why he should have been so certain, no one can tell. It must have been his instinctive adjustment to the conditions of a world that was too much for him. Self-preservation must have forced him to that certainty, for without it self-preservation would have been impossible. Man had to have faith in himself, or die—and he would not die.

So he had faith—and developed religion.

2

RELIGION is not all of faith, but only a part of it. By the word faith we mean that indispensable—and therefore imperishable—illusion in the heart of man that, though he may seem a mere worm on the earth, he nevertheless can make himself the lord of the universe. By the word religion, however, we mean one specialized technique by which man seeks to realize that illusion. It was by no means the first such technique to be invented by man; and it may not be the last, either. Long before man thought of religion, he tried to control the "powers" of the universe by magic. When the "dawn man" became sufficiently awake to be conscious of his life and of the innumerable hazards that threatened it, he did not first pause to examine those hazards; no, instead he first set out to avert them. He saw on every side of him the fell and bewildering "powers," and illogically (but naturally) his first concern was not how they worked but how they could be avoided. If he speculated about them at all, he probably decided the very objects he saw had an animus against him—the actual storms and streams and preying beasts. Only later, much later, did he advance sufficiently to be able to think of those "powers" not as the objects themselves, but as invisible spirits inhabiting them. Primitive man was utterly unable to draw fine distinctions between soul and body, between spirit and matter. He merely knew trees that crushed him, caves that smothered him, mountains that roared and belched lava that destroyed him. That was as far as his puny mind could carry him.

But at last the day did come when, like the stealthy climb of a slow dawn, that idea of the spirit crept into man's head. It came to him almost unavoidably. Of a morning he awoke, looked up bewilderedly at the familiar rocks of his cave, and gasped, "Hello, that's

MOUNTAINS THAT ROARED AND BELCHED LAVA

queer!"—or sounds to that effect. For there he was, just where he had been when he had stretched out and fallen asleep the night before—and yet he knew he had wandered very far from that place during the interim. He was quite certain of it! Very vividly he remembered fighting huge beasts during the night, or hurtling down ravines, or devouring whole mastodons, or flying. . . . And yet there he was, still lying in his smelly cave, for all the world as though he had never for a moment left it! . . .

Of course, we civilized folk would explain the mystery by simply saying the fellow had had a dream. (Which is perhaps not so much of an explanation at that.) But he, poor savage, could not even remotely guess at such an explanation. The idea of a dream was as foreign to his mind as the idea of a monocle or a wardrobe-trunk. No, the only acceptable explanation he could offer himself was the obvious one that he was dual: that he possessed not merely a body but also a spirit, and that while his body had that night remained decently at home, his spirit had gone a-roaming. . . . Why not?

There were other experiences which that answer seemed to explain. There was, for instance, death. Here was a body erect and vibrant one moment, and prostrate, inert, the next. What had happened to it? . . . Obviously the same answer fitted: its soul had fled.

Just what was the soul and what the body, the savage could not be certain. He rather thought the soul might be the breath, since that always fled at death. (And that is why the Japanese word for soul used to be "wind-ball," and the one for death, "breath-departure." Similarly, that is why the Hindu word for soul it still *atman,* parent of the German word *Ahtem,* meaning "breath," and of the English word "atmosphere.") But the savage had to imagine the soul might also be something else than the breath, for he saw souls in unbreathing things, too. Indeed, he saw souls in all the things he came across. His whole world thronged with souls.

Historians nowadays call that stage in the development of religion the "animistic," from the Latin *anima,* meaning "spirit." There are millions of savages in the world even today who still remain bogged in that animistic stage of religion. They dwell in India and Africa and other far-away places, clinging there to a primitive faith which once must have been the faith of all human beings.

3

EVEN at the dawn of the animistic stage there could have been little in the heart of man save fear—and the hate born of fear. Only two kinds of spirits did the savage then seem to know: those that were neutral, and therefore demanding no attention, and those that were hostile, and therefore to be driven away or circumvented. For instance, almost everywhere the ghosts of the dead were considered hostile. Because such ghosts were thought to hang like wraiths over the bodies they had once occupied, corpses were always put away with the most fearful and painstaking thoroughness. And after the burial the survivors usually tried to disguise or hide themselves so as to escape the ghosts. They would paint themselves white (if they were black) or black (if they were white); and they would bar the doors of their huts or hide in caves. (That is why we still "go into mourning" when a relative dies, putting on black garments and drawing down the blinds on the windows.) . . .

Not for a long time, it seems, did man cease to assume that the active "powers" were all unalterably hostile, and therefore to be driven away. Not until many centuries had passed did it occur to him that some spirits might really be friendly, or that even hostile spirits might in some way be won over and *made* friendly. But once that change did come, a complete revolution in the practice of religion ensued. Instead of spending all his time inventing ways merely of driving the spirits away, man now began to try to bring some of them near. And therewith a new era opened in the history of the race. The first stirrings of confidence began to warm the blood of man, and slowly his cringing back began to straighten. Fear received its first decisive setback, and the promise of civilization drew its first breath. For then at last man dared to think he could actually *exploit* the spirits! . . .

Now there were two main ways in which man tried

to exploit the power of a spirit. One was to conjure it into some individual, a medicine-man, or as he was called in primitive Siberia, a shaman. Originally the shaman was probably an epileptic, a person given to fits which could be explained only on the ground of "possession." The shaman was esteemed to be "possessed" by a strange spirit, a formidable and perhaps violent spirit that could do things both foul and fair. So if a man had a fever he went to his tribal shaman, and the latter tried to drive it out by pitting his own "familiar spirit" against the fever-spirit in the patient. If he failed on the first attempt, he tried again, using a more elaborate ritual the second time. Perhaps he made the patient smear himself with excrement, or do something else equally extraordinary. Then he, the shaman, would go off into a fit in which he would dance madly, utter ghastly shrieks, beat fiercely on a tom-tom, or shake a horrid-sounding rattle. Perhaps he would carry on in that manner through a whole night, raving, dancing, and making faces, all to drive the bad spirit out of the patient. And the more elaborate he made the performance, the more wonderful and powerful he appeared in the eyes of the patient. Failure seemed altogether impossible after such efforts—and often was.

But the shaman was not employed solely to drive out the evil spirits. More often, perhaps, he was employed to drive them *into* people. Because of the spirit that was supposed to be at his beck and call, the shaman was thought to be able to do evil as well as good, to send disease and defeat and death to one's enemies, as well as bring relief and life to one's friends. That was why the shaman usually became the tribal leader. The braves

stood in constant need of him, for without his "medicine," without his spells and curses, they believed themselves lost in war as well as in peace.   He seemed the one
effective instrument with which they could bludgeon the
"powers" arrayed against them, the one valid means by
which they could master the universe.   So they clung
to him with all their might and main, fearfully doing
homage to him because of the magic power he was supposed to possess.

Of course, the moment the falsity of a particular shaman's pretensions was definitely established, the poor
fellow was never forgiven.   The savages turned on him
mercilessly and put him to death, perhaps with the most
fantastic tortures.   They had no use for medicine-men
whose medicine didn't work. . . . For that reason it was
only the conscious charlatans among the shamans who
succeeded most and survived longest.   The rest, the inno-
cent ones who were fools enough really to believe that
they could command the spirits, were easily exposed
and soon snuffed out.   They were not shrewd enough
to see the essential falsity of their own claims, and therefore they were totally unable to keep others from seeing
it.   And, amazing as it may sound, that situation proved
to be of vast benefit to mankind.   As Sir James G.
Frazer remarks in his great work, *The Golden Bough,*
honest fools must have worked far more mischief
in primitive society than clever knaves.   Only the
individual who was sufficiently superior to his fellow-
men to be able to think of cheating them, was able
at the same time to help them.   Without any conscious
desire on his part, the good resulting from such an individual's sagacity almost inevitably outweighed the evil

accomplished by his guile. The emergence from the slime of primitive stupidity of a class of cunning shamans was therefore of genuine advantage to civilization. It took the direction of tribal affairs out of the hands of the old (whose only distinction was their age) and the strong (whose only distinction was their brawn) and put it in the hands of the shrewd and far-sighted. Indeed, the rise of shamanism was perhaps the most fundamental factor in the whole development of early government. . . .

4

BUT shamanism was only the less common of the two ways by which primitive man tried to exploit the spirits. The other, fetishism, was far more widespread because far more easily handled. The word "fetishism" comes from the Portuguese *feitico*, meaning a saint's medallion or relic worn as a good-luck charm. It is now the technical term for the belief that an active spirit dwells in some particular object, and that the mere possession of the object brings with it the power to control its spirit. The first fetishes were probably pebbles with markings which happened to attract the eye of the savage because of their extraordinary color or shape. (Millions of people in the most civilized lands still believe in such "lucky stones.") Later on, however, fetishes were manufactured. Frequently they were little pouches containing objects with reputedly magic properties. The hair of a lion was put in to give courage, a bit of human brain for cunning, an eyeball for keen vision, a tiger's claw for ferocity, and so forth. The savage gathered a whole collection of such fetishes on a string, and hung

them around his neck, or fastened them over the door
of his hut. (Some scholars say our wearing of crosses
around the neck, or fastening of horseshoes and mezuzoth to the door, is but a survival of that savage fetishism.) With those amulets on his person, the savage

WITH THOSE AMULETS THE SAVAGE WAS NOT AFRAID

was no longer so afraid. He felt himself better able to
fight off the hazards of life and imagined himself more
of a match for the universe. When in need, he simply
called on one of his fetishes for help; and if the help
was not soon forthcoming, he angrily upbraided the
thing for its laziness. If it still remained obdurate, he
simply flung it away and got himself another.

It took only a little while, of course, for the manu-
facture of fetishes to become a sacred profession. For

one reason and another, certain individuals came to be looked on as the makers of the most potent fetishes. They made them not alone for the individual members, but also for the tribe as a whole. And thus it came to pass that even in lands where shamanism was unknown the professional holy man, the priest, made his advent. He was inescapable. . . .

5

TRIBAL fetishes, like private ones, were originally natural objects: for instance, boulders of a peculiar color, or trees of a strange shape. The Kaaba Stone, still worshipped by Moslems in Mecca, was originally just such a tribal fetish.) Later, however, even these tribal fetishes were also manufactured. The boulder or tree-trunk was carved in some significant manner by the fetish maker, and became—an idol. It is impossible to say just where fetishism ends and where idolatry begins. The one grows into the other as the child grows into the youth.

Probably the idol was used in the beginning solely as a sort of scarecrow to drive the evil spirits away. Later, however, it was so carved that it had a less fearsome appearance, and was used for other purposes. Even more than to scare the evil spirits away, it was used now to bring the good spirits near. The idol was smeared with blood or oil, in the hope that some good spirit might come and lick the redolent bait—and perhaps remain. And then periodically the smearings were renewed in order to hold the good spirit fast. Again and again they were renewed, until in time the practice became a fixed rite. After that, in the place of mere smearings of blood, whole carcasses were offered to the good spirit lodging in the idol. And thus sacrifice began. . . .

Food was brought, the rarest and richest obtainable, and the priest ceremoniously offered it to the spirit resident in the idol. As to a dread chieftain, it was offered with many bowings and scrapings and ceremonial songs. And with many words of praise, too, for the spirit was thought to be vain as well as hungry. And thus prayer was born. . . .

In time a shelter was considered necessary for the idol: a cleft in a rock or a shady tree at first, and later a rude hut. And thus the first church was built. . . .

THIS WAS THE FIRST CHURCH BUILT

It was all a most natural process of development. Once man took it into his head that in order to live he must master his universe, then animism, fetishism, idolatry, priestcraft, sacrifice, prayer, and the church—all these were nigh inevitable. Primitive man, drowning in fear, clutched desperately at the spirits, as a man drowning in a stream might clutch at the reeds by the bank. Of course, one after the other the spirits failed him—even as the reeds break in a drowning man's hands. But still the savage continued to clutch at the spirits. It was almost instinctive with him. He could not help it. . . .

6

BUT the savage by no means imagined it was safe to clutch at *every* reed by the side of his tarn of fear. On the contrary, most of them he considered highly dangerous, and he tried with almost panicky care to avoid them. Those harmful spirits were what the savage in the Malay Archipelago still calls *taboo*, "marked." A sort of fiendish electricity was supposed to be in them, so that if one touched them they maimed or even killed.

All sorts of objects and actions were considered taboo: some because they were so holy, and others because they were so demoniac. Usually the name of the god was taboo, and therefore it dared not be uttered save at certain holy moments by officially holy men. (That primitive superstition still has its finger on the lips of man, holding him from speaking God's name in ordinary conversation.) The flesh of certain holy or of certain particularly unholy animals was considered taboo, and therefore might not be eaten. (That primitive superstition is responsible for the aversion to pork which marked the ancient Egyptians, and still marks the Jews and Moslems.) Marriage with a close relative, touching a corpse, killing one's fellow-tribesman, wearing clothes of mixed wool and cotton, stealing a fellow-tribesman's

DEAD BODIES WERE TABOO

wife, kindling a fire on a holy day, cursing one's own father, uncovering the head before an idol—all these acts and myriads of others, some of them socially criminal, most of them socially meaningless—were in one religion or another considered taboo.   Or their very opposites were occasionally considered taboo.

Certain taboos were temporary, as for instance the one branding a woman as contaminated for the length of the menstrual period.   Others were permanent, as for instance the one outlawing a man guilty of accidentally killing a fellow-tribesman.   In some cases, the tribes themselves were required to attend to the punishment of the transgressor; in others, punishment was supposed to be dealt in some magic way by the violated spirits directly.   The transgression of certain taboos entailed

disaster to every member of the tribe to which the transgressor belonged; in other instances punishment was confined to the transgressor alone.   In some cases punishment could be evaded by elaborate penance and cleansing
on the part of the transgressor; in other cases immediate death was inescapable.   The variants were innumerable. . . .

Even today most people are inhibited by taboos.
Superstitiously they dread to do all sorts of meaningless
little things.   They refuse to sit thirteen at a table, or
walk under a ladder, or light three cigarettes with one
match.   They are thrown into a panic if a mirror breaks
in their house, or a black cat crosses their path; and they
dread to tell of their own good health without "knock-
ing on wood" or mumbling "Unbeschrieen."   Even
people otherwise quite intelligent will sometimes be
terrified by one or another of these stupid taboos.   No
wonder, therefore, if the savage suffered himself to become altogether taboo-ridden.   Poor child that he was,
his whole life settled down into an incessant and frantic
struggle to keep away from all that was "marked." . . .

II. RELIGION

YEARS, centuries, millennia passed, and falteringly man
and his thinking advanced.   The savage changed his
mode of life from that of a wild hunter roaming the
jungles alone to that of a shepherd belonging to a tribe.
And his risks changed accordingly.   He had to worry
now not simply about himself: in addition he had to
think of his fellow-tribesmen, and of the herds off which
he and his fellow-tribesmen lived.   That meant an increasing interest in wells where the herds could be

watered, and in the sun, moon, and sky which seemed to control the rain. Thus a process of selection and elimination set in among the spirits he worshipped. Some of them (for instance, the spirits of the sun and sky and desert springs) rose to a place of supreme importance, while others (such as the spirits of the arrow and the jungle tiger) fell into neglect and were in time even forgotten.

That process was of course greatly accelerated once man made his next great change—from shepherd to farmer. It rendered his dependence on the elements complete, and the spirits dwelling in the elements perforce became his supreme deities. As a shepherd he had still been a little independent, for he had been able to move his flocks about to catch the rain. He could hardly do that now, however, for he had fields and not flocks any more. So he had to sit by and patiently wait for the rain to catch *him*. Or else he had to try to *force* the rain to catch him.

In the beginning he did literally try to force the rain to come to him and his fields. With the aid of his shaman or his fetishes he resorted to all sorts of magic practices. But later, when he got it through his head that not even with his shaman or fetishes could he unfailingly *coerce* the rain, he tried instead to *cajole* it into falling. And only when that happened did religion really begin. So long as man was still naïve enough to believe that by the possession of some fetish or the utterance of some spell he could force the spirits to do his will, man had not yet advanced beyond unqualified faith in magic. Not until the sharp bludgeonings of repeated failure rendered him a meeker and wiser man, did he begin to put his faith in what may be strictly termed religion. Not until he had grown up sufficiently to suspect that some attempts at coercing the spirits were doomed inevitably to failure, did he begin to try to persuade them instead.

Of course, religion never displaced magic entirely. Man could never bring himself to surrender *all* his faith in the old technique, and to this day no historical religion on earth is without its adulterations of magic. In all of them there survive at least the relics of old coercive rites; and in all of them there exist originally persuasive prayers that have since taken on the character of coercive spells. The belief, for instance, that the whole substance of a bit of bread and a cup of wine *must* change into the body and blood of Christ—that belief is quite flagrantly the relic of an old magic rite. Or the belief that any prayer is *only* efficacious if uttered in a certain place at a certain time in a certain tongue by a certain person, or is *particularly* efficacious if concluded with the words "We ask it in Jesus' name" or some similar formula— such a belief reveals quite obviously the degeneration of a one-time religious petition into a mere magic spell.

But though the technique of religion never managed entirely to supersede the technique of magic, it did succeed in making it of secondary importance. As man's wisdom increased, his over-assurance deserted him, and he resorted more and more to persuasion in his efforts to get the spirits to do as he desired. In time of drought he offered sacrifices of food and psalms of praise to the sun and moon and sky, or to whatever other spirits it seemed to him might exercise control over the water he needed. (In Egypt, for instance, the sacrifices were offered to the spirit of the Nile, for it was altogether on the annual flooding of that river that the people depended for the watering of their lands.)   But man offered them humbly.   The naively imperative tone was gone now.   Man had grown up and had learnt that he could not get far with magic. . . .

On the whole, man seemed to get along fairly well with the help supposed to come as a result of sacrifice. Of course, in unfavorable climates even sacrifices proved of no avail, and there man was of necessity compelled to remain a nomad.   But wherever the climate was not too severe, and of fair regularity, sacrifices seemed to be admirably potent.   Nowhere, however, was the climate so mild and the soil so generous that man felt able to dispense with sacrifices entirely.   Droughts occurred occasionally and crops failed, even in the most favorable regions.   As a result man never quite lost his dread of the tyrannical spirits, or his conviction that they had to be courted perennially. His confidence in their friendship was ever coupled with a lively fear of their fickleness.   Indeed, his faith in them was no more secure than that of the pickpocket in the policeman he has just bribed.   The primitive husbandman made no move without first casting a furtive glance to see if the "powers" were still well disposed toward him.   He never quite got to feel that his hard toil alone was enough to make the earth yield its riches.   No, he imagined the spirits unfailingly took a hand in the business, and he made no move to cultivate the soil without pausing first to cultivate *them*.   Agriculture with him was more a matter of religion than of science. . . .

AGRICULTURE WAS A MATTER OF RELIGION

2

NOW, it was quite natural for man the farmer to be particularly concerned about the spirits at particular seasons in the year. Spring, when the seed was sown; summer, when the first fruits were gathered; and autumn, when the crops were harvested; these were periods of extraordinary religious importance. It was then that the primitive farmer felt he must make his mightiest efforts to persuade the "powers" to be good to him. And thus arose the seasonal festivals. . . .

The ritual on these festivals was at first almost unprintably lewd. The savage imagined that the spirits brought forth the crops much as he himself brought forth children. And for fear the spirits might have forgotten the process of reproduction, or be too bashful to initiate it, he himself went out into the fields and showed the way. Sexual license was therefore religious virtue at most of the seasonal festivals. Either all the men and women went out into the open and lay together under the heavens, or in more advanced communities the priest and one or more virgins went into the temple and lay together before the idols. . . .

But the ritual on these festivals did not consist solely of sex orgies. Usually it included also sacrificial offerings, either human, animal, or cereal. At first these offerings were quite crude and direct. Sacrifices to the water-god were simply thrown into the streams, those to the earth-god were buried in the soil, while those to the sky-god were burned on altars so that the smoke might rise and tickle the nostrils of the heavenly one. But in the course of time, such simple practices were discovered to fail occasionally, and to remedy this, complications were invented. This sinew, let us say, was removed from the sacrificial carcass, or that organ was exposed; the blood was drained off and sprinkled on this or that side of the altar; prayers were recited at this or that stage in the ceremony. . . . So intricate, indeed, grew the etiquette to be used in approaching the gods, that in time it became impossible for the ordinary man to master it. He had to call on a specialist in the ritual code, a professional sacrificer, to make his offerings for him. Just as men had earlier been forced to employ a shaman or a fetish-maker to perform their magic rites for them, so now they had to employ a priest to fulfill their religious duties. And thus priestcraft came into its fullest power. . . .

Much the same logic that led to seasonal festivals during the year led also to periodic ceremonies during the individual's lifetime. It was felt that at birth something had to be done to win for the newcomer the favor of the deity, and to that end a sacrifice of one sort or another was usually offered. (It is possible that circumcision, common in Africa, Australia, Polynesia, as well as in Semitic lands, was originally such a sacrifice.) Then at puberty, when sex proclivities first made themselves markedly evident, it was felt that something more

had to be done to ensure the favor of the spirits. Elaborate initiation ceremonies were held, and the youths were usually put through ghastly ordeals to prove them worthy both of membership in the tribe, and of protection from the tribal gods. (Confirmation among the Christians, and Bar Mitzvah among the Jews, are really survivals of those old initiations.) Then at marriage it was thought well to invoke the blessing of the spirits. After all, marriage had for its prime purpose the bringing forth of children, and it was believed that, unless the spirits were properly placated to begin with, that prime purpose might be defeated. (That is why some people still regard connubial life to be improper unless ritu-

THE IDOL

ally consecrated by a minister or priest.) . . . And
finally at death it was believed dreadfully dangerous to
give umbrage to the spirits. In many places burial rites
became almost incredibly elaborate, giving rise—for instance, in Egypt and China—to whole religious systems. . . .

And thus originated the sacraments. . . .

3

FINALLY we come to the creation of the great gods.
Just as the tribal chieftain in time became a king, so the
tribal fetish in time became a god. It was a natural evolution. The wild spirit once thought to dwell in a tree
or hill was first conjured into a portable fetish, so that
the wandering tribesmen might enjoy its protection
wherever they moved. (Readers of the Bible will remember how the spirit of Jehovah—or more properly,
Yahveh—dwelling in Mt. Sinai, was transferred to a
portable "ark" which the primitive Hebrews carried
with them on their wanderings.) Later on, when such
shepherd wanderers settled down and became farmers,
their nomad spirit sometimes settled down with them.
(The old "ark" of the bedouin Hebrews was given a
resting-place at last in the temple at Jerusalem.) This
did not always occur, however, for the mortality rate
among deities was exceedingly high during the transition period from pastoral to agricultural life. And even
the spirits that did manage to survive, came through
completely altered in character. Their functions thenceforth were new ones, and often their names were new,
too. Only telltale little atavisms in the ritual remained
to betray their nomadic origin.

But even the lives of the deities surviving that great transition still remained precarious. Indeed, if anything, the mortality rate among them then increased. For now came greater changes than ever before occurred among men, and consequently greater changes had to occur among the gods. Tribes fused. The task of resisting invasion, or of building irrigation dams, compelled many clans to merge, and their customs, myths, and gods had to merge, too. Gods appeared on the scene who were obviously composites, with composite names and composite rituals. And as the population increased, and certain villages grew to be towns, city-states, nations, and finally empires, the jurisdiction of these composite gods grew also. They began to gobble up the little gods of the tributary lands, and thus in time became the almost undisputed lords of millions of worshippers.

Many centuries still had to run their course before anyone could imagine a deity who was the One God of the Universe. Men still continued to be polytheists, believing in many gods. They might pay homage only to one, the god of their own particular tribe. They might consider him the mightiest god of all and picture him as did the Hindus in their grotesque idols, as having arms that reached everywhere and eyes that saw all. But they never denied the existence of other gods sustaining similar relations to other tribes.

Significantly, however, even the mightiest god could not strike so much terror in the heart of civilized man as the rudest idol did in the heart of the savage. Time had dealt hard with fear. Man was still far from able to control his universe, but at least he showed signs of beginning to cope with it. And as a result the "powers" of the universe became less terrifying. Man began to say they were his allies and partners, and if he exalted them extravagantly he did so largely in order to exalt himself. The gods of the nations became simply the divine leaders of the nations, the heavenly kings. . . .

4

THE idea that the gods were heavenly kings had at least one implication of tremendous importance. Earthly kings were naturally expected to see to the enforcement of the laws of the nation. It was their task to see to it that crime was detected and that criminals were punished. But always certain crimes occurred that could not be detected, just as ever and again some criminals escaped without punishment. Particularly was this so in the newly swollen cities, where policing in the form of neighborly prying was no longer possible. In those new capitals, with their milling, thronging, turbulent populations, morality seemed to have no chance. The taboos which had been strictly kept in the compact little clan came to be transgressed in the cities almost with impunity. For a while the breakdown of society seemed inevitable.

But the idea that the gods were heavenly kings saved the day. By the logic of analogy it was reasoned that as earthly kings punished crime that was detectable, so heavenly kings punished that which was *un*detectable. So there really was no chance of avoiding justice ultimately. Neither might nor cunning was of any avail, for even though one escaped the judgment of the earthly king, there was another, the inevitable and inexorable judgment of the god, still to face. The god in the sky

THE GOD IN THE SKY SAW ALL

52

saw all and knew all. Not a taboo or a law existed but
he was concerned with its enforcement. (Indeed, he
was the actual author of all taboos and laws—at least,
so it was soon said.) So there was no chance for the
transgressor—he could never escape.

And thus was born the idea of sin. Crime, which
was really an offense against society, came to be thought
of principally as a sin against the god. And because
often no one could put his finger on the punishment
visited upon the offender by the god, the idea of the
conscience arose. The god, it came to be believed, punished the wicked in secret ways, sending evil spirits into
them to gnaw at their souls and give them no rest.
And when it was seen that many of the wicked seemed
quite untroubled by evil consciences, quite unperturbed
by secret punishments, then the idea of future suffering
was advanced. It was claimed that, even though some
of the wicked went scot free in this world, in the next
they would not be nearly so fortunate. No, indeed!
After death they would get even more than their just
due, roasting in flames—according to the dwellers in
torrid lands—or freezing in ice-floes—according to the
inhabitants of arctic regions.

The actual course of development out of which were
evolved these ideas of sin, conscience, and post-mortem
retribution, was, to be sure, not nearly so simple as is
made out here. For centuries man fumbled about to
lay hold of these ideas, blundering off into the most
pathetic errors, and beating his way back only with the
horridest pain. But finally the great task was accomplished, and morality, at the cost of being religionized,
was preserved.

It was no small price to pay. Religion proved in time rather too effective a preservative. It sheltered too extensively and indiscriminately, keeping alive not merely the morals necessary to the life of society, but also every scrap of ancient ritual and savage taboo. Religion developed a tendency to hold on to everything with equal tenacity, allowing for no difference between the slightest rite and the gravest law. Or if it did admit any difference, its verdict was usually in favor of the rite. Priestly teachers were inclined to tell the people that ritual, the proper treatment to be accorded the gods, was decidedly more important than ethics, the proper treatment to be accorded to mere men. What was more injurious, they often taught that all offenses, both against rite and right, could be atoned for in but one way: by sacrifice. Justice, they declared, could always be tempered, and the guilty might perhaps even go scot-free, if only enough rams and fatlings were offered the heavenly judge. . . .

That teaching, naturally enough, proved in time a gigantic obstacle in the path of civilization. Indeed, the whole career of religion among civilized folk is in a measure the story of the struggle to remove that obstacle. In essence it is the story of prophet warring on priest; of him who would moralize religion wrestling with him who had ritualized morals. . . .

5

BUT though religion may have exacted a high price for its saving of morality, still—*it did save it*. That is something many people are inclined to forget. They are accustomed to dwell only on the evils, on the thwartings and frustrations, which certain forms of religion in later days brought upon civilization. But it is well to remember that, had it not been for religion and its underlying faith that the universe and its fell "powers" could be controlled, there would not have been any civilization to frustrate. Civilization is but another name for man's increasing victory over fear—and the first phases of that victory were attained almost solely through religion. Religion was the boot-strap by which man raised himself out of savagery. Or, to return to a metaphor we have already used, it was the bank of reeds to which man clung as often as the dark waters of fear threatened to flood over him. In a very real sense it was his salvation. . . .

It was the salvation of society, too. Not merely did religion make it possible for one man to live by himself, but even more did it make it possible for two men to live together. Even the beginnings of society would have been rendered impossible by man's innate fear simply of the dead—let alone of the living—had religion not come into high standing in the world. At the sight of death, the natural reaction of the savage was flight. Instinctively he wanted to burn the whole village in which the corpse lay, and run! And at first probably he did follow that instinct, and for centuries no camp ever lasted more than a few weeks or months. . . . But then was born the idea of burial rites to placate the spirits of the dead, religious rites that firmly rooted the survivors to the place where the dead were buried. Religion found a way to rob death of a little of its ghastly frightfulness. Villages were now actually created around graves, instead of being burnt down over them. Man, once so terrified by the ghosts that he fled at the least suspicion of their presence, now dared to go right up to them and implore their aid. Ancestor-worship arose. Tribes often depended for their solidarity upon the sole bond of supposed descent from a common ancestor. Failing that, the tie that served to hold them together was a common ritual. Ceremonies at birth, puberty, marriage, and death were the things that bound those clansmen into a compact group. The same was true of the annual festivals. And thus, by and with religion, the living together of men was made possible. . . .

More than that: by and with religion the living together of men was made not merely possible, but also desirable. Religion clothed and adorned the cold nakedness of primitive existence with shreds and patches of beauty. All that grace and color which transmutes mere existence into Life—in a word, all Art—may truly be said to have arisen out of religion. Sculpture had its origin in idol-making, architecture in temple-building, poetry in prayer-writing, music in psalm-singing, drama in legend-telling, and dancing in the seasonal worship of the gods. . . .

It may seem to us incredibly rude, this conglomeration of terrors and hopes, of clutchings and gropings, of stupidities and yearnings, which for want of a better name we call Primitive Religion. But for all that it was holy—for it saved mankind. . . .

BOOK TWO

HOW RELIGION DEVELOPED IN THE ANCIENT WORLD

BOOK TWO

HOW RELIGION DEVELOPED IN
THE ANCIENT WORLD

I. THE CELTS

1: The primitive gods—Druids—the mistletoe cult. 2: The festivals—the great holocausts—Beltane—Lugnasad—Samhain —ghost worship.

II. THE BABYLONIANS

1: The Semitic goddesses—how the Babylonian gods arose —trinities. 2: Ishtar and the sex rites—holy prostitution— astrology. 3: The priesthood—its vices—and virtues. 4: The defects of the religion—polydemonism—a ritualized morality—Shabatum and mythology—contrast with Hebrew versions of same—fear.

III. THE EGYPTIANS

1: Original animal-worship—the growth of the gods—the priests. 2: The idea of monotheism emerges. 3: The reformation under Ikhnaton—reaction 4: The religion of the masses— Osiris—the future life—why the pyramids were built. 5: The dead—the Judgment Day—the resort to magic.

IV. THE GREEKS

1: The Minoan religion—how the Greek gods arose—the Olympian cult. 2: The Olympian cult fails—the learned take to philosophy. 3: The masses take to magic—and the "mysteries"—the savior-god idea—how men tried to become divine. 4: The desire for a future life—and how the mysteries satisfied it.

V. THE ROMANS

1: Original worship of household spirits—the state religion arises—and is intensified. 2: Why the state religion failed—the coming of the mysteries—Cybele—Attis—the other foreign cults. 3: Augustus restores the state religion—the god-emperor—the re-action—the Cynics. 4: Why decadent Rome took to the mysteries—Mithras—its significance. 5: Conclusion—Why these ancient cults cannot be called "dead"—the significance of their other-worldly appeal.

BOOK TWO

HOW RELIGION DEVELOPED IN
THE ANCIENT WORLD

THE story of how religion began has been made unconscionably short and simple in the book just closed. Fundamental elements have been treated in the sketchiest fashion, and many significant elements have hardly been touched on. But in so small a book it was impossible to do otherwise. To have gone into primitive religion with any thoroughness, to have given even in outline the myriad variants among the races of each belief and practice, would have required not a score of pages, but a whole shelf of heavy tomes. All that was possible here was an outline of the central plot, a hurried sketch of the main line of march followed by religion as it advanced through prehistoric centuries.

Unhappily, that outline reads as though given with complete assurance. Despite all the "perhapses" and "probablys" scattered throughout the story, it still reads as though the writer knew for certain just what had happened. Actually he knows nothing of the sort. All he knows is what many learned anthropologists, after much painstaking research, have *surmised* to be the truth.

Of course they may have surmised quite badly. Their underlying theory may be entirely wrong, and religion, instead of having been originally created to elude or conquer fear, may have arisen quite independently of it. Religion may be an altogether primal instinct in the human race—something just as old and fundamental and innate as fear itself. Who knows? . . .

To go into that question, however, would serve only to add confusion to what is already too confused a story. Many sets of guesses have been made as to how religion began, but in this little book there was room for only one of them—the one that seems (to the writer) the most reasonable. And that having been given, we must hurry on. . . .

Happily for us the development of religion is not nearly so veiled in mists of doubt as is its beginning. Fairly detailed accounts of many ancient cults exist, and from these we can plot out an almost clear line of pro- gression. Beginning with the animism of the barbaric Celts, and continuing clear through to the Mysteries of the last of the Romans, we can follow almost step by step the slow march of early religion.

I. THE CELTS

THERE is no particular reason for beginning our study of ancient religion with the Celts save that records of their rites and beliefs have come down to us with comparative fullness. Two thousand years ago the Celts were but one of a horde of Aryan peoples just come up out of the night of savagery into that fitful fore-dawn which we call barbarism. Their religion, therefore, was still no more than a pathetic gesture that wavered between the brave but foolish clawing of the savage and the meek but hopeful reaching-out of civilized man. It was not altogether a dependence on magic rites, for the Celts had already discovered that magic alone was not enough. They were already sufficiently advanced to have learnt that the "powers" controlling the universe, the spirits supposed to dwell in trees and stones and other natural objects, could often be moved far more effectively by petition than coercion. Yet they did not stake all their faith on petition, either. Their priests were still covertly shamans, and their sacrifices were at least implicitly half-coercive spells. Perhaps the word "cajolery" best describes the technique wherewith the Celts sought to win over their deities.

They had many deities to win over, for every natural object of any impressiveness seemed to them to contain a spirit to be conjured with. And certain of these spirits had already been sufficiently detached from their physical bodies to be thought of as remote gods and goddesses. Names had been given to them—Ogmius, Maponus, Bridget, and the like—and whole mythologies had been spun around them. A sacrificial ritual had grown up, and a priestly class had been established. There seem to have been no temple edifices, however, but only unroofed circles of stone pillars—Stonehenge in England is the ruins of one of these circles—and groves of sacred trees. Within these circles and groves the priests (who were called Druids, "Wise Ones") offered **up** sacrifices and cast spells at regular times, and the priestesses—of whom there seem to have been not a few—performed rites of decidedly dubious respectability.

STONEHENGE

Idolatry had not advanced far among the Celts, and their images of the gods were rudely carved logs or simply weapons of one sort or another. Their chief ceremonial object was the mistletoe, that white-berried creeper which has captured the imagination of primitive peoples all over the world. Sir James G. Frazer, in that most fascinating book in all the literature of comparative religions, *The Golden Bough,* has tried to give the reason for the peculiar veneration attached to this plant. He maintains it is because the mistletoe has no roots in the polluted earth but seems to grow magically between heaven and earth. By that sorry clutching at conclusions which is all that primitive man has of logic, this plant, dangling down from the sky, is therefore thought to be endowed with magic properties. Wherever the

Druids discovered it growing on an oak tree, they would approach with great awe and ceremonial pomp and cut it down with a golden sickle. They would be dreadfully careful to catch it before it fell to the earth, and then they would use it to make a potion for the fertilizing of barren women and cattle, and for the cure of epilepsy, ulcers, poisoning, and almost every other human ailment.

2

REGULAR festivals were held three times in each year, and with especial elaborateness once in every five years. They were largely fire festivals, and were directly intended to make the spirits fertilize the soil. Julius Caesar has bequeathed to us our earliest description of those gruesome quinquennial festivals, when scores of criminals—that is, persons who had transgressed taboos —and prisoners of war and animals would be herded into colossal images of wicker-work, and then ceremoniously burnt to death. It was imagined that the greater the number of victims, the greater would be the fertility of the land, and once all northern Europe reeked with the smell of such holocausts. Originally the ordinary annual festivals were also bloody scenes of human sacrifice; but by historic times they had been rid of that savage factor. But fire still played a large part in the conduct of those festivals, and their obvious purpose was still the magic fructifying of the land. On the eve of the first of May, when the Celts held their festival of Beltane, bonfires of oak-wood were lighted under sacred trees or poles. A "king" and "queen" were chosen to lead the processions into the fields, and then for hours there was a mad flaring of brands plucked from the bonfires, and a wild swirling and dancing in orgiastic revelry. Men and women lay together in the fields, and behaved as did all other primitive peoples at their religious festivals. Simple barbarians they were, and they did what they did in all good faith that it would suggest to the sun and the other gods what they in turn ought to do: make things grow. Not until the Christian idea of morality was brought to them did the Celts grow conscious of any wickedness in their old rites. And even then they did not give them up at once. Indeed, to this day their descendants have not given them up entirely. They have merely pruned and refined and Christianized them into the eminently respectable—but reminiscently very naughty—Maypole dances of modern times. . . .

The two other Celtic festivals of the year were Lugnasad held on the first of August, and Samhain held on the last day of October. Both were marked by rites rather like those of Beltane, and both have persisted to our time, the one as Midsummer Night and St. John's Day and the other as Hallowe'en and All Saints' Day. Samhain was the more important of the two, for even as in the Christian calendar it was regarded as the day when the souls of the dead foregathered with the living. Food was laid out in the huts of the Celts and cheery fires were lighted on the hearths, so that the shivering hungry shades of the dead might prepare themselves against the wintry months just coming to the world.

The Celts were inordinately interested in the dead. They knew little about another world save that there was somewhere in the Western Sea a "sweet and blessed isle" reserved for heroes and demigods; but nevertheless they cherished an abiding faith in an afterlife even for the lowliest tribesman. Nervously they imagined the dead to be shades that hovered in the gloaming, intangible wraiths that yet could do great hurt or kindness. Perhaps their great fire-festivals, those ghastly holocausts of men and beasts, were but desperate efforts to drive away the more malevolent of the shades. For those poor Celts, forever harried by storm and drought and pestilence, had brought themselves to believe that the dead were, in part at least, the doers of all mischief. The dead and the spirits of nature together seemed the ultimate masters of the universe, and all of life for the living seemed to depend on their mysterious favor. That was why religious rites played so large a part in Celtic thought and conduct. They were primitive rites, crude, blundering, almost absurdly naive—but *they had to be kept up*. Even as a sick man, though he may reject one medicine after another, never can quite bring himself to reject physicians entirely, so the ancient Gaul and Briton often forsook one spell for another, but never dared to forsake the Druids. They were afraid . . . afraid. . . .

II. THE BABYLONIANS

TO trace the further advance of religion we must now shift the scene to a land far distant from the primeval forests of the Celts. We must go to ancient Mesopotamia, that verdant region between the great rivers of the Near East, where dawn had already broken what-time night still reigned in the West. The religion of Babylonia, even though far more ancient than that of the Celts, was in almost every respect far more advanced. From long before the beginning of recorded history, religion seems to have been further advanced in the East than in the West. For reasons which we cannot at all make out, the Orientals, especially the Semites, seem to have had a peculiar genius for religion. They were bedouins, those Semites: a lean, hungry, harried race forever roaming the desert vastnesses of Arabia in search of another place and another time to die. And it was they, most probably, who laid the foundations of Babylonia's religion. Thousands of years ago, when some of them struggled out of the barren desert and obtained a foothold in the lush meadows of Mesopotamia, they brought with them their old desert religion. It was then little more than a crude animism,

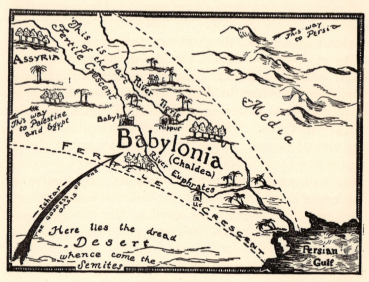

BABYLONIA

with Ishtar, "Self Waterer," the spirit of the oasis, as the chief deity. Ishtar, who was a goddess, probably had the spirits of the wind and sun and moon as husbands: and certainly she had Tammuz, the spirit of the date-palm, as her lover. We cannot be certain, but it seems rather likely that most of the other important deities then were also goddesses. This must have been because the primitive Semites were still in the matriarchal stage of pre-civilization. Wherever the heads of their families and clans were the mothers, not the fathers, quite naturally the chief spirits were imagined to be goddesses, not gods.

But once the invaders from the desert came to feel at home in verdant Mesopotamia, and began to mingle more or less freely with the non-Semitic natives, their religion took on a quite altered aspect. The matriarchal form of society gave way to the patriarchal, and as a natural consequence the goddesses were changed to gods. The chief deities chosen for the newly created cities were usually masculine. Sometimes they still retained the feminine names by which they had been known in earlier days, as is seen in the case of Ningirsu, literally "Lady of Girsu," who was the very masculine god of the city of Lagash. Or if the deities managed to persist in the new social order as females in fact as well as name, they took on altogether new functions. A population no longer living in the desert, for instance, had no longer any reason to worship the spirit of the desert oasis— so a star instead of an oasis was given to Ishtar as a home. . . .

But the Babylonians by no means contented themselves with merely remodeling the old gods. They

manufactured new ones, too—hundreds of them. Even
to list the chief of them—Ningirsu, Bel, Shamash,
Nabu, Marduk, Anu, Ea, Sin, and the rest—would be
quite tiresome. The idea of one great god with universal sway seems hardly to have occurred to the people.
Again and again, as one city after another became dominant in the empire, one god after another became chief
in the pantheon. For instance, so long as Babylon was
the capital of the empire, Bel-Marduk, the god of
Babylon, was considered the superior deity. But never
more than superior: never One alone, and beyond challenge. Occasionally not a single god, but a group of
three together was worshipped as superior: Anu (sky),
Bel (earth), and Ea (sea); or Shamash (sun), Sin
(moon), and Ishtar (the star Venus). . . . Age after
age new trinities of that sort arose.

2

BUT from beginning to end, one deity remained su-
premely popular at least among the plain people of
Mesopotamia. That deity was Ishtar, the great mother
of the gods, the spirit of sex and fertility, the very principle of life itself. Many other early peoples worshipped
some such mother goddess, for the power of reproduction among plants, beasts, and men, remained unflaggingly the most vital and engrossing power of all. To
be able to control it meant to live; to fail meant to die.
Little wonder, therefore, if everywhere in the world, in
Mexico and the Congo, in Ireland and the Malay isles,
we find the people groveling at the feet of some sex-
dealing, life-breeding spirit.

In Babylonia and throughout the Levant the people

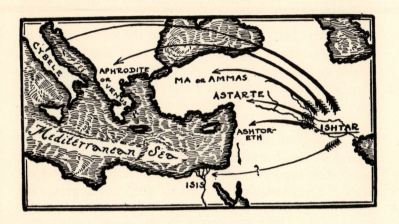

THE GREAT MOTHER GODDESSES

seem to have bowed down to it inordinately, and sex rites in honor of Ishtar—or Astarte, Ashtoreth, Isis, Cybele, Venus, and Aphrodite, as the goddess was known in the various lands—were counted of primary importance. In Babylonia itself it was required that every woman, rich or poor, should submit at least once in her life to the embraces of a stranger. She had to wait in the courts of a temple of Ishtar until some man bought her for an hour, and then she had to dedicate to the goddess the wages earned by her harlotry. Without performing that rite a woman was imagined to be incapable of bearing children, and was therefore unfit to marry. As a result, the temple-courts were simply choked with desperate virgins; and the priests of the Ishtar cult, who often were paid to play the part of the welcome stranger, grew enormously rich. . . .

The difference between this Babylonian cult of Ishtar
and the primitive Celtic cult of Bridget was entirely one
of degree, not of kind. Both were inspired by dread of
the same evil, sterility; and both sought to attain one
end, fecundity. But one, the Babylonian, was far less
primitive than the other—far less wildly promiscuous
and bestial. The Babylonian rites were conducted within
the confines of stone temples, not out in the furroughs
of the torch-lit fields; and they were hedged in with
a thousand rules and watched over by a myriad of priests.
Between those priests and the Celtic Druids there was
again a difference only of degree. The Babylonian holy
men were merely shamans of a more advanced type.
They still were little more than magicians and medicine-
men; but they had evolved a highly intricate technique,
and had developed a grotesque psuedo-science to support
it. They had somehow hit on the idea that the constant changes in the heavens bear some subtle relation
to the happenings here on earth. Not merely to the
vast geographic happenings on earth (that much would
be scientifically quite valid), but even more to the petty
fortunes of all the creatures swarming over it. All
human souls were believed to be hitched for weal or
woe to stars, and the chief concern of the priests was,
therefore, star-gazing. That sorry deceit called astrology, which still lures the feebler-minded among men,
had its first development back there in Babylonia almost
four thousand years ago!

3

BUT the Babylonian priesthood did not confine its
interests to the stars in the heavens. On the contrary,

it also reached out and tried to control the most mundane things on earth. It truckled to the conceits of the rich and preyed on the terrors of the poor. It owned magnificent and costly brick temples that rose to the very heavens in ornate terraces—veritable Towers of Babel they were—and regularly sacrificed to the idols that stood in them. There were many divisions in the priesthood, each with its own particular function. Certain of the clerics awoke the gods in the morning, washed and dressed them, and offered the elaborate sacrifices; others sang the hymns and chanted the spells; to others was assigned the task of fructifying the barren women who waited in the temple courts; still others read horoscopes and told fortunes. That many of the priests were fools and more were knaves, is to be taken for granted. That many gouged the widows and forgot the orphans, is to be expected. After all, religion to the Babylonian was not a matter of noble sentiment, but a sort of complicated insurance business; and its priestly solicitors and agents were, as Americans would say, out to get "all there was in it for them." Their extortions, especially for fortune-telling, sometimes grew so flagrant that kings had actually to pass laws to control them. Inscriptions tell us that already before 2800 B. C. King Urkagina had to legislate against priestly profiteering! . . .

But it must not be imagined for a moment that the great priesthood of Babylonia was unrelievedly lecherous and low. One cannot read their ancient hymns without realizing that at least some among their band were men of what we vaguely call "spirituality" and "religious insight." Most of those hymns are mere med-

leys of magic phrases, but others are poems of amazing
beauty.   Indeed, certain of them ring with tones that
are strikingly reminiscent of the Hebrew Psalms.   For
instance:

> The sin which I sinned I knew not;
> My God has visited me in wrath.
> I sought help, but none took my hand;
> I wept, but none gave ear.
> To my God, the merciful God, I turn and pray;
> How long, O Lord! . . .
> O God, cast not away thy servant,
> But turn my sin into a blessing.
> May the wind carry away my transgressions.
> Seven times seven are they—
> Forgive thou them! . . .

Now that is no ordinary bit of primitive liturgy.
It reveals a reverence for the deity, a humility in the
worshipper, and above all a freedom from magical formula that would lead us to think it all a forgery did
we not have the very stone on which the Babylonian
priests engraved it.   Such lines may not be even remotely typical, but they are authentic.   And because
they are authentic, and they and other lines of like
quality were ever written in Bel-Marduk's courts, the
cult of Babylonia must be seen to mark a distinct advance in the evolution of religion.

4

BUT we must not exaggerate the extent of that advance.   Babylonia's cult was distinguished for the in-
tricacy of its priestly organization, the ornateness of its

temple ritual, and most especially for the elaborateness of its astrology. In other words, it was distinguished for its legal, aesthetic, and psuedo-scientific features. But in the highest concerns of religion, in theology and ethics, it was still woefully primitive. Somehow it never progressed beyond polytheism; never really far beyond polydemonism. The Babylonians imagined the whole earth to be peopled with demons—with evil genii that stalked and afflicted men with floods and plagues and darkness. The gods themselves were often regarded by the priests as mere snivelling wretches forever hungering for scraps from the temple altars. (That was but natural, for no god can be a hero to his valet.) In one of the Babylonian scriptures the gods are actually compared to the flies that buzz around the sacrificial carcasses. In another place, where the story of the Flood is recounted, they are spoken of as dogs:

> The gods were frightened at the deluge;
> They fled, they climbed to the highest heaven.
> The gods crouched like dogs;
> They cringed by the walls! . . .

And ethically the Babylonians were just as primitive. Ritual scrupulousness seemed to them far more important than human rectitude; sacrificial omissions seemed to them far more heinous than moral offenses. Taboos dogged their every step in life, and "bad luck" threatened them at every turn. Every seventh day was regarded as somehow "evil," and on it special sacrifices were fearfully offered and all manner of special taboos were observed. For instance, the princes were forbidden to go forth on journeys on that day, or to eat meat cooked over a fire. Every fourth of those "evil seventh days" was particularly dreaded, for it marked the beginning of the waning of the moon's power. On it desperate efforts were made to placate the demons, and thus avert the unluckiness otherwise certain to come with the day. Significantly enough, the Babylonians called it *Shabatum,* a name strikingly like that given by the Hebrews, to their holy day, the Sabbath. It is highly probable that the Hebrews actually got their Sabbath from the Babylonian Shabatum, for we know they paid little heed to its observance until after they had lived in exile in Babylonia from 586 B. C. to 536 B. C. But note how differently the Hebrews regarded the day. To them it was holy, not evil. The Hebrews told themselves that the Sabbath was a divinely appointed "day of rest," and though they observed on it many of the old Shabatum taboos, they did so not out of fear of the genii but out of respect for their God. Their New Moon festival was an ocassion for rejoicing, not for added trembling and dread.

The contrast is no slight one. It reveals glaringly the inferiority, the essential primitiveness, of which religious thought in Babylonia never quite rid itself. The Babylonians developed a vast mythology, but they graced it with no ethical meaning. They told many tales about their gods, about the creation of the world, the first man, the great flood, and so forth. But these tales were almost unrelievedly wild, crude, even foul. When we meet them again in the Old Testament—for those stories, like the Shabatum taboos, seem to have been taken over from the Babylonians by the Hebrew exiles—we find them changed almost beyond recognition. In the Bible they are no longer mere bawdy romancings told for the mere joy of their telling, but passionate sermons recited to bring home certain moral ideals. Ethically the Babylonians were little more than grown-up children. Fear still had hold of them and kept them slaves. Even though they were rich and powerful, even though they were the lords of the green earth and thought themselves the masters of the starry skies, still they remained cravens in their hearts. Beneath all their bluster they were timorous and worried. They were afraid . . . afraid. . . .

III.   THE EGYPTIANS

TO trace the further development of religion we must go now from Babylonia to ancient Egypt. Of course, in very early times the Egyptians, like the rest of the primitive peoples of the earth, were simple animists. All things around them seemed to be animated by certain wilful spirits; and to these spirits the Egyptians paid terrified homage. Only a few of the spirits were thought to dwell in natural phenomena such as the sun, the moon, and the great River Nile. The majority were imagined to have their habitation in various species of animals and birds. Each tribe—there seem to have been forty-two of them in Egypt about seven thousand years ago—worshipped the spirit inhabiting some particular species of living creature, and looked to it for protection. One worshipped the ram, another the bull, a third the lion; others worshipped the serpent, the cat, the goat, the ass, the falcon, the hippopotamus, the pig, and the vulture. Evidently the earliest religion of Egypt must have been a totemism rather like that of the American Indians, each tribe being named after the animal which it held sacred, and which it may have looked on as its spiritual ancestor.

But as civilization advanced among the Egyptians, the primitiveness of their totemism began to disappear. The "powers" began to be thought of no longer as mere animals but rather as gods *symbolized* by animals. The idols, which originally may have been simple images of beasts, were now carved to represent bodies whose heads alone were those of beasts. Or occasionally—as in the case of the sphinx—the body was still that of an animal, but the head was human. And when, after much wandering, the tribes settled down at last in what became their fixed provinces, these half-animal gods became localized. For instance, Amon, who was symbolized by a ram, became the god of the village of Thebes; Ptah, the bull-god, became the deity of Memphis; Set, the ass-god, became the protector of the village of Ombos. In every town the stone temple of the local god towered over the mud hovels of the people. It was literally the "house of the god," and the priests in it were called the god's servants. Morning, noon, and night they waited on the idol that glowered in the terrifying dimness of the inner sanctuary. They washed and dressed it in the morning, gave it food, and flattered it with hymns. At night they removed its vestments and figuratively put it to bed. Stony and immobile as it was, the idol nevertheless seemed to them the dwelling place of the most dreadfully potent force in the world. Perhaps the more astute of the priests, those who had served longest and profited most by the cult, knew better. But certainly the people did not. The people,

the myriads of sweating serfs and starving peasants—
they believed. Unalterably they believed that lodged in
the idol there was a spirit that could bring them life
or death. Probably the majority of the priests believed
likewise, for the proverb "as the people, so the priest"
states a truth that holds for all races, not merely the
Hebrews. Rare indeed, therefore—and silent as night
—must have been the doubters in those days of un-
bridled faith. . . .

2

BUT what happened later in many other lands happened of course in Egypt, too. Though the fear of
terrorful spirits never ceased to be a stark and ominous
reality, the exact identity of those spirits wavered and
continually changed. The fusion of the Egyptian tribes
brought with it a fusion of the tribal deities. The
temples became the houses not of single gods, but of
whole families. Usually the original spirit of the temple
was given a neighboring goddess for a wife, and a
minor godling for a son. Or sometimes he was given
two goddesses as wives. And that tendency, begun on
so small a scale, was carried on until at last one god
was exalted over all the rest in Egypt. Centuries before
the Hebrews came up out of the night of desert savagery,
we find the Egyptians already groping their way toward
the idea of a monotheism, a One God. It was political
rather than philosophical considerations that impelled
the Egyptians in such a direction. As soon as some
tribal chieftain managed to fight his way to the throne
of the land, so soon did he try to set his tribal god on
the throne of the heavens. And to give permanence to

the arrangement, he naturally was driven to attempt the destruction of all the defeated but still menacing gods. Usually he tried to wipe them out by declaring them to be merely so many vagrant manifestations of his own deity. Or else his priests invented elaborate mythologies to prove that his god had been the very first in the universe, and had actually created all the other deities. Century after century such stratagems were resorted to. Every king cherished the same futile hope of establishing his dynasty forever, and for that reason every king tried to prove his god to be the only one worthy of worship. . . .

3

BUT no one of the attempts ever quite succeeded. Even the valiant attempt of the famous King Ikhnaton came to naught. This Ikhnaton, who reigned in Egypt from about 1375 to 1350 B. C., has not unjustly been called the first individual in human history. With amazing clarity of vision and singleness of purpose he set himself the task of making the religion of Egypt an absolute monotheism. He broke completely with the polytheistic past, denying all the favorite old gods and suppressing their cults. Only Aton, the Sun-God, was recognized, and to Him every human knee was made to bend, and every tongue to give homage. The king gave up the name, Amonhotep, by which he had been known all his life, simply because it contained the name of the old god, Amon. Instead he called himself Ikhnaton, which meant "Spirit of Aton." Because his old capital was the center of Amon worship, the king gave that up, too. He built himself an entirely new city, calling it

Akhetaton, meaning "Horizon of Aton." He tried to
revolutionize every phase of Egyptian life, spurning all
the old conventions and creating by fiats even a new
art and literature! . . .

Of course, the priests of the fallen gods fought him
bitterly, for he had taken the bread—and honey—right
out of their mouths. But they could do little, for the
power of Ikhnaton was absolute in all his empire. He
sent stone masons all through Egypt to erase the names
of the old gods from the temples and pyramids. He
caused even his own father's name to be obliterated because it contained the name of Amon! And in his new
capital he built a splendid temple to his One God, Aton,
adoring him with sumptuous sacrifices and with hymns
of surpassing beauty.

> Thy dawning, O Living Aton, is
> beautiful on the horizon. . . .
> O, Beginning of Life, Thou art all,
> and Thy rays encompass all. . . .
> Manifold are Thy works, One and Only
> God, Whose power none other possesseth;
> the whole earth hast Thou created
> according to Thine own understanding.
> When Thou wast alone didst Thou create
> man and beast, both large and small;
> all that go upon their feet, all that
> fly on wings; yea, and all the foreign
> lands, even Syria and Kush besides this
> land of Egypt. Thou settest all in their
> place, and providest all with their
> needs. . . . [though] diverse are their
> tongues, their forms, their skins. . . .
> O how goodly are Thy designs, O Lord,
> that there is a Nile in the sky for

strangers and for the cattle of every
land. . . . Thou art He who art in my
soul; Thou art the life of life;
through Thee men live!

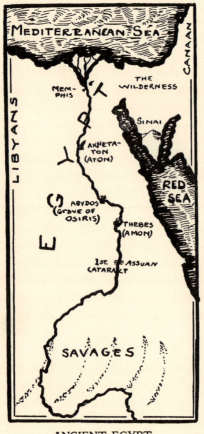

ANCIENT EGYPT

So did he sing, that great Egyptian heretic, centuries before ever a Hebrew psalmist had appeared on earth!

But none there was to sing so after him. When Ikhnaton died, Aton also died. The priests of Amon and Re and the other old gods quickly came into their own again, setting up their old altars, and chanting their old spells. The very son-in-law of the man who so zealously altered his name from Amonhotep to Ikhnaton thought it wise to change his own name from Tutenkhaton back to Tutenkhamen. Once more Thebes was made the capital, and its priesthood waxed fat with might. Two per cent of the entire population (one out of every fifty Egyptians!)

became actual slaves in the temples; and a seventh of all the arable soil in the realm became temple property. The high-priests grew more powerful year by year, and in the end one of them actually seized the crown! . . . And thus was all the labor of that royal heretic, Ikhnaton, made to come to naught.

Yet a vestige of that impetuous reform did endure. The idea of a monotheism, of a single God in all the universe, was never quite blotted out from Ikhnaton's day on. Somehow the idea lingered in the land, persistently affecting at least the language if not the life of the priests. More and more the old gods were merged together; even their names were hyphenated. Amon and Re were spoken of as one from then on—Amon-Re. And what was more important, this composite god was now thought of not as a spirit animating merely a golden disc in the heavens, but as a spirit flaming in the hearts of men. Not merely in the hearts of kings, but in the hearts of men—*all* men! . . . So the impatient heretic, the tyrant reformer, Ikhnaton, though he failed, nevertheless succeeded. A little, perhaps the veriest trifle, of that which he had preached while he was yet alive remained on after his death. But it was an enduring trifle. . . .

4

THE leaning toward monotheism was not, however, the chief distinction of old Egypt's religion. One must realize that the tendency in that direction was marked only in the upper levels of religious thinking in Egypt. It arose partly out of philosophical reasoning and largely out of political necessity, and therefore it did not even touch the life of the plain people in the land. So

far as the Egyptian masses were concerned, no tendency
toward monotheism was even existent.   The masses
laboring on the banks of the Nile, like the masses everywhere else, were not much given to abstract theologizing.
Harried and hounded by a myriad terrors, they could do
no more than reach out into the blue for help, and then
trust to luck that they had clutched for it in the right
direction.   The masses had neither the time nor the
brains to speculate on the nature of the spirits who gave
the help, or the manner in which they gave it.   Questions of such a nature had to be handed over by them to
the priests and learned men to solve.   It was not the
peasant's part to reason how; his was but to fear and
bow. . . .

From first to last, therefore, the masses of Egypt continued to worship their innumerable half-animal gods,
paying heed neither to the fiats of kings nor the dis-
quisitions of priests.   Of course, the mob had its favorite
gods, differing at various times and in various localities;
for with the unconscionable fickleness characteristic of
mobs, it dropped its favorites about as fast as it took
them up.   Only one god, Osiris, managed to hold his
place in the affections of the people throughout Egypt's
long history.   Originally this Osiris seems to have been
the spirit who made the crops grow, the god of vegetation comparable to Tammuz of the Babylonians.   As
such he was of great importance almost from the beginning, for the Egyptians were an agricultural people who
depended on the crops for their very life.   As time went
on, therefore, Osiris assumed a place of more and more
importance in the minds of the people, until at last they
came to look on him as the Divine Lord of the Nile

Lands, the God of Justice and Love and nurturing Light. In large part his exaltation to this rank was due to the spread of a significant myth among the people. The story was told how once on a time Osiris, this god of nurturing Light and Good, was treacherously put to death by Set, the god of withering Darkness and Evil. When Isis, the loving wife of Osiris, learnt of the murder, she went up and down the land to find the body of her lord, lamenting sorely as she went, and weeping until the Nile actually overflowed its banks. Isis found the body at last and buried it; but not very carefully. As a result, while she was away looking after her fatherless son, Horus, the corpse was stolen from its grave. The wicked Set got possession of it, dismembered it thoroughly, and then hid each fragment in a different place. So then Isis had to traverse the land a second time, seeking out the pieces of the body, and burying them more safely this time in a sealed tomb. And thereupon Osiris came to life again! He was miraculously resurrected from death and taken up to heaven; and there in heaven, so the myth declared, he lived on eternally!

Obviously that myth had its origin in an attempt to explain the annual death and rebirth of vegetation. Every autumn seemed to witness the foul murder of all that was good to man, and every spring seemed to mark its resurrection. And the Egyptians, like most other races, came to look on that recurrent rescue of the earth from bleakness, cold, and famine, as the most wondrous miracle in the universe. Even the dullest serfs could not fail to be bewildered by it; even the most cloddish minds could not but be eager for some story explaining it.   And having agreed upon such a story, those fellahin felt impelled for some reason to dramatize and enact it year after year.   Every spring at Abydos the drama of Osiris was enacted by the Egyptians in a stirring passion play, much as the peasants in Oberammergau enact the drama of Jesus even today. . . .

There is small cause to wonder that in time this folk-drama, rooted as it was in the earth's greatest mystery,

PYRAMIDS BY THE NILE

became the very core of Egypt's religion.   Somehow its plot seemed to give the key to the whole riddle of life and death.   The Egyptians reasoned that if it was the fate of the god Osiris to be resurrected after death, then a way could be found to make it the fate of man, too. Of course!   All one had to do was be buried properly. If only a man's soul were committed safely into the hands of Osiris, and his body embalmed and preserved in a tomb, then some day of a surety the two would get together again, and the man would walk the earth as of yore. At least, so it came to be believed in Egypt as long as four thousand years ago.

In the beginning, however, only the kings were believed to stand a chance of resurrection, for they alone were thought to have souls. That was why in those days the kings alone were embalmed and mummified. Huge pyramids were built to shelter their royal bodies against the day of their resurrection, enormous structures of brick and stone that still stand today, and no doubt will still be standing centuries hence.

But finally the day of the despotic pyramid builders came to an end, and a spirit of democracy crept into the land. The bliss of immortality that had formerly been reserved only for kings was then promised to all men. It came to be admitted that every man had a soul that lived on through the winter of death; and for that reason every man's body had to be preserved in the hope of ultimate resurrection. Even the bodies of those animals that were deemed sacred to the various gods, the bulls and rams and cats and crocodiles, were preserved in that hope. At Beni Hasan so many mummified cats were laid away that nowadays the cemetery is used as a quarry for fertilizer!

5

THE dead were thought to lead a curious double life, one on earth and the other in heaven at the same time. The earthly existence was carried on by the mummy in the tomb, and its conservation demanded that food be laid out for its nourishment at regular intervals. The horridest fear in the heart of the dying Egpytian was that his heirs would neglect to perform that service, and often contracts were made with utter strangers, with professional tomb-tenders or neighboring priests, to keep the mummy's larder replenished. And for fear that even these solemn contracts might be broken, the tombs were carved with piteous verses begging the passer-by to offer if not a meal at least a little prayer—"which costs only the breath of the mouth"—for the neglected dead. . . . The heavenly existence of the dead was carried on in the realm of Osiris, and it was described in considerable detail by the Egyptian theologians. It was believed that on death the soul of a man set out at once to reach a Judgment Hall on high. Evil spirits tried to waylay it on the journey, but any soul adequately provided with magic formulae could evade them all. With these spells the evil spirits could be dodged or fought off until finally the soul attained the Judgment Hall and stood before the celestial throne of Osiris, the Judge. There it gave an account of itself to Osiris and his forty-two associate gods. Any soul that could truly say: "I come before ye without sin, and have done that wherewith the gods are satisfied. I have not slain, nor robbed, nor stirred up strife, nor lied, nor lost my temper, nor committed adultery, nor stolen temple food. . . I have given bread to the hungry, clothes to the naked, a ferry to him who had no boat"—if in sincerity it could say all that, then the soul was straightway gathered into the fold of Osiris. But if it could not, if it was found wanting when weighed in the heavenly balances, then it was cast into a hell, to be rent to shreds by the "Devouress." For only the righteous souls, only the guiltless, were thought to be deserving of life ever-lasting! . . .

It was an extraordinary set of beliefs, and reveals a moral insight on the part of the Egyptians that must have been unmatched in the world of four thousand years ago. No other people in that day seems to have been capable of conceiving a Judgment Hall where a life of moral innocence, and not merely of ritual propriety, decided the soul's fate after death. Of course, certain elements in the conception were distinctly primitive; for instance, the idea that no soul, however righteous, could ever reach the Judgment Hall unless well armed with magic formulae to protect it on the way. Such a flaw could not but leave an opening for the introduction of all sorts of superstitious practices. To be on the safe side, coffins were literally lined with those magic formulae, or were packed tight with rolls of parchment on which mystic spells were written. The practice was relentlessly opposed by King Ikhnaton, the heretic, and during his reign it was rarely if ever observed. But once he died, it returned and flourished more rankly than ever before. The ancient Egyptians were not yet so free of primitive fear, or of primitive measures of defense against it, that they dared to rely on their moral guiltlessness alone to win them paradise. They still clung to the notion that there were many evil spirits in the universe which could not be fought off by virtue, but only by magic. They even entertained the notion that the good spirits, too, could be controlled by magic. Certain of their spells were designed for the express purpose of helping sinful souls to dodge the verdict of the Heavenly

Judges and sneak their way into Paradise despite their guilt. . . .

It is not unlikely that the priests winked at these relics of a bygone age, if only because their vogue tended to give them great power. For the priests alone knew how to write the magic formulae, and thus they alone controlled the keys to heaven. At different times they gathered many of those formulae together, and made of them sacred tomes which later came to be known as the "Book of the Dead," the "Book of the Other World," and the "Book of the Gates." In them were set down, not merely magic phrases, but also maps and travel instructions for the dead. They were, so to speak, Baedeckers to the Next World. . . .

So this chapter on the religion of Egypt must end much as did the one on Babylonia. Religion advanced in the valley of the Nile to unprecedented heights. There earlier than anywhere else in the world—at least so far as we know—the idea was conceived of One God ruling in all this Universe. There too was first told the legend of a Lord of Light who died at the hands of Darkness, only to come to life again and go up to Heaven to receive all the righteous there into his embrace. Those were no inconsiderable heights for an ancient people to attain. . . . But the pity of it was that, though those heights were attained, they were not held. Perhaps that decline occurred because the Egyptians sank too completely into thralldom to the priests. (Save for Ikhnaton, Egypt in all her five thousand years of history produced not a single prophetic spirit. And prophetic spirits alone can keep a people on the heights.) But more fundamentally the Egyptians must have failed because they were still too close to the primitive. Crude fear still had too strong a hold on them. With pathetic earnestness they tried to put their trust solely in the goodness of the spirits; but always they remained a trifle uncertain, tucking away a spell on their person or in their tombs in case of need. They tried hard to believe that virtue alone would win the favor of the gods; but inevitably they added a little incantation, just to be "on the safe side." They could never quite keep from slipping down into the slough of magic. No matter how hard they tried, they could never for long hold to the heights. For even they were still not at home in the universe—even they were still afraid . . . afraid. . . .

IV. THE GREEKS

AND now we come to Greece, that little land of broken valleys and sea-swept cliffs wherein ancient civilization climbed and climbed until it reached its very zenith. In the beginning its religion was naturally a terrorful worship of the spirits supposed to dwell in stones and trees—just such a worship as obtained everywhere else in savage times. The inhabitants of the land then were people whom modern scholars call the Minoans, a race whose writing has not yet been deciphered, and whose history and religion are consequently but little known. Judging from remains discovered in Crete and the Aegean Islands, the chief deity of the Minoans seems to have been a goddess who, like Ishtar of the Babylonians, was an impersonation of the principle of fertility, or motherhood. But the Minoans had numerous other deities besides her, some of them gods and most of them goddesses. Only with the coming of the Indo-European Greeks does the religion of the peninsula become better known to us. These invaders were of the same stock as the Hindus and the other Aryans, and when they swept southward from Central Europe sometime before 1200 B. C., they brought with them their sky-god, Zeus Pater, and all their other old Aryan deities. But once established in their new home, they speedily merged their religion

ANCIENT GREECE

with the one already existing in the land. They adopted the deities of the native Minoans, calling them all relations of their own sky-god, Zeus Pater. The great fertility-goddess of the Minoans was named Rhea and called the mother of Zeus; another goddess, Hera, was made his wife; a third, Athena, was called his daughter. Two of the native gods were named Poseidon and Hades, and were given to Zeus for brothers; another, Apollo by name, was declared his son. Even the crude idols of the Minoans, obvious sex symbols sacred to the goddess of fertility, were taken over by the newcomers. And thus a new religion came into being. In part it was a fear-riddled, magic-mongering cult rooted in the half-civilization of the Minoans; and in part it was the shallow, light-hearted, myth-making cult of the barbaric Greeks.

For many centuries the second element remained dominant. When the minstrels of classic Greece sang of the gods, they sang of glorified men: gay, lustful, brawling heroes, who sported about on Mount Olympus without giving the slightest heed to morality or property. And there seems to have been no thought of any compelling tie between the people and the gods. Even centuries later the philosopher Aristotle solemnly wrote, "to love God would be improper."

But if the early Greeks did not love their deities, neither did they greatly fear them. The tales that are called Homeric reveal almost no trace of any terror of the gods. The people seem to have regarded Zeus and his divine family with a measure of fondness, perhaps even with a measure of awe—but nothing more. Perhaps this was because the priesthood never attained any great power in ancient Greece. A well-organized priestly caste inevitably succeeds in hammering the "fear of the gods" deeply—usually too deeply—into the hearts of the people. But no such caste ever existed among the Greeks. The priests in the land were but minor state officials who differed very little from laymen, save on the rare occasions when sacrifices had to be formally offered to the gods. The images of the gods were carved by artists who thought only of beauty, not by holy men bowed in terror or reverence. The cult was solemn and dignified, but far from intensely moving. The ornate sacrificial etiquette that marked the religions of Babylonia and Egypt was largely unknown in early Greece.

2

BUT though that shallow, light-hearted cult managed to persist for a while, ultimately it had no alternative but to fade away and be forgotten. For it lacked warmth and fervor. It had too little of that commingled terror and hope, too little of that blasting fear and febrile yearning, which is the stuff whereof enduring faiths are made. Essentially the cult was without point, without much value or helpfulness in the business of keeping alive. It held out neither a comforting hand nor even a threatening fist to man. And therefore it could not possibly keep alive itself. Had it possessed an elaborate ritual and a politically powerful priesthood, no doubt it could have subsisted much longer than it did. (Well-intrenched ecclesiastical systems have protracted the life of many an outworn religion.) But the Olympian cult, as we have already seen, had never been able to develop such a preservative for itself. For a while it hung ripe on the bough of Greek thought, and then the people allowed it to fall to the ground and rot there. Both sage and boor, aristocrat and slave, turned from it in despair. None of them found it to be the indispensable viand that sustains life and makes it worth while. To none of them could it bring salvation. So it died. . . .

But it did not die of a sudden. Already by the sixth century B. C. the vanity of the Olympian cult was sensed by the keener minds in Athens and the other city-states of Greece. But not until the fourth century did it really give up the ghost. And during all those years of its slow disintegration, new approaches to salvation were being discovered by the Greeks. The learned took to philosophy, for they were far advanced in mentality and fully able to extract satisfaction from such a discipline. Had primitive fear swirled higher around them, of course they would never have been capable of being sustained by philosophy. They would have resorted instead to magic spells for help, and gone clutching bewilderedly at mythical spirits. But the flood of fear had subsided, and only a slough of despond was left. It was not terror, therefore, so much as disquiet that spurred the learned folk of Hellas to go seeking salvation. The advance of the race out of the hazards of the primeval forest had already made life *possible*—but it had not yet made life *reasonable*. As a result, the Greek sages were intent not so much on *self-preservation* as on *self-realization*. . . .

And that was why they turned from the childish vanities of the Olympian cult to the rigors of philosophy. Through philosophy, that trying discipline of the mind which indefatigably gropes and claws its way in the hope that at last it can uncover the *why* of all things— through philosophy the learned of Greece sought to attain that sense of security which we call salvation. A whole galaxy of sages deployed their forces in the realm of the spirit, each of them bent on finding a means not of material protection but of spiritual satisfaction, each of them grailing not so much for *a* way of living as for *the* way of Life.

We are tempted to go off here at a tangent, and speak at length of the great philosophers that ancient Greece produced. There was first of all Thales, who lived fully twenty-six hundred years ago; then there were Pythagoras, Xenophanes, Heraclitus, and Empedocles; there were Socrates, Plato, and Aristotle. Each of them, in his own way and according to his own lights, went groping, searching, after that sense of security without which life is either terror or vanity. For the most part they did not even bother to discuss the old religion and the old gods. They simply shrugged their shoulders at their mention, and passed them by. Occasionally a dramatist, like Euripides, stopped to take a fling at them; but the philosophers, as a general thing, let them alone. They struck off along paths that led to new gods, or rather, to a new idea of god, of the One God, whom their new-found logic told them must be the ultimate source of power in all the universe. Almost without exception the sages seem to have been conscious of some such unifying God. Thales called Him "the Intelligence of the world." The Stoics described Him as "the Help-ing of man by man." Plato called Him "the Idea of Good." And so most of the other philosophers. . . .

3

BUT the plain people, the masses, could not follow along the steep, narrow paths of hard reason up which the philosophers clambered. Indeed, they sometimes resented the temerity of those philosophers, and violently dragged them down. They exiled Anaxagoras, and

Protagoras, and put the great Socrates to death. They could not fathom what those philosophers were after. The plain people of Greece were, after all, still quite primitive. They were not yet capable of wondering as to the ultimate reason for living; they still wanted to know just how to keep alive. With them the vital problem was not self-realization, but still self-preservation. For they were still not at home in the universe. They were still afraid! . . .

Quite naturally, therefore, the plain people fell back on magic. The old Minoan element, that dark mumbling of spells between chattering teeth, came sweeping back over the land in a mounting wave of hysteria. Even in the gay, sunny days of Olympian worship there had always been among the plain people a cowering worship of ghosts. There had always persisted a rooted belief in the power of certain evil spirits to maim, sicken, and kill; and always there had been the desire to placate those spirits with sacrifices, or drive them away with spells or a good beating. But now that primitive demon-worship no longer lurked in haggard woods or slum alleyways. It crawled out and began to flaunt itself in the open. And there was none left in all Hellas to drive it back. Like some loathsome nocturnal beast out of the jungle it bared its fangs and went ravishing through the land. . . .

And side by side with this demon-worship there came a second monster of faith: an ecstatic, drunken savior-worship. In origin it seems to have been foreign to Greece, an exotic thing from the hinterland and the orient; but for all that it did not want for prey. The ruck and scum of a hundred foreign populations had been dragged in chains to Athens and the other Greek cities. Hordes of serfs and slaves festered in crowded slums, or slaved in mines and fields and forests. And eagerly, frenziedly those hordes threw themselves in the path of this strange beast. Secret cults of mystic salvation arose in every corner of the land, little sodalities preaching a religion of ecstatic hope and orgiastic practice. They were called "Mysteries," and almost without exception they circled around the idea of a god who died and was resurrected. As we have already seen, that idea was obviously inspired by the sight of the annual death and rebirth of the crops. The idea was known and gave rise to cults not alone in Egypt, but in almost all the other Mediterranean lands. Indeed, throughout the world one discovers signs of its quondam prevalence. And that scattered dissemination was hardly due to widespread borrowing from a single source; rather it was the result of a widespread clutching in a single direction. No matter how far the races of man may be scattered across the face of the earth, they are all hounded by similar dangers and cursed with similar fears. As a consequence they have all been forced to hit on more or less similar means of defense. Mankind everywhere, in Mexico and Iceland, in Zululand and China, makes more or less the same wild guesses in its convulsive effort to solve the riddle of existence. And that is why we find this complex idea of a slain and resurrected god common in many parts of the world. It was one of those guesses. one of those blindly hopeful snatches after security, which a race drowning in insecurity instinctively felt forced to make, no matter where it dwelt.

In very early times that idea flourished not alone

among the Babylonians and Egyptians, but also among the barbaric tribes in and around Greece. Among the latter it gave rise to a whole farrago of myths telling how some god—Dionysus, Zagreus, Zabazius, or Orpheus—had once upon a time gone madly careering through the woods, had been torn to pieces and destroyed, and then had been magically restored to life again. And as a corollary of those myths there had arisen the companion belief that by imitative magic every human being could repeat that divine experience. Every mortal could take on immortality simply by doing as the god had done. A man had only to eat the flesh and guzzle the blood of the animal sacred to his savior-god, whirl around in orgiastic passion, hack at his own flesh in madness, and shout, scream, howl to the skies, and then in a moment of frenzy—an "enthusiasm" it was called in Greek—he was of a sudden overwhelmed by the conviction that he actually *was* the god! He had to experience a mystical orgasm that sent silver, sensory storms sweeping through his flesh, that set a diapason of nerves quivering in his rigid body, that lifted him up, up, up, till with a sob of unendurable ecstasy he felt all the evil literally gush out of his being . . . and then he knew himself at last to be— divine! . . .

4

SUCH was the wild flame that burnt in most of the mysteries; and one cannot wonder that myriads in Greece went flocking to it once the sun of Olympian worship could no longer warm their blood. It gave them hope and cheer; it won them Paradise. It gave them life—life in some other and better world—life immortal and ever-blessed. And that was, after all, the ultimate want of the submerged masses in Greece. They had given up this world as hopeless, as utterly barren of all chance of joy for them. Those wretched helots, ground in the dust beneath the heel of the upper classes, could not possibly see any remaining hope of peace for them in this vale of tears. But being still human, still charged with that insensate Will to Live which is life's primal spark in man, they could not sit supinely by and let death overtake them. No, they had still to want for life, for restful, blessed, enduring life. Only they had perforce to want it in some other world. . . .

Now the old Olympian worship had done nothing to satisfy that want. Only the half-divine heroes—and not all even of them—were assured a life in the Elysian Fields when death took them from this earth. Ordinary men, no matter how righteous and worthy, were all consigned to Hades after death. There in dank subterranean realms their spectral forms, bereft of bones and sinews, swept "shadow-like around," and chattered tonelessly like so many bats. They knew no bliss, no rest, no peace—only unbroken gloom and misery. No wonder Achilles cried: "Nay, speak not comfortingly to me of death, O great Odysseus. Far rather would I live on earth the hireling of another, with a landless man who is himself destitute, than bear sway over all the dead that be departed!" . . . But the new worship, these mysteries come down from Thrace or across the sea from Egypt and Asia Minor, told a far different tale. They declared that for every man, no matter how poor or vicious, there was a place in heaven. All one had to

do was to be "initiated" into the secrets of the cult, puri-
fying oneself by baptism in blood or water, dancing
the sacred dances, partaking of the sacred offering, and
finally gazing on certain very sacred and mysterious
cult objects. Once a man performed those rites, then
salvation was assured him, and no excess of vice and
moral turpitude could close the gates of paradise in his
face. He was saved forevermore! . . .

Perhaps as early as 1000 B. C. the Greeks were already
practicing what were called the Eleusinian mysteries;
but these were of a relatively sober and formal character.
Not until the sixth century B. C. do we hear of more
violent and primitive mysteries in Greece, and then they
are associated with the name of Orpheus. They were
imported largely from Thrace, where they had long been
indulged in by barbaric tribes; and the faith-hungry
Greeks took to them with avidity. For one thing, there
was the element of dread secrecy about these strange
mysteries—and secrecy has always been enormously attractive to inferior minds. Only those who were solemnly initiated into the cult could have any knowledge
of its secrets, or enjoy the immortal bliss which that
knowledge was supposed to confer. All others were
condemned to writhe forever in a foul, loathsome
hell. . . .

These Orphic mysteries therefore flourished luxuri-
antly, as did the many other mysteries that later invaded
Greece. When the cults of the Egyptian Osiris and of
the Phrygian Attis were introduced, they too won initiates by the thousand. It was inevitable that they
should do so, for the lure they held out was irresistible
to the people. Before the eyes of a mob of low-caste

peasants and slum-dwelling slaves they dangled a high promise, a glittering hope. They offered divinity, immortality, paradise, and all at the price of orgies which seemed in themselves a delirious delight. How then could they possibly be resisted? . . .

And the vogue of those irresistible mysteries brought the ancient religion of ancient Greece to an end. Only the mysteries survived, increasing in complexity generation after generation, and spreading throughout all the lands bordering the Mediterranean. Even after Christianity came they still flourished. Indeed they almost made Christianity itself another mystery.

But that is another story. . . .

V. THE ROMANS

THE religious history of Rome was in many respects strikingly like that of Greece. It began, of course, in the universal primitive belief that all objects are animated by resident or roving spirits. But the chief of these spirits were of a peculiar type in Rome, being not tribal but family deities. That was because the early Romans were a farming folk divided not into large units like tribes, but into small families. Naturally enough, the primal aim of the religion was the perpetuation of these small families; and the principal spirits, therefore, were those which guarded the home. Each man was believed to have what was called a Genius, a spirit personifying his virility; and each woman had what was called a Juno, a spirit personifying her power to conceive. (The early Romans, like most other primitive peoples, were driven by their constant struggle against extinction to consider the power of reproduction a miraculous and highly divine thing.)   The threshold of every house had its guardian spirit called Janus, just as the hearth had its Vesta, the storeroom had its Penates, and the farm had its Lares.

The favor of these spirits was courted with simple ceremonies on fixed holy days, each family having its own altar on its own land, and its own priest in the person of the *pater familias,* the father of the family. Some of the spirits were also worshipped with minor rites observed in everyday life.   For instance, after every midday meal a sort of "grace" was offered to Vesta by throwing a salt cake into the hearth-fire.

But this simple family cult had to give way in time to a less primitive form of religion.   Harried by continual attacks of enemy tribes, the little family groups were forced to consolidate into the city-state of Rome; and then a state religion arose.   It centered chiefly around a god of war who was called Mars (it was just like the Romans to make a god of war their chief deity), and included the worship also of other gods, especially a sky-god, Jupiter, the Roman version of the Greek Zeus-pater.   The king of the city-state was the high-priest of this newer Roman religion, and numerous minor priests aided him at the state altars.   But there was no great fervor in the cult, for it was far more a political than a religious institution.   It was a formal, civic affair, and though many festivals were listed in its elaborate calendar, no demands were made on the people to take a passionate part in them.   Most of those festivals must have antedated the state religion, for they were marked by magic rites of evident primitiveness.   There was, for instance, the Lupercalia, a festival at which the worshippers smeared themselves with sacrificial blood from a dog or goat, sponged themselves with milk-soaked wads of wool, clad themselves in goat-skins, and then danced through the streets of the city, striking the women they met with bits of skin to make them fertile. . . . Then there was the Saturnalia, celebrated on the 25th of December, the signal for more wild dancing, and especially for giving gifts and lighting many candles. . . .

But the old family religion still persisted, despite the institution of this state cult. The worship of the hearth spirits still went on, and still a great concern was felt about evil ghosts and demons. For protection, fire-brands used to be tied to the tails of foxes, who were then let loose in the fields to frighten away the crop-devouring demons. For further protection, men and cattle were passed through fire so that they might be magically purified. Taboos of a thousand varieties to ward off as many sorts of danger were scrupulously observed in every house in the growing town. The religion of the city-state of Rome was only *supposed* to be the new state cult; *actually* the people still clung to the family cult of earlier days. . . .

A distinct change did occur, however, about the sixth century B. C. It came as an after-effect of the invasion of the Etruscans, a race with apparently higher capacities for civilization than the original Romans. They took over the state religion and made it a thing of far greater importance than ever it had been before. New gods were introduced: Minerva, Diana, and others. A college of priests was founded, and the priesthood was organized under a chief who was called Pontifex Maximus. For the first time in the history of Rome temples were built, and images of the gods were placed in them and worshipped.

But even then the state religion remained in large part a formal affair. It had too little emotional drive, too slight a relation to fear and hope, ever to be able to enter deep into the life of the people. The priests were more or less civic officials who were left to attend to the gods much as in constitutional monarchies the chamberlains are left to attend to the kings. The gods demanded that the vows the people made to them should be most scrupulously observed; but they insisted on very little else. They were not immoral or venal, like the gods of the Olympian religion, but neither were they puritanically moral or tyrannically strict, like, for instance, the God of the Hebrews. They seemed to be quite content with purely formal obeisance. . . .

2

OF course, such a religion, clean but not very exciting, proper but not very compelling, could not persist for long. Between 500 and 200 B. C. it deteriorated and sank into almost complete bankruptcy. The whole structure rotted away from corruption, and finally toppled to the ground. And with it toppled the family religion. Rome by that time had become a vast empire: rich, mighty, and not a little dissolute. Roman citizens had gone forth as soldiers or traders to the farthest ends of the known world, and had come back spoiled. The old Roman family, which had been so important a factor of social health in the early life of the people, fell into decay; and with it the old family gods went into the limbo. The priests became grafting politicians, and their training colleges mere political clubs.   And then the old order ended.

But as fast as the old gods fell away, new gods arose. For the most part they were the savior-gods of the Orient, those lusty relics of the savage past which were immortal in more than myth.   The Roman legions had gone out to conquer all the world, only to come back conquered by all its gods.   The mysteries that had spread like a plague throughout Greece in the days of its decay now found similar soil in which to flourish in Rome. As early as 200 B. C. the cult of Cybele, "the Great Mother of the Gods," was brought to the city.   Imported from Asia Minor, where it may have developed out of the old Babylonian worship of Ishtar, this mystery found its chief sanctuary on the Vatican Hill—almost on the precise spot where the basilica of St. Peters now stands.   There, and wherever else in the empire the cult had a following, spring festivals of almost incredible bestiality were held.   The people gathered around altars erected under sacred trees, and amid the thundering of drums, the screeching of flutes, and the clashing of cymbals, they wildly sought salvation of their goddess. First the lower priests, excited by the barbaric music, would begin to whirl themselves around convulsively. With mad eyes and streaming hair they would whirl themselves around until, rapt in a frenzy and insensible to pain, they would begin to hack at their own flesh— hack and slash at their own bodies until both altar and tree were red with their spurting blood.   And then the spectators, caught up and swept out of their minds by the tumult, would suddenly join in the dance.   A mad light would leap into their eyes at the sight of the blood and the sound of the throbbing music; jaws would open wide in their waggling heads, and limbs would swing out flail-like to the beat-beat of drums and cymbals. And then first one, then another, would suddenly tear off all his clothes, and with a manic shout would seize a sword from the heap ready at hand. Howling with ecstasy he would hack at himself until, exhausted at last, he fell and lay bleeding in a ditch.

Of course, such self-mutilation was not the ordinary act of devotion in the cult of Cybele. Only those of the extremest faith, those who desired to become actual priests of the goddess, ever went to such excesses. But even the common followers, the ordinary first-degree initiates, went through rites which were more than adequately gruesome. There was, for example, the rite called the Tauroboleum. The candidate was placed in a pit and then washed in the blood of a bull slaughtered over his head. He had to lave himself in the warm blood as it came dripping through the crevices between the planks covering the pit; he had to crane up avidly and receive it on his face, in his ears, his eyes, even his mouth. And thus he was initiated into the mystery. . . . Madness? No, merely logic gone wild because based on a wild hypothesis. The first axiom of primitive magic held that any quality could be acquired merely by consuming the proper part of a creature already possessing that quality. For instance, a man could take on his enemy's strength merely by eating his enemy's liver; he could acquire his father's cunning simply by consuming his father's eyes. So to acquire his god's immortality it seemed only necessary to quaff that god's blood—a feat not at all impossible because the god was usually imagined to be incarnate in some sacred human being or animal. Such was the logic, false but plausible, which led to blood-guzzlings like those in the cult of Cybele. Such was the reasoning, cracked but intensely human, which led men in Rome to seek salvation through the Tauroboleum.

Closely associated with this orgiastic worship of Cybele there was also the worship of her lover, Attis. This god Attis was believed to have been conceived immaculately in the womb of a virgin, and was said to have died of self-immolation at the base of a tree. Attis was of course but another version of Tammuz, Adonis, Dionysus, Orpheus, and Osiris, a god of vegetation who died and was reborn every year. His "passion" was enacted every spring in Rome, much as the "passion" of Osiris was enacted annually in Egypt. The festival began with a "day of blood"—the pagan Black Friday —commemorating the death of the young god; and *after three days* it reached a climax in the "day of joy," commemorating the god's resurrection. . . . But Attis was by no means the only one of the savior-gods to be imported into Rome. The Greek Dionysus, renamed Bacchus by the Latins, also had his myriads of followers, as did the Egyptian Osiris. Nor was Cybele the only mother-goddess, for many of the Romans preferred to worship Isis, or Ma, or Bellona, or some other of those whoring fertility-spirits common in all of the Orient. Indeed, it is quite impossible to give a definitive account of all the mystery gods and goddesses whose cults were permitted to flourish in imperial Rome.

3

OF course, none of these mysteries could make any great appeal to the learned among the Romans. The higher classes in the republic were forced to drift along without any faith whatsoever. The old state religion had long lost its power to hold them, and they looked on the ancient gods of Rome as either patent frauds or mere figures of speech. Among the higher classes even as much as among the lower, the old state religion seemed as dead as a carcass three days old. . . . But it was not. A spark of life still lingered in it, and in time there came a man with the will and power to breathe it into flame again. That man was Augustus, one of the outstanding figures in Roman history. In the year 31 B. C. he took hold of a republic in a state of advanced corruption, and by intrigue and shrewdness converted it into a sound and flourishing empire. It was solely in order to make that empire firm that he set himself the task of reviving the old religion. He could not possibly use the alien mysteries to attain that end, for those mysteries were in their very nature a divisive and not a cohesive force. They addressed themselves primarily to the individual, not to the group; they promised individual, not social, salvation. Besides, they had little concern with this world and its upstart empires. They were concerned only with the other world and its eternal joys. So Augustus saw no reason to favor the mysteries. On the contrary, he sought to drive them out of existence by lending all his power and prestige to the moribund state religion. He built great temples everywhere, equipping them with beautiful idols of the old gods.

He thoroughly reorganized the priesthood, making
himself its head. Then he went further—a long, long
way further. He realized that, though there were
already many gods, each with his own following in
the empire, there was no imperial God to whom all
might pay homage. So to supply the need he nominated
himself! By a decree of his own as Emperor, he made
himself the Deity Supreme! He commanded that the
guardian spirit of his own person, his "Genius," be worshipped in every city throughout the empire; and poets
and writers were hired to invent legends telling how he,
Augustus, had been originally fashioned in heaven and
miraculously brought to the world to save it. And
as long as he lived, this religion he built around himself
flourished everywhere in the empire—everywhere save,
of course, in Palestine, where dwelt the Jews.

But even the revival under Augustus could not stay
the debacle of the old religion. On the contrary, it may
perhaps have hastened it. It but opened the way for
one more corroding element: the human gods. Suc-
ceeding emperors emulated Augustus, deifying themselves, and sometimes also their wives, their mistresses,
even their lewd boy-companions. In time there were
almost forty names on the roster of these monstrous
gods! . . . And meanwhile more and more of the gods
of the East came pouring into the imperial city. . . .

There seemed to be but one sane element left, the
Cynics. The word cynic—with a small "c"—now con-
notes a disillusioned, sneering, hopeless individual; but
in the days when its initial letter was capitalized the
word connoted an altogether different sort of man. The
Cynics of that time were preaching philosophers, exalted

souls who felt themselves called upon to drag the people out of the sinkholes of superstition in which they floundered. These Cynics stood on the corners of the market-place, or on temple steps, and harangued the people to abjure the wild existences they were leading and go back to the simple, natural life. They assured them there was but one way of Salvation: common sense. They summoned the people to be brave and wise; to be virtuous; above all, to be calm and exercise good horse sense! . . .

4

BUT, despite all their devotion and eagerness, it was impossible for those Cynics to work any profound change in their fellow-men. The people could not be satisfied with the little joys afforded by common sense. They were tired, exhausted. Their forbears had wandered off to all the ends of the earth, traversing seas and mountains and deserts and swamps, invading, besieging, despoiling, and laying waste. For centuries on end they had been running to and fro across the face of the globe. And now the stock was run out. Their decadent offspring were in no mood for calm common sense; they had no appetite for staid virtue. They wanted passion, excitement! . . . And so now even more than before they took to the mysteries. It is true that the cults of Cybele, Isis, and Bacchus began to wane a little in their popularity; but that was only because a new cult had come to take their places. It was the cult of Mithras, imported from Persia, where it had arisen out of those primitive elements which the prophet Zoroaster had failed to stamp out. It had spread since from one land to another, from Persia to Babylonia, from Babylonia to the Ionian Isles, and from the Ionian Isles finally to Rome. It entered there about the first century B. C., and so ready were the Romans to receive it that soon it was almost dominant in the empire.

The root of the mystery was an ancient Persian legend which told of a divine hero named Mithras whose miraculous birth had been witnessed only by a few shepherds come from afar with gifts to adore the wonder-child. Mithras grew up to be the most strenuous champion of the sun-god in his war against the god of darkness, and the climax of his career was a life-and-death struggle with a mythical sacred bull. By finally slaying this bull and letting its blood flood the earth, Mithras gave life to the soil, and earned immortality for himself. Straightway he was exalted to the abode of the Immortals, and there he dwelt as the divine protector of all the faithful on earth. . . .

Long before the advent of Christianity we find a significant religion and an elaborate ritual crystallizing around that legend of Mithras. To this day there exist along the Danube and in Northern Africa certain subterranean caves in which are statues and carvings depicting scenes in the tale. Those caves were the secret churches of the Mithraists, and in them all manner of magic rites were once performed. Three times a day, with especial elaborateness on the Sun-day and the twenty-fifth of December, the Mithras priests offered services in the caves. Libations were poured, bells were rung, hymns were chanted, and many candles were burnt. Above all, holy sacraments were administered to the initiated. The flesh of a sacrificial animal was eaten, and its blood was drunk, and thus the celebrants were thought to take on the divinity and immortality of their blessed lord, Mithras. By a primitive process of reasoning which we have already described in connection with the Cybele cult, the Mithraists galloped to the comforting conclusion that the mere consumption of the supposed flesh and blood of the god assured them of life everlasting. When they died on this earth they expected to ascend to Heaven through seven gates, unlocked by seven keys which the Mithras priests possessed, and in Heaven they hoped to dwell with Mithras until the final Judgment Day. All the unbaptized, both living and dead, were to be totally annihilated on that Judgment Day. Only the redeemed were to be saved, and Mithras, come to earth a second and final time, would administer to each of them a last sacrament, and then cause them to inherit the world in peace and blessedness forevermore. . . .

Such in brief was the theology and ritual of Mithraism. It was in all respects a purer mystery than those that had proceeded it. It had a distinct ethical content, and showed little tendency to encourage riotous and orgiastic practices. As a result it showed promise of persisting far longer than the other cults. Though equally fervent, it was less hysterical than its rivals; though just as certain of its validity, it was far less given to emotional excess. By the first century A. D. it loomed up as the foremost religion in the Empire; by the second century it seemed destined to become the lasting religion of all the Western world. And perhaps it would have actually fulfilled that destiny—had it not been for Christianity. . . .

But again, that is another story. . . .

5

AND with Mithraism in Rome we close this book of
the religions of the ancient world.   There were other
religions that had their beginnings in that ancient world;
but we shall have to tell of them later, for unlike the
ones already described, they lived on.   Neither the
decay of civilizations nor debacle of empires could destroy those other religions.   Again and again they were
rent and broken; again and again they were well-nigh
wiped out.   Century after century they were changed
almost beyond recognition.   But nevertheless they lived
on.   And that is why we have to leave their stories to
be told separately and at greater length. . . .

As for these religions whereof we have already
spoken—they died.   They did not entirely disappear,
of course.   No, fragments of them survived.   Isolated
rites, festive days, theological notions, even some of
their god-names, persisted.   They took up their abode
—albeit furtively, clandestinely—in the religions that
endured.   And there they persist to this day. . . . For
that reason one cannot well refer to those cults of Babylon, Egypt, and the rest as the "dead religions."   Actually they are not dead at all, for the echo of their
ancient thunder is still to be heard reverberating in
almost every form of faith existing today.   They are
dead only in name. . . .

But that is not their only, nor their most urgent,
claim on our attention.   Those ancient cults would
deserve to be studied even if not one of their rites or
myths still survived in the world.   For the development
of those cults marked the development of an entirely
novel idea in religion.   Until the advent of the Osirian

and the other mysteries, the whole aim of religion was the wresting of *terrestrial* favors from the gods.   Primitive man uttered spells and offered oblations solely because he desired to make his life *here on earth* less fearful and insecure.   But when man advanced beyond the primitive, and for the first time paused to consider just what chances he really had of satisfying his desire, he slowly began to realize how naive and foolish he had been.   And then despair overwhelmed him.   Like a day-dreaming boy suddenly brought face to face with the harsh, sharp, exigent realities of life, his heart sank and he stood ready to give up the fight.   It was hopeless, he told himself.   This world was irredeemable and this life utterly vain.   There was no chance, not the slightest, of ever attaining peace and security here on earth.   All the spells and prayers and sacrifices imaginable could be of no worth in this vale of tears. . . .

But still he could not surrender utterly.   The hunger for self-preservation was still mighty in the bones of man, and he could not possibly lie down and let himself be annihilated.   No, instead he was forced to fly back to his old illusions, assuring himself that despite all realities he still could attain peace and joy.   Only now man began to look for those blessings not in this life but in some other.   Bowing to what seemed the insuperable tyrannies governing the natural world, he now comforted himself with the tale that his triumph must come in a *super*-natural world.   With that inevasible life-lust which is at once the sorriest vice and the mightiest virtue of mankind, our ancestor incontinently transferred all his hopes from a tangible earth to a hypothetical heaven! . . .

The social effect of that great religious change can hardly be overestimated. For one thing, it made it possible for the few to exploit the many with unprecedented ease and impunity. So long as the credulous masses were content to look to some other world for their triumph, the crafty few were safe to enjoy their triumph in *this* one. So long as the meek were concerned only over their treasures in heaven, the strong were left free to steal all the treasures of the earth. And to such an egregious degree has this other-world hope fattened the crafty at the expense of the simple during these last two thousand years, that nowadays there are some who maintain it was from the very first simply a stratagem devised by the crafty to attain that very end. Of course, such a theory cannot be taken seriously. It is obviously pure romance to imagine so human a hope to have been deliberately foisted on humanity by a handful of greedy priests or princes. Undoubtedly such men did take all possible advantage of the hope—once it had come into being. But that was all. They no more created that belief in another world than they created the belief in ghosts or gods. The poor man's dream of heaven was but one more of those wild clutches after security which make up the whole spiritual history of the race. And it was as unpremeditated, as thoroughly natural and inevitable, as the thirsty bedouin's sight of a mirage. . . .

But all that is a matter of secondary importance. Our main concern is the nature, not the origin or even the effect, of this other-world hope. Quite clearly it differed in kind, not merely in degree, from the more primitive hope confined to *this* world. Perhaps it was even due to a different impulse. The Celt was driven to religion by fear; but the "civilized" Greek and Roman was moved rather by despair. The former wanted to know merely *how* to keep alive on earth; but the latter desired rather to know the answer to the question *why*. Even the exploited pleb sweating in the slums of Rome was advanced enough to wonder what it was all about. Why was he here on earth? Where was he going? What did it all mean anyway? . . .

And therein lies the one truly fundamental advance marking the development of religion in the ancient world. The whole impulse to believe took on a changed character. Men were no longer driven to the gods by the common animal hunger for self-*preservation*; they were moved rather by the high human yearning for self-*pacification*.

And that was no slight advance. . . .

BOOK THREE
WHAT HAPPENED
IN INDIA

BOOK THREE

WHAT HAPPENED IN INDIA

I. BRAHMANISM

1: The primitive Aryan gods—the Vedas. 2: The Aryans move to the Ganges—caste—the brahmins. 3: The Upanishads —the Over-Soul—transmigration—Nirvana—the growth of asceticism.

II. JAINISM

1: Mahavira—his gospel. 2: How the gospel of Mahavira was corrupted—Jainism today.

III. BUDDHISM

1: The story of Gautama. 2: His gospel—its implications— the Law of Karma. 3: How Gautama spread his gospel. 4: Early history of Buddhism—deification of Buddha—Asoka— the new Buddhism in China—Tibet—Japan—India—Ceylon.

IV. HINDUISM

1: The dominant religion in India today—caste—the trinity— the divisiveness in Hinduism. 2: Vishnu—the avatars—the Bhagavad-Gita—Krishna—theology in Vishnuism. 3: Shiva— his popularity—the Tantra—sex in religion. 4: Hindu philosophy—yoga—the mystic ecstasy. 5: The religion of the lower classes.

118

BOOK THREE

WHAT HAPPENED IN INDIA

I. BRAHMANISM

NO ONE can say for certain, but it seems probable that before the first white man entered India, the land was populated entirely by a snub-nosed, black-skinned people. By what means those black savages tried to cope with the universe, by what illusions they tried to make their life livable, no one knows. Nor does anyone know, save very vaguely, the nature of India's religion even during the first centuries after the coming of the white man. The first white invaders of India belonged to what is loosely termed the Aryan race: the stock that also produced the Persians, the Greeks, the Romans, the Celts, and most of the other peoples of Europe. About four or five thousand years ago they broke through the passes of the Hindu Kush Mountains, and then settled down in the fertile valley of the Indus. They were warriors and shepherds, a crude, simple folk who seemed to be only slightly less uncivilized than were the black men whom they drove before them. Their religion was a low fear of many spirits, among them being "three and thirty

119

gods" who were worshipped with oblations of beer—
soma it was called—on a spread of straw. It was,
therefore, an advanced form of animism, a nature-wor-
ship in which the more important spirits were no longer
thought to animate mere sticks or stones but rather vast
phenomena such as the sun and the sky.

The most important of these spirits was one called
Indra, usually pictured as a boasting, gluttonous,
drunken brawler controlling the wind and the rain.
Besides him there were several other deities who had
most seriously to be reckoned with: Dyaush Pitar (related to Zeus Pater and Jupiter), who was the sky-god;
Asura, the "Wise Spirit of Heaven"; Agni, the god of
fire (the Sanskrit name is related to our English word
"ignite") ; Mithra, a sun-god (the remote ancestor, of
course, of the Roman mystery-god Mithras) ; Soma,
the principle of intoxication become a god; and various
others.

Certain of these gods the Aryan invaders must have
brought with them from the unknown cradle-land
whence they had come; others quite clearly must have
been developed in the new home. Most of them, however, must have been worshipped only by single tribes,
for so soon as the tribes began to merge, many of those
gods disappeared. From early times there seems to
have been a steady drift in Aryan India toward a syn-
thesis, an amalgamation of the gods.

In the beginning the means by which the Aryans
courted the favor of these gods was exceedingly simple.
The father of each family was the priest, and the mother
was the priestess. There were no temples, and indeed
no permanent holy places of any kind. . . . But what

happened in the rest of the world soon happened also
in India.   In the hope of cajoling the gods more effectively, the ritual was gradually elaborated.   Then professional sacrificers arose—priests whose services at the
altar were imagined to be somehow more efficacious
than the services of ordinary men.   And by these priests
the ritual was elaborated and complicated still further.
They created a vast literature of psalms and magic spells
to recite at the altars in order to get a firmer hold on
the gods—a literature still preserved in what are called
the Vedas.   The word *veda* is related to the English
word "wit," and the German word "wissen."   Broadly
interpreted it means "knowledge," but refers specifically
to that sort of knowledge which will aid a man to win
the protection of the gods.   There are more than a
hundred books in existence which are called Vedas, but
many of them are little known even to the most erudite
scholars today.   Of them all the oldest and most important is called the Rig Veda, a collection of over a thousand hymns which date back perhaps as far as 2000 B. C.

2

THIS Vedic literature—or much of it, at least—was
developed while the Aryan population was still confined to the valley of the Indus.   Many years passed in
that fertile region before overcrowding forced the white
men to penetrate further into the land; but then a heavy
migration began southward toward the valley of the
Ganges.   There it halted for a while, and there a new
civilization arose.   The life of the Aryan took on an
entirely new character in this changed environment.
For one thing the distinctions between the various classes

of human beings had to be emphasized as never before. The white invaders grew terrified lest in time the identity of their stock might be lost in the welter of the far larger black population. It was the ancient hunger for self-preservation manifesting itself once more, the old, old hunger for continued life for the race as well as the individual. And to satisfy that hunger the Aryans resorted to the most desperate expedient imaginable. They raised up a towering religious and social barrier of caste to protect themselves from the blacks. (In Sanskrit the one word *varnu* means both caste and color.) And across that barrier they forbade not merely intermarriage, but also every form of social and religious intercourse. White was white and black was black, and ne'er the twain were supposed to meet. . . .

Of course, the expedient failed to accomplish its purpose, as we can see from the fact that all Hindus today, high-caste as well as low, are black. But though it failed utterly in that direction, it proved all too successful in another. Though it could not keep whites physically separated from blacks, it was soon all too effective in keeping whites socially separated from each other. For once the idea of caste took root in the land, it began to spread like a veritable plague. Soon it began to distinguish not merely between whites and blacks, but also between white priests and white chieftains, and then between white chieftains and white farmers, and finally between white farmers and white serfs. It was natural. of course, for the priests—the brahmins they were called —to emerge at the very top of this monstrous social system. As long as they alone were deemed able to placate and cajole the gods, so long were they alone able to command the highest respect of men. Even the rajahs, the princes, had to rank below them. . . .

With great power there came as a matter of course the opportunity of acquiring great wealth. Riches literally flooded into the coffers of the brahmins. From every sacrifice to the gods the priests were permitted to take no mean portion for themselves; and besides they did not scruple to accompany even their most poetic prayers and loftiest adorations with open bids for extra "bakhsheesh." . . . And with great wealth came the opportunity of acquiring still greater power. In time the priests, not content with their supremacy over men, began to covet supremacy over the very gods. And they actually managed to achieve it, too! They began by exalting the importance of the ritual, saying: "The whole world was created by the sacrificial rite; from the sacrificial rite the very gods are sprung. . . . Assuredly the sun would not rise if the priest did not make sacrifice." And from that they went to exalting themselves, saying: "The whole universe is subject to the gods, the gods to the spells, and the spells to the brahmins; therefore the brahmins are our gods!" They came to look upon the gods almost with disdain, and treated them like so many hungry tramps. "As the ox bellows for the rain," they presumptuously declared in their holy writ, "so yearns Indra for soma." . . . It was a development which had mounted so outrageously high that it had toppled over into absurdity.

Of course, such a religion could not hold sway forever. The masses, finding the protection afforded by the brahmin gods to be prohibitively costly, began to bargain instead for the much cheaper protection of unorthodox demons. Out of the depths of their ancient savage heritage, or from the slime of the black native animism around them, they dragged up scores of fell spirits to dread or cling to. . . . And in time the priests, too, began to question the sincerity of their over-ritualized religion. In the same Brahmanas, the "Priestlies," in which the clerics dared to assert their claims as the lords of the religion, they also had to betray their lurking doubts as to the validity of the whole religion itself. Of course, they did not dare confess those doubts openly, for that would have cut the ground from beneath their own feet. It would have put an end to their inordinate power by destroying the whole system which gave it to them. So, as always happens when men no longer believe but cannot afford openly to disbelieve, the brahmins tried to ease their consciences by developing an apologetic theology. With suspicious anxiety they tried to strip the ritual ceremonies of their obvious absurdity by interpreting them as beautiful symbols and allegories. Theology very frequently is no more than an effort to prolong the life of moribund ideas by reinterpreting words which no longer mean what they used to say— and when theology is that, it is invariably a confession of secret distrust and skepticism. Quite obviously whole sections of the Brahmanas were intended to be stout ropes of ingenious rationalism by which the priests might save themselves from drowning in doubt.

But despite the stoutness of those ropes, and the craft with which they were plaited, they nevertheless failed to be of much avail. The priests went down. Down, down they went in the dark and muddy waters of doubt and dismay. With frozen fingers they still held on to

the ropes, tugging at them again and again in vain effort
to stay their sinking.   But down they went nevertheless, down, down until at last their feet touched bottom
in the ooze of blackest pessimism. . . .

3

PERHAPS the physical conditions of life at the time
had a share in this drowning of Vedic hopefulness.
Things had profoundly changed since the old days in
the valley of the Indus when the Vedas had been
created.   The Aryans by now had become Hindus.
Despite all the thickness of the wall of caste, the black
blood of the aborigines had seeped into the veins of the
white men.   And synchronously with this coloring of
the skin, the evil climate of the Ganges Valley had in-
duced a darkening of the soul.   A new spirit, a sepul-
chral spirit of hopelessness, took possession of the erstwhile white men.   It found its expression in a new
literature, a vast collection of philosophic tractates
called the Upanishads, the "Séances."   It is difficult to
say just when the Upanishads were written, but according to the best authorities it was probably during the
two centuries stretching from about 800 B. C. to about
600 B. C.   Their burden was an entirely new understanding of man's chance of ever attaining rest in the
universe.   In the first place, they threw all the old gods
and the old rites overboard, frankly confessing that they
were quite without essential reality.   Only one thing,
they insisted, was real: the Brahma, the "Self," the One
Absolute, Infinite, Impersonal, Indescribable "It."   And
all deeds and words, all creatures, even all gods, were
but fleeting manifestations of this "It."   As a logical

consequence, therefore, there existed but one way by which man could ever attain ultimate peace. Obviously he had to lose himself in the "It." He had to cease being just a mere manifestation, and become at last an integral part of Brahma.

Now all that was by no means unique. Many peoples other than the Hindus have at one time or another taken refuge in the thought that this world is but an illusion, and that salvation can be obtained only on some other plane of existence. But no other people ever carried that thought to so rigorous a length as did the Hindus. Most other folk halted with the hope that death would immediately open the door to salvation. They told themselves that, though life in this world was unutterably vain, death was approaching, and with it the assurance of real life in some other and more glorious world. But the Hindus could not cherish so easy a hope. Death seemed to them anything but a way out. In the dread valley of the Ganges, where existence meant perpetual struggle beneath a sun that seared one's flesh and in an air that strangled one's courage, even death did not hold out any immediate promise of peace. The fell idea of transmigration, of a weary round of endless life, had taken hold of the Hindus. Death seemed to them but the beginning of more of this same old torment which is earthly life. The souls of the dead might escape for a little while to the moon; but just as soon as the influence of their good deeds was exhausted, back they sank to the earth like so many spent balloons. And then they were reborn as persons or animals or even plants. If their preceding life had been extraordinarily good, on their return they became perhaps as much as princes or even

brahmins; but if they had done evil, then they returned
to live as dogs or pigs or even slimy weeds at the edge
of swamps.

There seemed to be but one effectual way of escape
from that terrible cycle of unending life, and that was by
absorption into the "It." If only a man could annihilate his individual self, could utterly destroy his little
"it," then at last could he be free of life and attain the
release called Nirvana. Nirvana was not a place but a
state of mind, and therefore it could be attained only by
means of the mind. Mere acts, good or bad, could not
help in the least; nor could even the very gods be of
assistance. As the Upanishads explicitly declare:
"Whoever thus knows 'I am the Brahma!' becomes the
Brahma. Even the gods have no power to hold such a
man from becoming thus, for he becomes their very
Soul." Therefore mere striving after moral perfection
or even after ritual propriety could never win for man
the blessedness of Nirvana; no, only the total abolition
of striving itself could do it. For striving, desiring—
that was the very source of all illusory life. To desire,
to want, to cherish even the least flicker of a petty wish—
that was the vicious stuff whereof the ever-reincarnating
self was made. Without desire the individual "it"
would be lost, and only the Brahma, the Over-Soul, the
One Universal "It" would be left. So logically there
was but one sane purpose left in life: to cease desiring! . . .

One wonders if this nihilistic philosophy of the Upanishads greatly influenced the life of the masses in India
twenty-six hundred years ago. Probably it did not, for
it must have been far beyond the comprehension of those

MEN FLED TO THE JUNGLES

masses. But that it profoundly affected the learned is quite beyond doubt. The desire to end desire simply ravished the higher classes in that day. Asceticism, the voluntary slaying of appetite in all its forms, became rife in every temple and princely court. Men fled away into the mountains and far into the jungles, there to live as anchorites and strangle every last vestige of normal desire. In incredible misery they dragged out their days, hungry but for one thing—the extinction of hunger.

And then came the heresies. . . .

II. JAINISM

IT was inevitable that heresies should arise, once asceticism began to spread in old India. It may be laid down as an axiom that a man who does not live the life of the mob will not think its thoughts either. He cannot but become unorthodox in spirit as well as conduct, looking out on life from an angle of his own, and drawing his own conclusions. Therefore it was but natural for the advent of asceticism in India to be accompanied by the advent of heterodoxy. In the sixth century B. C., India literally swarmed with heresies. Sects arose in a night and perished in a night; prophets were hailed and forgotten between the phases of a moon. Indeed, only two of all the movements initiated in that century endured long enough even for their names to be remembered. But those two endured well—passing well. . . .

The less important of those two was the sect now known as Jainism. Its founder was a young prince named Mahavira, a man who lived until the age of thirty the riotous life of an Indian rajah, and then of a sudden turned ascetic. "I shall for twelve years neglect my body," he vowed; and, casting off his fine clothes, plucking out his hair in five handfuls, he went off into the jungles. And after those twelve years of self-denial had passed, he reached Nirvana. From then on he was called the Jina, the "Conqueror," for of all men he seemed the most thoroughly to have conquered every last form of human desire. And abandoning his solitude thenceforth, he began to go up and down the Ganges Valley to tell his fellow-men just how he had attained salvation.

Now Mahavira was certain that he had become the Jina, the "Conqueror," without the help either of the gods or the brahmins. He did not believe in the gods, and he scoffed at the very idea of prayer. "Man! Thou art thine own friend!" he cried. "Why shouldst thou crave a friend beyond thyself?" He derided the Vedas and decried the entire caste system. All he believed in was the willful annihilation of the self, the rigorous and unsparing destruction of every desire save the desire for no-desire. He demanded of his disciples that they do injury to no living thing, that they remain ever poor and ever meek. "Dish-water, barley-pap, cold sour gruel, water in which barley has been washed: such loathsome food the mendicants should never despise." He forbade his followers to hate, and he also forbade them to love, for Mahavira considered the one as earth-binding as the other. And especially did he warn them against showing any favor to women. It is a pity we know so little that is authentic concerning the life of Mahavira, or we might be able to discover just what it was that made him so bitter a misogynist. Lust must naturally have been a frightful thorn in his spoiled princely flesh, and perhaps that was why he so unjustly branded woman as the cause of all sinful acts. He commanded the true follower not to "speak of women, nor look at them, nor converse with them, nor claim them as his own, nor do their work."

But above all he forbade his monks to kill. "This," said Mahavira, "is the quintessence of wisdom: not to kill anything!" And of all the prohibitions, this was the one most scrupulously observed. Solicitude against destroying life—and life was thought to be not merely in man but also in animals, plants, even grains of dust— drove the followers of Mahavira to the most grotesque of excesses. Some of them sat immobile for years, refusing to stir a limb or even breathe deeply, lest thereby they destroy aught of those small insects with which the air of India swarms. They refused to wash their teeth, or cleanse their clothes, or scratch their bodies when the vermin nipped them. To this day they maintain hospitals for animals, caring even for sick snakes and rats and even lice! . . . Only one form of destruction was permitted: self-destruction. As death approached, the holy Jain might make his one last effort to sunder the chain of transmigration by bravely crushing all desire for sustenance and starving himself to death! Then at last he was free. . . .

2

MAHAVIRA, the founder of Jainism, was born in 599 B. C. and died in 529. According to tradition he preached untiringly during all the last thirty years of his life, and when he died he left many disciples to carry on his work. But those disciples were smaller men than the Jina, and at their hands his gospel came in for profound and sorry perversion. In the first place the personality of the Jina was exalted until he was made out to be almost a god. Legends sprang up around his name, fantastic stories recounting the miracles attendant on his birth and death. And before many generations had passed he actually *was* declared to be a veritable god! That gentle, quiet anchorite who had given more than half his life to preaching the worthlessness of gods and the futility of prayers was himself deified and prayed to. By the year 400 the Jains were already setting up idols of Mahavira, and building beautiful temples in which they burnt regular offerings of flowers and incense. Then, not satisfied with one god, the Jains created twenty-four other Jinas to adore. They said that Mahavira was only the last and greatest of a long line of divine "Conquerors," and they surrounded his image with images of all the twenty-four others. Even then they were not satisfied, for later they added many female divinities to the pantheon. Century after century the people took up new gods and spirits to worship and cling to, until finally Jainism became almost as crudely polytheistic as the old Vedic religion it had once set out to reform. The brave atheistic spirit in which Jainism had been conceived seeped out of it entirely, and the highest heresy preached by Mahavira was the one most flagrantly betrayed.

Of course, that was all but inevitable. Once Jainism began to spread among the plain people, its first principles simply had no chance of surviving. Mahavira had preached a gospel utterly beyond the comprehen-

sion of ordinary men. He himself had been one of those
mighty souls for whom the consciousness merely of
living the right life was enough. He had not needed
gods to cling to. Right Faith, Right Knowledge, and
Right Living—called by him the "Three Jewels"—had
by themselves been enough to win him salvation. . . .
But those who came after him were weaker men. In
their blind eyes the Three Jewels seemed worthless without a setting in a tinsel plate of theology. Those followers were not courageous enough to stake all on their
own strength of will. They simply *had* to have gods
to aid them. . . .

But that was not the only issue in Mahavira's gospel
which his followers surrendered. Mahavira had revolted
against the whole caste system, declaring that all men,
low-caste as well as high, were equals once they entered
the *Sangha*, the "Congregation." But as soon as he
died, that heresy died too, and before long even the
very gods were divided into distinct social classes. Only
the commandment against killing was not openly betrayed; but as we have already seen its observance was
carried to the absurdest extremes. Save for that, Jainism became hardly distinguishable from orthodox
Hinduism. The religion took unto itself gods, idols,
temples, priests, sacrifices—every one of the old means
of salvation which Mahavira had most scornfully re-
jected. . . . But what else was to be expected? After
all, the common folk in India—like the common folk
everywhere else in the world—were (and are) still too
weak to look to their own selves for salvation. They
needed reeds to cling to, gods to believe in. For they
were (and are) afraid . . . afraid. . . .

III. BUDDHISM

BUT Jainism was only the less important of the two great heretical religions that arose in India in the sixth century B. C. When Mahavira was already almost forty years of age, there was born in India a male child destined to found the far greater religion of Buddhism. The name of this child was Siddharta Gautama, and his father was a wealthy rajah in the valley of the Ganges. Gautama in his birth was therefore strikingly like the man who founded the earlier heresy; and, as we shall see, in his life he was even more like him. At an early age Gautama too was married off to a beautiful princess; and until he was almost thirty he, too, reveled unrestrained in princely luxury.

But then of a sudden something came over him. Exactly as had happened to Mahavira, a revulsion against pleasure took hold of this young prince so that he no longer could abide the lusts of the flesh. His eyes were suddenly opened to the unutterable misery of all life, and the sight so burnt its way into his soul that he nevermore could be at ease in his palace. One night he arose and, tiptoeing into the room where lay his sleeping wife with their new-born child in her arms, he took one last fond look at them both, and fled. Off into the night he sped, with his trusted charioteer by his side. Very far he rode, not halting until the rising of the sun had shown that he had already got far beyond the lands of his clan. Then he dismounted, cut off his flowing locks, tore the jewels and ornaments from his clothes, and giving them together with his horse and sword to the charioteer, commanded that they be

returned to his wife. Gautama himself did not go back,
but turning his face toward the hills, he went off alone
on foot. But even then he did not feel free. Not until
he had exchanged clothes with a beggar he met on the
road did he feel himself loosed at last from all attach-

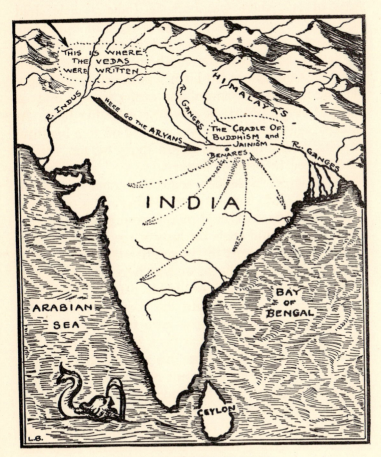

WHAT HAPPENED IN INDIA

ments to the world of vanity. Not until he stood there on that dusty road a ragged vagrant without a possession on earth did he feel himself able at last to go forth undistracted in search of salvation.

Southward Gautama took his way into a range of hills where dwelt certain hermits in caves. He had long known of these hermits, for their fame had spread throughout the countryside. They were not ordinary ascetics frantically starving their bodies, but rather devoted philosophers trying to enrich their minds. Most of their time was spent in the pursuit of knowledge—not knowledge about the facts of life, however, but about the destinies of the soul. They did not poke about in laboratories as do our modern investigators; rather they sat under trees and talked. Long and earnestly they conversed about those metaphysical things our material world does not know. Their great concern was how to lose themselves in the Brahma, in the universal Over-Soul which was the only reality they knew. They were sick of this futile, finite, tortured existence called life. They wanted to cut away from it, cut clear away from the individual self and attain a sense of finality and security through absorption into the universal All. They craved release from the vicious round of transmigrating life; they craved everlasting extinction. Eyelids are heavy in the sweltering tropics, where the wet jungle heat breeds life too rankly; and these unhappy hermits wanted to sleep—to sleep forever. And because Gautama, too, wanted to sleep forever, he joined himself to their company. And Gautama came and took part in their conversation.

But the wandering prince did not tarry with them

long.   His mind was keen, and it took little time for
him to discover how empty was the ratiocination of
those talky hermits.   They tried to drag their petty souls
to Brahma by strings of words—but Brahma Itself, he
discovered, was also a mere thing of words.   He saw
through all the arguments, no matter how smoothly
and plausibly they were put, and he realized that
Brahma, the great "It," was essentially no more real
than man, the little "it."   So, taking five of the hermits
with him, he went off into the jungles to try another
road to salvation.   With all his being he now gave himself up to years of self-mortification, striving, as had
Mahavira before him, to reach Nirvana through pain.
For six years—at least, so we are told—he practiced
austerities the like of which had never before been seen
in the land, living on a grain of rice a day, or on a single
sesamum seed.   But, unlike Mahavira, no success attended his efforts.   Despite all Gautama's austerities,
those six years were "like time spent striving to tie the
air into knots."   So finally he gave up the vain struggle.
He had to confess to himself at last that senseless and
irrational self-affliction was not enough.   In despair he
had to admit that the dismal path of mere denial could
never be for him the way to peace.

And so once more Gautama set off alone, far unhap-
pier now than ever before.   He had tried the ordinary
life of the prince, and it had left a taste as of ashes in
his mouth.   He had tried the life of the philosopher, and
that too had brought him no peace.   And then he had
tried the life of the ascetic, only to find that even in that
there could be no release.   So now he was lost, utterly
at sea on a night that seemed to hold no faintest gleam
of light, no slightest promise of dawn.

And then of a sudden light broke on him. He was seated one day beneath a banyan tree, his spirit at its lowest ebb, when all without warning salvation came to him. In an instant his spirit leaped up in ecstasy; his whole being became suffused with joy. He felt himself released at last, released from life and the fear of life. He felt himself free at last, free and safe and secure.

BUDDHA WAS SEATED BENEATH A BANYAN TREE

. . . For a day and a night, so tradition declares, he continued beneath that tree, sitting there and pondering on the wondrous thing that had happened to him. Then he arose to his feet, and went off to tell men what he had learnt.

2

IN essence what Gautama had learnt was the folly of all excess. It had come to him in that moment of illumination that it was just as stupid to go mad with pain as it was to get drunk with pleasure. He had suddenly come to see that asceticism inevitably overshot its mark, that it missed the very thing it was after because it went after it too wildly. He had discovered that the frantic excess with which the ascetics strove to curb desire meant only that they were letting desire run away with them. . . . So Gautama came forward with a new gospel which he called the Four Truths. They were these: First, both birth and death bring grief, and life is utterly vain. "The waters of the four great oceans," he declared, "are naught compared with the tears of men as they tread the path of life." Secondly, the vanity of life is caused altogether by the indulgence of desire. Therefore, thirdly, the vanity can end only with the ending of all desire. But fourthly—and herein lay the whole originality of the gospel—all desire can be ended not by excessive asceticism but by sane and intelligent decency! The road to salvation, according to Gautama, was therefore not the tortuous trail of bodily self-destruction, but rather the "Middle Path" of spiritual self-control. It was the Eightfold Noble Path of "Right Belief, Right Resolve, Right Speech, Right Action, Right Livelihood, Right Effort, Right Thought, and Right Meditation." Nirvana was, after all, not a physical condition but a state of mind, and therefore it could be reached not through physical torment but mental discipline. The blessedness of freedom, of everlasting passionless peace, of Nirvana, could be attained only by destroying the three cardinal sins: sensuality, ill will, and stupidity.

Now the implications of such a gospel were grave and revolutionary beyond words. In the first place, they left no room whatsoever for gods, priests, or prayers. "Who is there that has ever seen Brahma face to face?" cried Gautama scornfully. Or with regard to prayer: "Could the farther bank of the river Akirvati come over to this side no matter how much a man prayed it to do so?" Thus it scouted the whole sacrificial system of the brahmins. It condemned outright that shameless ritualization of morality which the priests had introduced with their Brahmanas. Indeed, it condemned not alone ritual but religion itself—that is, in its narrower connotation. Gautama's gospel countenanced none of those common instruments—gods, sacrifices, priests, or prayers—wherewith the religious technique is always practiced. . . . But in the broader connotation of the term, the gospel was itself a religion. It tried desperately to find a way of escape from the insecurities of life, and to that extent it was most generously a religion. It tried earnestly to rid man of fear, to make him feel *at home* in the universe—and for that reason it deserves its chapter in the story of this believing world. . . .

But opposition to the gods was not the only radical implication of Gautama's gospel. A second and perhaps just as radical implication was its opposition to all caste divisions. According to Gautama there were no valid distinctions between high-born and low-born, for men could be judged only according to their deeds. Very

explicitly he declared: "A man does not become a
brahmin by his family or by birth. In whom there is
truth and righteousness—he is blessed, he is a brahmin.
O fool, if within thee there is ravening, how can'st
thou make the outside pure?" Gautama, who had belonged to the princely caste, realized all too well how
empty were all distinctions of birth. Though born and
reared in a palace, life for him had been no whit less
futile and troubled than the life of the lowest serf in his
wattle-and-daub hut. So how could he respect the
trumpery social distinctions of the brahmins?

But the revolt against the gods and the revolt against
the castes were neither of them unique to Gautama's
gospel. Mahavira had urged them just as emphatically
when Gautama was still a child in arms. What alone
was original in the younger heresy was the emphasis
Gautama laid on social ethics. Mahavira had insisted
that each man could attain salvation for himself by going
off alone and afflicting his own body. But the younger
prophet declared that all individualism was sinful, and
that one's own salvation could be found only in the
effort to bring salvation to every one else. "Go ye
now," he commanded his followers, "out of compassion
for the world and the welfare of gods and men . . .
and preach the doctrine which is glorious." And thus
he cut at the very root of selfishness. One's own peace,
he declared, could be found only in seeking peace for all
humanity. . . .

Now Gautama arrived at that conclusion from a
rather startling and original premise. Unlike all other
Hindu thinkers of his day, he did not believe in the
individual soul. Just as some modern psychologists

claim the soul to be no more than the name for a certain
class of subtle muscular reactions, so Gautama claimed
it to be no more than a name for the totality of human
desires. As he himself put it: the chariot is made up
of wheels, shaft, axle, carriage and banner-staff, and
has no real existence when these are removed; and just
so the soul is made up of desires and psychic tendencies,
and disappears the moment these are taken away.
Therefore, argued Gautama, all this pother about the
transmigration of souls was sheer folly. Only the
deeds, not the doers, lived on from generation to generation. So no matter how anxiously a man looked
after what he called his soul, no whit of good could
possibly result from it. Only if a man diligently
watched his deeds could he possibly attain salvation.
For there was an inexorable Law of Karma, an inescapable "law of the deed," in the universe. The effects
of all actions lived on perpetually, good breeding good,
and evil breeding evil. And these effects could never be
eluded. "Not in the sky, nor in the midst of the sea,
not in the clefts of the mountains, is there known a spot
where a man can be freed from an evil act." So every
man's fate depended not on what he was but what he
did. Only if he did that which was righteous in the
eyes of men, only then could he throw off the ball and
chain of evil consequence and attain the blessed release of
Nirvana. . . .

3

SUCH in brief was Gautama's gospel after the revelation came to him beneath the banyan tree. He sought
to communicate it first to the five disciples whom he had

left behind when he forsook asceticism. But these men looked on him as an apostate, and would not even receive him on his return. Only after much persistence could Gautama get them to give ear to his doctrine, and then he had to argue with them five days long. But in the end he won them over. With one accord those five men then hailed him as the Buddha, the "Enlightened One," for they had become convinced that he could not but be another of those chosen souls, the Buddhas (in Jainism they were called the Jinas), who from time to time were supposed to descend into the world to speak celestial truth. And then a little holy brotherhood was created around the person of this new Buddha.

India was then swarming with restless souls in search of a faith that might comfort them; many of these came and found it in the words of Gautama. They gathered in the Deer Forest near Benares, and built themselves little huts around the dwelling-place of the Buddha. And when they were as many as sixty in number, their master commanded them to go forth during the dry months of the year and carry his comforting message to the people. He told them to carry abroad the good tidings that salvation was free, and that all men, high and low, learned and ignorant, could surely attain it if only they practiced justice and righteousness.

Buddha himself went out into the country with that evangel. For twenty years he wandered far and wide, winning disciples wherever he moved. Early in his ministry he went back to his own home, and there converted his long-deserted wife and son to the new faith. (His son even became one of his preaching monks, and his wife joined an order of Buddhist nuns which was soon organized.) And thus, the center of an ever-growing movement, Siddharta Gautama, the Buddha, lived out his days on earth. To the end he continued to instruct the disciples that gathered during every rainy season in the Deer Forest near Benares. Indeed, the very last words he uttered were addressed to them. "Work out your own salvation!" he told them with his last breath. And then he died. . . .

More than twenty-four hundred years have passed since Siddharta Gautama passed away, and it is not easy for us to appreciate how revolutionary his doctrine must have been when first he uttered it. Never before had it been said in India that salvation was obtainable in any wise save through scrupulous sacrificing, or profound philosophizing, or extravagant asceticism. In other words, never before had it been asserted that those who were too poor to offer sacrifices, too dull-witted to indulge in philosophy, or too human to set up as anchorites, could possibly be saved. Only when Gautama the Buddha took the field was that assertion made. Until then salvation, and even the hunger for salvation, had been deemed privileges open only to the few. But with the coming of Gautama they were held out to the many—to all. According to him even the lowliest in the land could attain Nirvana, if only they followed the Noble Eightfold Path. . . . And though that gospel was afterward distorted and corrupted and changed out of all likeness to what it had been when it came fresh from the lips of the Buddha, nevertheless it did endure and spread until its light was known over all the East.

4

BUT his gospel did not spread at once. For years Buddhism remained an obscure and unimportant sect, probably just one of many heretical movements fermenting away in the troubled India of those centuries. For a while it was no more than a mere ascetic order similar to Jainism. The very selfishness which Gautama had most bitterly attacked, took hold of his professed followers, and they became far more concerned about the peace of their own little souls than the peace of all mankind. But about the third century B. C. there came a revival of Buddha's world-saving spirit, and monks once more went out to preach a gospel in his name.

Only now it was no longer the simple ethical gospel of Gautama. Theology had crept in, and it became a religion in the very narrowest sense of that word. Time had dealt hard with the memory of Gautama, and by the third century he was no longer imagined to have been a man but a god. A new school of Buddhist thought called the Mahayana, the "Greater Vehicle," arose, and according to its teaching Buddha had been from the beginning a divine being. The earlier school, the Hinayana or "Lesser Vehicle," had been content to picture Gautama as altogether a human creature. It had frankly told in its writings how the master had occasionally suffered from wind on the stomach, and how once when he ate a meal prepared by a blacksmith he was attacked by dysentery and almost died. But the new school was totally incapable of such realism. It told instead how the Blessed One had been conceived supernaturally and had been born without pain. It described him as a sinless being who had been sent from heaven as the savior of gods and men. It further declared that his divine spirit continued regularly to return to the earth, incarnating itself generation after generation in certain exceptionally holy men called Bodhisattvas, "Living Buddhas." And thus it opened a way for the incursion of a whole troop of extra gods. And finally it allowed idols of Buddha to be set up in splendid temples, and even encouraged the offering of sacrifices of flowers to those idols. Just the very elements in the old Brahmanic religion against which Buddha had most directly rebelled came sidling over to the protestant faith, and through the Mahayana took possession of it.

And now, bedizened with idols and made colorful with myths, Buddhism began to spread at last. Power and riches began to flow to the sect, and before long the tiny huts in which the preachers had been wont to shelter themselves during the rainy season were replaced by imposing and costly monasteries. The rajahs of India were just then struggling to wrest supremacy for themselves from the hands of the long-dominant priestly caste; and these rajahs began to see the value to their cause of this virile caste-destroying movement. Especially did one of them, a certain low-caste adventurer named Chandraguptra, see its usefulness. By war and intrigue he had managed to carve out for himself a vast empire in northern India, and because the anti-caste doctrine of Buddhism promised to help him retain his power, he endowed its monasteries with vast estates and enormous riches. And his grandson, the famous King Asoka who became emperor of India in 264 B. C., devoted a great share of his energy during all his reign to the spreading of the Buddhist religion.

Asoka is esteemed by many scholars to have been the noblest monarch in history; and if the criterion is the number of souls that still revere his memory, then certainly he was a far greater figure than any other in the whole world's catalogue of kings. By acquiring one state after another he built up an empire that included a large part of the East; and every inch of it he won by faith and not by the sword. Asoka sent out Buddhist missionaries to Ceylon, to Kashmir, and to the uttermost ends of the earth known to him. Eight and twenty years he carried on his far-flung missionary work, and before he died he had managed to make Buddhism the dominant religion in his half of the world.

But of course it was not the simple ethical gospel of Gautama that was carried to these strange lands. Rather it was an intricate theological dogma that translated Buddha into a God. Gautama had preached a religion of morality; but these successful missionaries rather preached a religion that made a morality of ritual. Mere obeisance to the god Buddha was deemed enough to save one's soul. Nirvana, which to Gautama had been entirely a state of spiritual peace attained by following the Noble Eightfold Path, was now interpreted to be a physical post-mortem heaven won by much kissing of an ikon's toe. And these corruptions were marked not merely in the Mahayana school of Buddhism which spread to China and Japan, but later also in the Hinayana school which throve especially in Ceylon. The farther Buddhism traveled, the more it changed. On the northwestern frontier of India, where the Hellenic and Hindu worlds touched, the Buddhist idols came to look exactly like the idols of the West. Hariti, a pestilence-goddess whom Buddha was supposed to have converted, was carved to look very much like Isis, the mother-goddess of Egypt. She was even pictured as holding the infant Buddha to her breast, exactly as Isis held the infant Horus and—much later— Mary held the Christ Child.

In China Buddhism took on much of the character of Taoism, and in Japan it was greatly influenced by the national religion called Shinto. Then contact with Christianity began to have its effect, first through the efforts of the early Nestorian preachers, and much later through the activities of Protestant missionaries. Buddhism in Thibet very early took on a distinct Christian coloring, accepting into its ritual such Christian symbols and instruments as the cross, the miter, the' dalmatica, censer, chaplet, and holy-water font. The Buddhist religion in Thibet has developed a most elaborate hierarchical system, with a pope, the Dalai Lama, ruling the whole land from his palace at Lhassa, assisted by bishops and priests officiating in vast cathedrals cluttered with images and pictures, and by myriads of monks busily spinning prayer-wheels in high-walled monasteries. And also in Japan Buddhism has more recently taken on Christian coloring, though here of a Protestant shade. Modern Japanese Buddhists are reported to have congregational worship and hymn-singing, Sunday Schools for their children, a Young Men's Buddhist Association for their men, and Buddhist temperance societies for their women! . . .

In India itself, Buddhism simply withered and died

out. A thousand years after the death of Gautama, it
had become very largely Brahmanized. The plain
people fearfully cried to the idols for help, and the
leaders earnestly wrangled about the proper size and

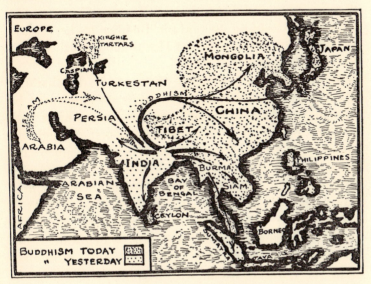

HOW BUDDHISM SPREAD

cut of their ceremonial robes. When therefore a new
religion, Islam, invaded the land, it swept all before it.
Although there are perhaps a hundred and fifty million
Buddhists in Asia, no more than two thousand of them
now remain in all of India.

Buddhism is still the religion of Burmah, Siam, and
Ceylon, but in those lands it has fallen back almost to
sheer animism. Everywhere in Ceylon one can hear the
bellman at sundown calling the naked brown folk with
glossy black hair to the service in the temple.   They

bring candles—if they can afford them—and flowers to the yellow-clad priest; and the latter solemnly offers them to some fetish, perhaps a putative tooth of Buddha, nestling in an innermost shrine. Then there is much praying—praying to gods, devils, angels, demons, saints, and all manner of other spirits. . . . And all the while there stands within that land a mighty tree whose seed came from the very banyan under which Gautama received the revelation. There in Ceylon it still stands, the oldest tree known to history. During nearly twenty-two hundred years it has been tenderly watched and watered; its branches have been stoutly braced, and its soil has been terraced to give room for the gigantic roots to grow. And there it thrives still today, a pitilessly ironic monument to the pitiful stupidity of man. For that tree, a mere thing in nature, has been most carefully preserved and nurtured, while the faith which alone gave it meaning, long, long ago was allowed to perish. . . .

IV.   HINDUISM

BUT despite the rising of Jainism and Buddhism in India, the old priestly religion rooted in the Vedas was never completely ousted. Even though for a while it lost the favor of the rulers, never for a moment did it lose its attractiveness to the ruled. Of course, inwardly it changed from century to century, taking on new gods and forgetting old ones, acquiring strange rites and neglecting native ones; but at least in its caste structure and priestly character the old religion of the Hindus never wavered from first to last. At the present time well over two hundred million souls in India—more

than the number of Protestant Christians in all the
world—still call themselves Hinduists!

To define Hinduism is very nearly impossible.
Actually it is not so much a religion (in the narrower
sense of the word) as a religio-social system. Although
Hinduism contains a whole farrago of theologies, philosophies, and sacrificial systems, nevertheless its one
dominant note is that of caste. An elaborate tissue of
ancient religio-social laws has hardened until by now
it seems altogether indestructible. That tissue was first
built up by a series of law codes, most prominently the
Code of Manu, which were compiled about the time the
Buddhist heresy was at its height. These codes set out
to do for Hinduism what the Talmud in a later day
did for Judaism. They tried to build a wall of law
around the faith so that none could stray from it. Of
course, the stoutest buttresses of the Hindu wall were
naturally the caste distinctions, and these therefore received the most careful attention of the law-makers.
The superiority of the brahmins and the inferiority of
the laborers were declared to be ordered in heaven according to a divine plan "for the prosperity of the
world." A man's caste, like his breath, was with him
incessantly from birth to death; indeed, unlike his
breath, it was even supposed to follow him into the
grave.

But save for these laws regulating caste there is no
other unifying element in all Hinduism. There are
two major sects in the religion, and at least fifty-seven
sub-sects, each seeking to attain salvation with the aid
of its own gods and ceremonies. Christianity, which
is even more intensively divided, is at least united by its

unanimous recognition of the uniqueness of Jesus. Hinduism has no such common doctrine. It is true that
about 300 A. D. an attempt was made to create such a
doctrine by combining the three main Hindu gods into
a universally acceptable trinity; but the attempt failed
dismally. Brahma, the chief god in that trinity, never
became popular save with the priests and philosophers.
He was not nearly concrete enough a deity for the plain
folk to grasp and believe in, and there are now only two
temples in all India that are devoted to his worship.
And Vishnu and Shiva, the two other gods in the
trinity, always remained distinct and separate, continuing to attract distinct and separate followings. . . .
But though Hinduism has never been united on any
creed or rite, its divisiveness has rarely if ever led to
bloodshed. Unlike the Christians, who again and again
have resorted even to wholesale slaughter in order to ex-
tirpate all heresy, the Hindus have rarely persecuted
divergence of faith. They have been wise enough to
see that each man has a right to worship as he himself
sees fit, and that no man is justified in seeking to force
his doctrine on his neighbor. Therefore the worshippers
of Vishnu and those of Shiva have dwelt side by side for
centuries without bitterness, and countless sub-sects have
arisen and disappeared in India with very little violence
or acrimony. No matter how many evils may be debited
against Hinduism, at least this one virtue must be listed
to its credit: it is tolerant. . . .

2

ONE of the two most popular gods in India today is
Vishnu. Originally a minor Vedic sun-god, he has

since risen to superlative importance largely because he
has been credited with the power of incarnating himself
occasionally in human form. One can easily understand
why that propensity should have made Vishnu attractive to the people. Through those periodic incarna-
tions—those "avatars" as they are called—Vishnu became real, tangible, almost human to all sorts of Hindu
people. The trouble with a god like Brahma, for
instance, was that he was no more than a cold,
impersonal, philosophical deduction—a blank. But
there was no such chill impersonality about Vishnu. On
the contrary, he was believed to share in every joy and
sorrow of his followers, and their distress and sin were
supposed to be his incessant concerns. It was said, indeed, that whenever the people became wayward Vishnu
was so solicitous that he actually came down to earth
in human form and himself led the way to reformation. Many epics were written to tell how the god
had thus incarnated himself as a man and worked great
wonders. Indeed, two of those epics, the Mahabharata
and the Ramayana, form the final and most popular
chapter in all of Hindu sacred literature.

The Mahabharata tells the adventures of Vishnu incarnated in the body of a great hero named Krishna,
and in it is to be found that famous tractate called the
Bhagavad-Gita, the "Song of the Adorable." This
little tractate, which has often been called the New Testament of Hinduism, has been translated and distributed
by societies with just the same missionary zeal wherewith tract associations distribute the Bible. Actually
the Bhagavad-Gita is an exceedingly confused and repe-
titious little work, and one greatly marred by bewilder-

ing inconsistencies. Perhaps that is why it has been so popular, for in its frequent stretches of vagueness and confusion one can find confirmation of almost any belief on earth. One can say of it as the Rabbis said of the Bible: "Turn it over and over, for in it is everything." But, despite all that, the Bhagavad-Gita is a work of rare grandeur. In spiritual tone and exalted ethical import it is hardly inferior to any other scripture in the world. Nowhere is a nobler note struck than this one which rings out in the "Song of the Adorable": "He who does all his work for my (Vishnu's) sake, who is wholly devoted to me, who loves me, who is free from attachment to earthly things, and without hate to any being, he enters into me." . . .

Krishna, the god-man, whose adventures are celebrated in the Mahabharata and whose wisdom is set down in the Bhagavad-Gita, is considered the most important of Vishnu's avatars. Indeed, in the hearts of millions of Hindus today he has actually come to occupy the place of Vishnu himself. Just as many Christians turn to Christ much more frequently than to God, so do many Hindus bow to Krishna rather than Vishnu. And it has been suggested that Krishna—whose name in some of the northern dialects is pronounced Krishto—may bear some significant relationship to Christ. That theory, however, cannot be substantiated by facts. In all probability Krishna and Christ are akin only to the extent that both arose out of a similar passion of the human race: the passion that sublimates its hero until it has made him more than mortal and has exalted him to the skies. It may be that originally Krishna was a beloved tribal chieftain and religious reformer who dur-

ing his lifetime taught his people to worship a god
called Bhagavata, "Adorable." So wondrous a character may he have been that after he died his followers
were not able to resist thinking he had actually been
the god himself. Therewith arose the cult of Krishna,
the man-god; and as soon as it grew powerful the
priests of the old order shrewdly threw a cloak of Brah-
man orthodoxy over it by saying Krishna was none
other than an incarnation of their old god Vishnu. . . .

That, however, is mere speculation. All we know
for certain is that somehow the people did begin to
believe that the god Vishnu from time to time came to
earth in the form of avatars. Krishna was only one
of these. Rama, whose exploits are detailed in the epic
called the Ramayana, was almost as great; and innumerable chieftains, milk-men, even elephants and tigers,
are included in the long list of lesser avatars. And
because the people thus humanized Vishnu, they could
believe in him with great intensity. They could look
upon him as a spirit enshrined in their own human
hearts, one that guided their own souls and ultimately
snatched them out of the cycle of life in order to carry
them up to heaven. At least, so could and did the people
consider Vishnu—before the theologians appeared.
Once the latter came on the scene, however, the nude
innocence of the popular doctrine was immediately hidden beneath thick folds of words. Terms were defined
and redefined, and at once schisms resulted. Acute con-
troversies were started over the very idlest questions.
To this day all followers of Vishnu are divided into two
denominations because of a dispute as to whether man
is saved by Vishnu as a new-born kitten or a new-

born monkey is saved by its mother. The new-born
kitten acts helpless and its mother has to grasp it by the
nape of its neck to carry it off to safety; but the new-
born monkey lends a hand in its own rescue, clinging
to its mother with all the strength of its little arms. (In
essence we have here those old antagonists, Predestination and Free-Will.) Even now that theological conflict rages, dividing the Vishnuites into two camps:
those who believe in the "cat-hold" theory, and those
who are strong for the "monkey-grip" belief! . . .

3

BUT Vishnu, even with the aid of all his avatars,
never managed to attract so vast a following as did
the third god of the trinity: Shiva. Originally this
Shiva may have been one of those gruesome demons that
had been conjured up in the fear-fevered heads of the
black aborigines, and that were still worshipped even
after the coming of the Aryans. He was (and sometimes still is) conceived to be a wild, morose deity,
malevolent and destructive, causing pestilence, storms,
and all manner of other horrors; and he is commonly
depicted as a monster bearing a trident and rosary.
(Christians did not learn of the rosary until they observed its use during the Crusades among the Moslems;
but the Moslems themselves had only a little earlier first
taken to it as a sacred symbol in imitation of the followers of this god Shiva.) In the trinity by which
the theologians tried to unite the Hindu sects, Brahma
stood for the principle of Creation, Vishnu for that of
Preservation, and Shiva for that of Destruction. Of the
three, Shiva became and remained the most popular.

The masses loved him because he was very much their own kind: passionate, violent, and licentious. And with him they loved his sluttish wife, Parvata the Terrible. To her glory the Thugs, a secret sect of pious murderers, used to commit unspeakable outrages; and in her name the Tantrists, a secret sect of pious perverts, still indulge in indescribable sex orgies.

There is hardly a village in all of India today where there is not at least one shrine sheltering the emblem of Shiva: an upright cylindrical block usually resting on a circular slab with a hole in its center. Curiously, the people do not seem to realize the crude symbolism of that emblem, and do not even remotely associate it with sex. Many of them even wear it as an emblem around their necks for good luck, or as a sign of their religious devotion. Of

SHIVA

course, sex does play a very real part in the worship of Shiva and his female counterparts. One denomination called Tantra is built around the alluring theory that only by riotous indulgence in passion can man ever cross the region of darkness which keeps him from utter union with Shiva. Passion, it is admitted, is poison; but the only antidote for this poison is more poison.   Therefore it is reasoned that only indulgence in the five vices that poison the soul of man—wine, meat, fish, mystical gesticulation with the fingers, and sex looseness—only veritable orgies of those five vices, can drive their poison out of the system and really purify the soul! . . .

Now, scholars are not lacking who maintain that *all* religion is merely a form of sex expression; and they have not a little plausible argument to sustain their theory.   It would be strange indeed if religion, which reaches down to the very depths of human consciousness, should not be greatly influenced by so pervading an impulse as sex.   Indeed, it must be freely admitted that even the most advanced and civilized of religious practices are colored by sex.   (But for that matter, so also are the most advanced and civilized of art forms and social systems.)

The religious practices of India, however, are, for the most part, far from being advanced and civilized, and it is therefore the more natural that sex should obtrude itself in them.   Indulgence in erotic practices is part of the worship not alone of Shiva, but also of Vishnu.   It is said that many of the minor sects adoring Krishna really adore his wife or mistress, or draw their inspiration from the wild tales that the Mahabharata tells of Krishna's dissipated youth.   One must remember that the average worshipper of Vishnu, like his fellow in the Shivaite sect, is still a relatively primitive man. He is still hungry for those animalic delights which alone seem to make his wretched life livable. . . .

4

BUT though Hinduism among the low-caste folk has remained revoltingly primitive, among the high-caste philosophers it has advanced until certain of its teachings are almost beyond comprehension. The Hindus as a people seem to be equipped with a deep and definite tendency to think rather than to act. Perhaps because of the enervating climate in their land they are much more given to hard labor in contemplation and meditation than to hard labor in conquering and creating with tools and machines. As a result their highest achievements have been in the realm of ideas rather than of concrete things. And the Western world, weary now of things and the frantic struggle to get them, has in recent decades come to take an inordinate interest in those mental achievements of the Hindus. Many Western souls too weak or too fine to stand the grind of our machine civilization have flung themselves with great—and often uncritical—enthusiasm into the pursuit of various systems of Indian metaphysics. They have joined New Thought churches, Theosophical Societies, Leagues for the Contemplation of the Over-Soul; or at least they have sat in fashionable drawing-rooms and listened entranced to the praise of one and another method of contemplation by turbaned yogi, swami, and other Hindu lecturers.

But for all that, it is hardly possible that Indian thought will ever be able to take deep root in the Western world. At its heart there is a hunger quite incomprehensible to the Western mind, the hunger for final death, for extinction, for utter release from the dread cycle of transmigrating life. To the Hindu thinker the bitterest woe in this woe-begotten life has always been the dread that there is no way out of life. Practically all of Hindu philosophy has been one protracted attempt to prove that there is indeed a way out. According to Mahavira the Jina, the way out is through physical self-denial; according to Gautama the Buddha, it is through spiritual temperance and moral rectitude. But according to the orthodox Hindu philosophers, the way out is rather through various physical and psychic exercises.

Most of these philosophers belong to the school known as "Yoga." The Sanskrit word *yoga* is said to be related to the Latin *jugum,* and the English "yoke"; and it means "union." Yoga aims to unite the individual soul with Brahma, the Universal Over-Soul, by the persistent suppression of all disturbing sense-activity. Various exercises which it provides enable a man to restrain even the slightest unnecessary action of his body, leaving him immobile, transfixed, almost breathless. There he is to sit like a stone image, no tremor in his flesh, no lustre in his eyes, with his mind riveted in concentration on the Over-Soul. And then of a sudden the mystic marriage is consummated. The little soul of the individual becomes suddenly at one with the great Over-Soul of the Universe. An ineffable bliss suffuses the devotee, a peace and rest such as he knew only in the womb of his mother. He feels himself somehow exquisitely exalted, deliciously carried out of himself, divinely disembodied. He becomes for a moment entirely a spirit, an ethereal floating part of the All, a yogi. . . . And then the trance snaps. With a sickening horror in his slow-beating heart, the devotee comes sinking down to earth again. And there he awakes to find himself earth-bound once more—but with a memory he cannot obliterate. From then on he is a changed man, for having once tasted of Nirvana his one consuming passion is to taste again. From then on he is lost completely to the world, caring neither for its virtues nor its vices. From then on he goes wandering lonely as a cloud, not worrying whether he does good or evil, not thinking whether he builds or destroys. For he is no longer an ordinary man—he is a yogi!

This is not the place for a detailed discussion of mysticism. No one can say with indisputable certainty just what it is, or whence it comes. Theologians and most of the older psychologists insist that the mystic ecstasy experienced by the yogi or the saint is a veritable glimpse into eternity, and that it is a gift from God; the newer psychologists are inclined to believe it is no more than a sublimation of sex desire. But though we may not know what the mystic esctasy is or whence it comes, no one can deny that it is a valid and genuine phenomenon. The fact that ninety-nine out of every hundred people who read this paragraph may never have experienced such an ecstasy does not in the least militate against its reality. Evidently there do exist in the world, especially in India, certain persons whose minds are peculiarly sensitive to what is loosely termed the spiritual. And when such persons heighten their sensitiveness by means of exercises like that of Yoga, it is no real cause for wonder if they experience the transcendent ecstasies whereof they tell. We ordinary mortals have hardly more right to challenge their testimony than we have right to challenge the testimony of astronomers who, with the increased sight afforded them by their telescopes, tell us of stars which our naked eyes have never seen.

Besides, even if the mystic experience be indeed a delusion and a lie, all that matters is that to the mystic it seems the only indubitable truth. All of life's earthly phenomena seem to him entirely illusory and unreal; only those fleeting moments of unearthly ecstasy seem to him to be valid and genuine. And in that faith he lives. Firm in the conviction that all the torments and hazards of earthly life are mere lies and fantasies, he can go through the world without fear. He can have no dread of this material universe because he tells himself it simply isn't there—and means it. Matter does not exist for him. Only Brahma, the Over-Soul, the "It," the Infinite Spirit—only that exists. His only concern is how to break jail out of this illusory world, and his whole religion is directed toward that release. In essence the mystic's religion is the technique by which he strives to rise to union with Brahma. It is, of course, in no wise like the ordinary religious technique. It lays no emphasis on prayer or sacrifice, for the Over-Soul is purely impersonal and cannot be moved by cajolery or petition. Nor does it lay any emphasis on morality, for since the Over-Soul is not concerned with this illusory material world, necessarily it cannot be interested in the goodness or badness of the illusory deeds performed in it. No, the religion, the technique of salvation, practiced by the Hindu mystic, lays emphasis only on certain psychic exercises. It demands only concentration, suppression of all sense activity, breathless medi-

tation—and then it guarantees Nirvana. It demands
that all action be put to death, and then promises everlasting inaction. And millions of souls in India have
been "saved" by that belief. . . .

5

BUT though many Hindus may have found comfort
in Yoga and the other philosophical systems, the vast
majority of the people have always taken refuge in less
abstruse beliefs. To this day the religion of the Hindu
serfs and peasants, especially in the south, is still almost
the primitive animism of the aboriginal blacks. It is
said that four-fifths of the people of India still worship
local spirits, usually female demons, with the most revolting of animal sacrifices. The orthodox Hinduism
of the brahmins is opposed to animal slaughter, and especially reveres the cow. But the naked masses out in
the jungles pay little heed to that taboo, and on occasion they even manage to engage fallen brahmins to
officiate at their animal sacrifices. Those wretched half-
starved peasants worship godlings, demons, and ghosts,
and carry on in the jungles much as did their black ancestors thousands of years ago. For they are still afraid.
They are not tired of life, as are so many of the higher-
caste Hindus. Actually those serfs have never really
lived enough even to *know* life, let alone be tired of
it. They've merely existed; they've been growing,
spawning, and dying, generation after generation, like
so many jungle rodents. And therefore they've never
been able to understand the philosopher's world-weary
appetite for annihilation. Those masses still hunger

for life—but life enriched and made brahminically luxuriant.

That is why the peasants flock to the temples with offerings of meat or flowers, and pray fearfully to the idols of wood and stone. They imagine that thus they can win for themselves an easier life in a higher caste when they are born again. Or if they dream at all of escape from the cycle of reincarnating life, it is never of escape into passivity and nothingness. Nirvana to them is not a mental state of utter imperturbability in this world, but a physical riot of joy in some other world. And the attainment of that lusty Nirvana is of course their highest hope. To win it they will go

IDOLS GROTESQUE BEYOND WORDS

to almost incredible excesses of piety. Millions of them when old and decrepit will c r a w l on their bellies to the River Ganges simply because the belief prevails that for drawing the last breath by the side of the Ganges, a dying man's soul receives c e r t a i n and immediate transportation to Shiva's heaven. Benares, on the banks of the Ganges, contains over two thousand temples a n d uncounted lesser shrines, all of them supported by such credulous Hindu pilgrims.

Benares, however, is not the only holy city in the

land, nor the Ganges the only holy river. Every corner of India has its own temples and shrines. Idols grotesque beyond description are to be found everywhere: elephant-headed bodies, three-eyed gargoyles, monsters with many heads, and all manner of other such fear-inspiring creations. And to these idols, which increase yearly in number and monstrosity, the millions of India give adoration. The priests, who are supposed to wake and wash and feed the idols, are still the aristocrats. Many a serf in India today refuses to break his fast in the morning save with water in which the toe of a brahmin has been dipped. Caste still has hold of the people with an iron grip. Its original four divisions have multiplied many fold, and the population is now broken up into hundreds of little sub-castes. And there are said to be fifty million men and women in the land who are considered too low to belong even to the lowest sub-caste. They are the outcasts, the "Untouchables," whose very crossing of the shadow of a brahmin is supposed to render him ritually unclean!

One wonders what will come of it all. Fear, organized and intensified by priestcraft, has led poor India into a quicksand whence there seems no escape. Century after century brave attempts have been made to reform the religion; but invariably they have met with failure. No matter how many prophets come to the masses to tell them to destroy their idols and cast out their priests, those masses will not obey. They simply *must* have their reeds to cling to, their spirits to believe in. For they are still afraid . . . afraid. . . .

BOOK FOUR
WHAT HAPPENED IN CHINA

BOOK FOUR

WHAT HAPPENED IN CHINA

I. CONFUCIANISM

1: The primitive religion of China—ancestor-worship—the state cult—the popular religion—burial customs—family festivals—why did China advance so early? 2: The story of Confucius. 3: The work of Confucius—his gospel—his place in history. 4: The deification of Confucius.

II. TAOISM

1: The life of Lao-Tze—the Tao-Teh-king—the gospel—was Lao-Tze a religious teacher? 2: The degeneration of Taoism —alchemy—gods and priests—the deification of Lao-Tze.

III. BUDDHISM

1: How it entered China—why it succeeded there—its rise and fall. 2: The Land of the "Three Truths"—popular worship.

BOOK FOUR

WHAT HAPPENED IN CHINA

I. CONFUCIANISM

 HAT may have been the earliest religion of China, no one seems to know for certain. Some scholars maintain it was almost or quite a monotheism, for from earliest times the Chinese seem to have worshipped a Supreme Ruler usually identified with Heaven. This theory of an early monotheism can hardly be accepted, however, for side by side with the worship of the Supreme Ruler, the Spirit of Heaven, there went on also the worship of numerous spirits of the earth. As far back as we can go, the Chinese seem to have reached out for help to the spirits which they supposed animated all natural phenomena, and especially to the ghosts of the dead. It is therefore safer to describe the earliest religion of China as an advanced animism rather than a monotheism—a peculiar animism rooted in the worship of the spirits of nature and the worship of the spirits of the dead. Perhaps originally those two elements, nature- and ancestor-worship were rivals for the allegi-

169

ance of the people; but later they were fused together by the belief that Heaven, the chief of the nature spirits, was the first forefather of the emperor, and therefore the chief also of the ancestor spirits.

Devotion to the dead was the outstanding characteristic of the Chinese religion from the very beginning. It was incumbent upon all men, high as well as low, to worship the spirits of their individual forefathers. The emperor worshipped the spirit of Heaven as his ancestor, and the regular sacrifices which he offered to it were the occasion of tremendous ritual display. In a wide deserted reach of sand just south of Peking there still stands the magnificent altar of pure white marble upon which the emperor, clad in robes as azure as the sky, kow-towed and made offerings once each year. It was believed that if the emperor should make the slightest error in those annual rites, lo, the whole world would straightway go to chaos! And for any other man in the land to presume to sacrifice to the spirit associated with Heaven was tantamount to a declaration of rebellion. The emperor was the religious head of the nation, and because the greater spirits were supposed to be his exclusive ancestors, their worship was deemed his exclusive privilege. Annually he made offerings to the spirit of the Earth, from which he also claimed descent. He made them in a second sandy, pine-dotted plain outside Peking, and with much the same pomp as was employed by him in worshipping Heaven. He also worshipped the spirits of the soil and the crops and the rivers, and if they did not respond properly, he deposed them much as he might depose a disobedient prince. Being "Son of

Heaven and Earth," he had the right to reduce or increase the number of spirits at will!

All this, however, was only the state religion. The ordinary people could no more approach the god called Heaven than they could approach the emperor, and they could no more share in the worship of Heaven than they could have a hand in the government. Necessarily, therefore, they cherished a separate religion of their own. Harried by the dangers and frustrations of life, they turned for help to the spirits of their own forefathers. Funerals were the occasion of the most elaborate rites and offerings. Clothes and food were put into the graves. Even retainers and relatives were sometimes slaughtered and buried with the corpse of a man of rank. The same thing, of course, was done in Egypt when a king died. The pyramids are stocked full with sumptuous furniture and other possessions. In early Greece, too, that practice was once observed, and there it was carried to such excess that the statesman, Solon, felt compelled to legislate against it. But in China, where the custom must also have threatened to become a serious menace to economic stability, it was curbed in another way. It was not suppressed there but allegorized. What was called the "make-see" device was introduced, and thenceforth the slaves buried with the corpse were merely wooden dolls, and the clothes were of paper! Mere pictures of food and furniture were considered real enough to be sacrificed and buried with the dead!

Perhaps that subterfuge was possible in China and not in other lands because the Chinese took a peculiar attitude toward those who had departed this life. In Egypt, Greece, and wherever else possessions were buried with the dead, it was frankly conceded that the practice was observed in order that the departed souls might be well taken care of in the next world. The Chinese, however, refused to make that admission. They knew nothing about any other world than this, and seemed not to have been interested enough even to speculate about it. There was a distinct belief in China that the dead did survive somewhere—but just where, no one troubled to ask. All that the Chinese were concerned about was that the ghosts of the dead should come back and help the living. To that end they offered regular sacrifices to the ghosts, worshipping them through the medium of living "personators" who sat stock-still throughout the ceremony, and then ate a share of the offerings. In later days simple memorial tablets of stone were made to serve as substitutes for these "personators." The higher classes built temples in which to keep their ancestral tablets; the lower kept them in the main (usually the only) room in their huts.

The sacrifices to the spirits of the dead were really family feasts. All the art and mystery of Chinese cooking went into the preparation of the sauces, relishes, little cakes, and condiments that were used. Divers drinks made from millet were set out with those dishes of food; and then the ceremony began. With the most scrupulous care each minute detail of the ritual was enacted, while drums boomed, flutes screeched, and huge stringed instruments let out their persistent ping-ping. Both men and women sang songs and danced pantomimic dances that were imagined to be entertaining to the ghosts in the room.   For hours the ceremony went on, sometimes outlasting the day.   And then finally the "prayer officer" would declare that the ghosts were satisfied.   Gravely he would bless the celebrant, saying: "Fragrant hath been thy filial sacrifice, and the spirits have delighted in the liquors and viands.   They shower on thee a hundred blessings, each as it is desired and as certain as law.   Thou hast been exact and earnest, and thou wilt surely be blessed with favors in the myriads and tens of myriads."   Whereupon bells and drums would raise a mighty din, and the spirits of the dead would politely leave.   Having sat in ghostly invisibility throughout the ceremony, having hearkened to the noise, smelled the punk, eaten of the food, and drunk till they were presumed to be full, the spirits would "tranquilly withdraw" to that unknown bourne where they had their permanent residence.   And the celebrants, exhausted but happy, would then arise and wearily set to clearing away the dishes. . . .

In no other part of the world did a religion of so bland a character develop.   The element of fear was either nonexistent in it, or kept effectively buried beneath a thick skin of courage and confidence.   There was no such thing as prayer for the benefit of the dead, for no Chinese dared to insult his ancestors by imagining them to be in any need of help.   Prayers were offered *to* the dead, and only in order to bring them near and secure their aid.   Of course, it must not be imagined that the Chinese peasants three thousand years ago knew no demons to fear or taboos to dread.   But it is safe to say that, of all ancient peoples, the Chinese were the least intimidated by such things. Perhaps that is why of all ancient peoples the Chinese were the first to dare push forward along that adventurous path which we call civilization. Perhaps it was because the Chinese lived largely without terror and altogether without priests, and that in an age when Athens was still a village and Rome was not yet built, when Britain was still outside the world and Gaul was but a wilderness roamed by savages, China was already a civilized land where people rode around in carriages, lived in well-built houses, dressed in silk, wore leather shoes, sat on chairs, used tables, ate food from plates, measured time by a sundial, and carried umbrellas! . . .

2

BUT if one dares to claim that the fearless, priestless religion of China was responsible for her early advance in civilization, one must admit it was responsible also for her early arrest. Today China is one of the most backward lands on earth, and it seems evident that her backward-looking ancestor-worship is in large part to blame for that condition. For ancestor-worship has remained the orthodox religion of China. Until the revolution occurred in 1912, it was still possible to see the emperor with his vast retinue go out to the great altars south and north of Peking, and sacrifice there to Heaven and Earth almost exactly as did his predecessors three thousand years earlier. And although the coming of a republic to China has brought an end to that imperial worship of Heaven, the old family worship of the ghosts of the ancestors still persists. It may be far less naive and crude today than it was when the night of barbarism had barely lifted in China; but of all the religions in the world it has suffered least alteration at the hands of time.

It is customary in the West to speak of the orthodox ancestor-worship of China as Confucianism. It must not be imagined, however, that the figure of Confucius is related to this religion as, for instance, Buddha is related to Buddhism, or Mohammed is related to Mohammedanism. Confucius was not at all the founder of the religion, or even its reformer. Rather he was its conserver, taking hold of it twenty-five hundred years ago, when it was just beginning to decay, and revivifying it so that it could remain the dominant force in the life of the Chinese from then on. He said of himself that he was "not a maker but a transmitter, believing in and loving the ancients"—and in hardly a word or act did he belie that description.

Confucius, whose Chinese name was Kung-fu-tze, lived in that amazing century, the sixth B. C., which produced Mahavira and Buddha in India, Zoroaster (perhaps) in Persia, and Jeremiah, Ezekiel, and the Second Isaiah in Israel. He was born in 551 B. C., and of his early life we know practically nothing. All we are told with any credibility is that at twenty-two he was already a teacher, and an extraordinarily popular one. But his following seems to have been quite unlike the following of most other young teachers who have left their mark on civilization. Those who sat at the feet of Confucius were not zealous rebels but pious students. For Confucius himself was in no sense a rebel. He was an antiquarian, a man who loved the ancients and devoted himself whole-souled to the study of their wisdom and their ways. Very early he acquired the standing of an expert in the ancient ritual customs, and he counted as one of the great experiences of his life the opportunity which once came to him to visit Peking and inspect the places where the great sacrifices to Heaven and Earth were offered.

For many years Confucius spent all his time collecting and editing the old writings of his people, and he was not called upon to apply himself to practical affairs until he was fifty years of age. In 501 he received the appointment of chief magistrate to a city named Chung-tu; and tradition declares that within a twelvemonth he had rid that city of every vestige of crime. He accomplished this miracle by subjecting all life to an elaborate etiquette. Even the food which different classes might eat was regulated. All living beings were regimented, and even the corpses were laid away in coffins of a prescribed thickness and buried in graves of a prescribed shape!

Whereupon, so goes the story, the duke of the province elevated Confucius to ever higher offices, finally making him the Minister of Justice. And as Minister of Justice, Confucius haltered the population so effectively with rules and regulations, that in a very little while the whole province became a model state, and all the laws against crime fell into disuse. "Dishonesty and dissoluteness were ashamed. Loyalty and good faith marked every man, and chastity and submissiveness graced every woman. Strangers in vast multitudes came flocking from other cities, and the fame of Kung-fu-tze, the idol of the people, flew in song from every mouth"—at least, so declare the not altogether unprejudiced biographers of the sage. . . .

But matters went too well to last for long. Neighboring princes, jealous of the prosperity and peace in the reformed province, seduced the mind of the duke with presents of fast horses and faster dancing girls. The wonder-working minister, suddenly finding himself out of favor, sadly—and very slowly, for to the last he hoped the duke might repent—shook the dust of the ungrateful p r o v i n c e from his feet. He began to make the rounds of China, going from one c o u r t to another and freely offering his services to every prince and minister he met. With naive assurance he told t h e m, "In a twelve-month I could effect g r e a t changes, and in three years I could perfect everything!" But there was none in the land to take advantage of his offer. He wandered about for thirteen long years without find-

KING-FU-TZE

ing a single ruler willing to give him employment. Evidently he was looked on with suspicion by princes and people, and at least once he was attacked by a mob and almost assassinated. Many a day he was forced to go without food, and many a night he was left without shelter. Yet during all those years his heart did not fail him. Stubbornly he remained confident that Heaven would protect him in his mission of truth, and despite every discouragement he continued to hope for a chance to save the world.

But at last there came the day when he could wander no longer. Life began to ebb from his old bones, and in sorrow he returned to his native province to spend his last days in the study of his beloved ancient scrolls. His body shrivelled into a dry yellow sack, and his courage withered and faded quite away. Perhaps he grew querulous toward the end; certainly he became plaintive and helplessly resentful. "The great mountain totters," he mumbled to himself as death came over him; "aye, the stout beam breaks, and the wise man wilteth like a plant! There is not one in the empire that will make me his teacher! Verily, my time has come to die!" . . . And thus ended the life of Kung-fu-tze. . . .

3

NOW it is obvious that this man, one of the greatest in all history, hardly deserves to be described as a religious prophet. Prophets almost invariably are rebels, holy heretics forever breaking with the past. But this man, Confucius, sought not to break with the past, but rather to heal the breach that had already been made. And he did heal it. By his diligent labor in editing the old sacred writings of China and establishing their paramount authority, he laid a yoke on his people that to this day they have been unable to throw off. . . . This is not the place to go into a discussion of the books, the five *king,* and the four *shu,* which he or his immediate disciples under him are supposed to have written.

For the most part they are made up of collections of
ancient ritual hymns, ceremonial laws, magic "permuta-
tions," historical chronicles, and proverbs.   Their importance to us rests not upon their own merit, but solely
upon the very real though nigh incredible fact that
almost to this day they have dominated the life and
thought of all learned China.   Upon that fact, too, rests
the importance of Confucius.   He was in no sense an in-
novator.   He did not contribute a single new idea or
practice or experience to the inherited religion of his
country.   But he was most effectively a conserver.   He
took hold of an already ancient and decadent religion,
and by dint of organizing its scattered traditions, managed to infuse imperishable life into it.   It is question-
able whether any other man in all history has had
more lasting influence on a people than that old sage
of Shantung who in his life could not even get a
job! . . .

But though Confucius organized and virtually established a great religion, he himself in the narrower
sense was not a religious man.   He knew very little about
the gods, and seems to have cared less.   When a disciple
asked about the service of the spirits, he is reported
to have answered: "So long as thou art not able to
serve men, how canst thou serve the spirits?"   Nor
had he a word to say about the next world.   "So long
as thou dost not know life," he declared, "how canst
thou know death?"   He saw no reason for prayer, and
scorned all interest in the supernatural.   "To give oneself earnestly to the service of men, and while respecting
the spirits, to make no great to-do about them—that
is wisdom," he said. . . . Quite clearly, therefore, Con-

fucius had little of that fear and none of that humility which drive men to implore the help of gods. He saw little need for gods, for he believed in himself, in his own might as a righteous man. "What a superior man seeks," he declared, "is in himself!" . . . It seemed to Confucius that if only a man conducted himself with propriety, then frustration and despair were impossible. He believed in the moral power of deeds quite as much as his savage ancestor might have believed in the efficacy of magic spells. Indeed, it is reported that once he declared the very stars were held in their courses solely by the moral propriety of man. Not unjustly, therefore, Confucius may be described as a shaman who relied on moral prescriptions rather than magic rites as the means wherewith to control the universe. His highest contribution was in the field of ethics, and his proverbs are quoted—and in the breach, at least, observed—still today. There is no extravagant idealism to be found in them, no exaggerated turn-the-other-cheekiness. There are proverbs for the guidance of all-too-human humanity, and other-worldiness has no place in them. "It is folly to withdraw from the world," Confucius declared, "and make fellowship with birds and beasts that are not our fellows. With whom should I make fellowship save with suffering mankind? . . ."

But it is important that we resist the temptation to exaggerate the majesty of Confucius even as an ethical teacher. The common tendency to class him with the great sages who came markedly to the front in Greece a century or two later is hardly warranted. It is true that they also were quite willing to bend the knee to any and every god so long as they were left to bend their thoughts as they alone willed.   But they differed from Confucius in that they bent their thoughts to the new, not the old.   They dared to venture out into virgin lands of the spirit, blazing trails through wildernesses no human minds had yet traversed.   But Confucius?   He deployed the forces of his reason only into the decayed and rutted moors of the past.   He may have doubted the existence of the ancient gods, but never did he doubt the validity of the ancient rites paid to them.   He held it incumbent upon all men to worship with the most scrupulous care, not so much for the gracious benefit of the spirits who were worshipped as for disciplinary benefit to the men who did the worshipping.   Propriety, regularity, exact and punctilious observance of the "three hundred points of ceremony and three thousand points of behavior"—these were the ultimate ends and aims of life.   Confucius himself, we are told, carried this ritual of regularity in his life to quite fantastic extremes.   Even his posture while asleep in bed was in accordance with a fixed ruling! . . . Everything had to be ordered, for "Order is Heaven's only law."   All change was injurious, and salvation could be obtained only if none tried to disturb the religious, social, and political order that already was established.   Of course, one had to go for the ultimate authority for the details of that order to the golden past. Whatever was *of* the fathers seemed to Confucius to be *for* the sons.   Filial piety, respect for the ancestors, was in his eyes the highest of all virtues.

And exalting that virtue, he died.

4

BUT then Confucius began to live anew. Devoted disciples set down his words in huge collections which are called the "Analects." The memory of the great sage began to grow in might, especially in the following century, when a new disciple, Mencius, arose to spread his doctrines. In the third century a successful usurper of the throne tried his best to u p r o o t the whole growth, for its uncompromising condemnation of all nonconformity and change made his rebellious l i f e indescribably hard. This emperor put forth systematic effort to destroy all the Confucian books, and to slay all those who knew them by heart. But he faīled, and when a member of an old-time dynasty regained the imperial t h r o n e, Confucianism b e g a n to flourish as never before.

A CONFUCIAN TEMPLE

Confucius himself was exalted until he became a veritable god. In the year 1 A. D., the old antiquarian was canonized. "Duke Ni, the All-Complete and All-Illustrious," he was officially named. . . . In 57 A.D., it was ordered that sacrifices be offered to him at all the colleges. . . . In the year 89 he was

raised to the higher imperial rank of "Earl," and in 267
it was decreed that more elaborate animal sacrifices be
offered to him four times a year. . . . In 492 even more
honor was done him, and he was officially canonized
"the Venerable Ni, the Accomplished Sage." . . . In
555 separate temples for the worship of Confucius were
ordered at the capitals of all prefectures in China, and in
740 his image was moved from the side to the center of
the Imperial College, to stand with the historic Kings of
China. . . . In 1068 he was raised to the full rank of
Emperor. . . . And finally in 1907 the Empress
Dowager raised him to the first grade of worship, rank-
ing him with the deities Heaven and Earth!

And thus it has come about that he who in life was
beaten and hounded is now a god for all China. He
who had no sheltering place now has over fifteen hundred temples to house his tablets; he who was starved
now has over sixty-two thousand animals offered to his
ghost every year. Worse still, he who saw no untoward
need for prayer has himself been made the object of
prayer, and he who had little use for gods has himself
been made co-equal with Heaven. . . . Irony!

II.   TAOISM

CONFUCIUS, the practical man, the organizer, the
high-priest of the meticulous, is frequently pointed to
as the personification of the entire Chinese character.
But that is not just. In the maze which is the Chinese
mind—as in the maze which is every other mind—
there are many paths shadowed by wild hedges of
mysticism. If China has made a god of the practical

Confucius, she has done no less by the mystical Lao-Tze. . . .

Unhappily we have almost no reliable data concerning the life of Lao-Tze.   His case is not like that of most of the other great men of the past—like the case, for instance, of Moses, Buddha, Confucius, Jesus, or Mohammed.   Concerning each of these men we have legends and traditions that offer at least a few nails not too loose to sustain the threadbare tapestries of "critical" biography.   But concerning Lao-Tze we have not even a half-dependable fact.   Our main source of information is a short sketch of two hundred and forty-eight Chinese words which were set down at least five centuries after the philosopher's death.

Lao-Tze, whose name may be translated the "Old Scholar," or perhaps the "Old Boy," is said to have been born in the year 604 B. C., and is supposed to have been the librarian at the court of the province of Chou.   There is an anecdote told of how Confucius, while staying once at this court, tried to learn from the then very aged librarian some obscure details concerning the outworn customs of the province.   But all he got for his pains was a severe drubbing, and he left the court saying Lao-Tze was as inexplicable and terrible as a dragon.   Confucius was completely bewildered by the old man, for in him he was confronted with a mind more unlike his own than seemed possible.   Lao-Tze was possessed of one of those tremendously inquisitive, speculative, adventurous intellects.   He was forever asking *why?* Unlike Confucius, Lao-Tze could not blandly take the world for granted, but had to know first who was granting it, and how, and why.   And he was old, and very tired, and very wise. The lust after earthly conquest had long seeped out of his brittle bones, and only the vanity of all life and striving filled his bleared little almond eyes. No wonder, then, if he had slight patience with the eager, hopeful, bustling young world-saver who came to consult him on the forgotten ways of the past.

The story is told of how in his very last days, Lao-Tze tried to flee from the province of Chou because of the anarchy into which the state had fallen. Like Confucius, the older man sorely lamented the "poverty of the people" and the "great disorder" and chicanery in the land; but, unlike Confucius, he did not feel himself called upon to try to remedy these evils. He told himself that "to withdraw into obscurity is the way of Heaven," and forthwith tried to clear out. But at the frontier the captain of the garrison halted the old man, and asked him to write out his philosophy of life before going into exile. And so there, in a little frontier garrison in ancient China, Lao-Tze wrote the book which is the Bible of the whole Taoist religion. The "Tao-Teh-king" the book is called, and although many scholars claim it was never written by Lao-Tze himself, it is reasonably certain that it contains many of the ideas which the old sage himself thought out. It is a very brief book, barely five thousand words in length, and could be set down here verbatim in less than twenty pages. No doubt its very conciseness, its severely ungenerous brevity, was responsible for the little understanding it received in later generations.

The book consists of two sections: the first, the Tao, sets out to tell the *why* of the universe, and the second,

the Teh, endeavors to tell the *how* of life. The word
Tao is almost untranslatable. A remote approximation
to it is the word "Nature" or perhaps "Way." Tao
is that which is behind all other things, the fundamental
reality, the "Way of the Universe." As Lao-Tze himself said: "There is a Something undifferentiated and
yet perfect, which existed before heaven and earth ever
came into being. I know not its name, and if I must
designate it, I can call it only Tao." The outstanding
characteristic of this Tao is that it does everything
without giving any sign of doing anything. It is a
great, inchoate, incorporeal, intangible Something that
never exerts itself, and never gets excited. It simply
is. . . .

And in that very passivity, said Lao-Tze, the Tao
sets the standard for the proper life of man. There is
but one Teh, one "Virtue," for man, and that is to
emulate the poise and inaction of Tao. It is vain beyond
words for any individual to try to accomplish anything
in a fever. Fussy meddling with the world, breathless
striving to reform or debauch it, are so much sheer folly.
There are but "Three Jewels" of character, and choicest
of them is *wu wei*, "inactivity." The true disciple is
everlastingly silent, even about Tao. He rejects all
learning and scoffs at all hunger for learning. He is a
thoroughgoing nihilist, refusing to trouble himself
sufficiently to believe anything or do anything. Even
to defend himself from injury is too much of a bother.
Confucius taught that reciprocity is one of the main
laws of ethics. The good should be requited with good
and the evil with evil. But Lao-Tze taught far differently. He declared: "To them that are good I am

good, and to them that are not good I am also good;
thus all get to be good.   To them that are sincere I am
sincere, and to them that are not sincere I am also
sincere; thus all get to be sincere." . . . Weakness
seemed to him the greatest strength.   "There is nothing
in the world more soft and weak than water," he said;
"yet for attacking things that are firm and strong
nothing surpasses it."   An extraordinary spectacle, this:
a decrepit old yellow-skinned sage sitting there in a wild
frontier camp in China five hundred years before Jesus
ever walked on earth, and calmly telling the world to
return good for evil! . . .

Next to inactivity, the most precious "Jewel" of
character is humility.   "When merit hath been achieved,
take it not unto thyself," said Lao-Tze.   "If thou dost
not take it unto thyself, behold, it can never be taken
from thee!"   Or again: "Keep behind, and thou shalt
inevitably be kept in front."   "The wise man is he
alone who rests satisfied with what he has."   "There is
no greater guilt than to sanction ambition; neither is
there any greater calamity than to be discontented with
one's lot. . . ."   And next to humility the most
precious "jewel" is frugality.   Just as out of weakness
comes strength and out of humility comes prominence,
so out of frugality comes liberality.   As Lao-Tze put
it: "The wise man doth not accumulate.   The more
he expends for others, the more doth he possess of his
own; the more he giveth to others, the more hath he
for himself."

Of religion in the narrow sense of the word, Lao-
Tze said nothing.   He did not believe in the gods, and
he was unalterably opposed to all forms of worship.

He thought sacrifice and prayer both vain and impertinent, for they endeavored to bring nature into harmony with man, when properly it was man's duty to let himself passively sink into harmony with nature.   Only once in the "Tao-Teh-king" is the Supreme god, Shang-ti, mentioned, and then only to make known that he is inferior to the ineffable Tao.   In the narrower sense of the word, therefore, Lao-Tze was distinctly not a religious man.

But in the broader sense of the word, Lao-Tze was superlatively a man of faith.   For all the eerie morbidness of his nihilistic doctrine, Lao-Tze was profoundly a spiritual being.   He saw with blinding clarity what Confucius never even remotely suspected—that all life is but an ark of bulrushes drowning in a swamp of vanity.   Desperately was he conscious of the need for security, of the need for something infinite in time and space to which finite little man might cling.   And that was why he was so attached to the idea of Tao, and taught that the one road to salvation for every man was utter union with that Tao.   In all the mystic literature of the world, it would be hard to find a warmer or richer glow than that in the "Tao-Teh-king."

2

OF course a teaching so aloof and unpractical could not remain undefiled and stand any chance of entering the hearts of ordinary men.   Tradition declares that when Lao-Tze had made an end to his writing, and was free to take up his journey once more, he went off into the world beyond, and was never again seen by man.   He died, and perhaps he was buried—though no man knows how or where. But his book lived, and soon many philosophers were to be found in the hills or far in the forests of China, striving there to live according to the teachings of that book. In caves and the hollowed trunks of trees they sat and labored to practice kenosis—the seeing, doing, and thinking of nothing.

And the plain people were, of course, tremendously impressed when rumors of the strange doctrines of the "Tao-Teh-king" reached them. And they were even more impressed by the extraordinary men who actually tried to live up to those doctrines. They imagined such men must be not merely saints, but also magicians. Whereupon not a few of those men, either out of knavery or self-delusion, did set up as magicians. The "Tao-Teh-king" degenerated in their hands from a source of spiritual wisdom into a textbook of magic formulae. They harried and fretted it to shreds in a mad hunt for the secrets it might contain. Emperors were fooled into spending fortunes on the hare-brained researches of so-called "professors of Taoism." In the third century A. D. one emperor actually sent out two huge expeditions to discover certain magic islands wherein, according to the "professors," the elixir of life might be found that would make all men immortal, and the philosopher's stone that could turn all metals to gold. In the middle ages another emperor actually died of drinking too much of an elixir of life! . . . Men of all classes spent their substance in a frantic hunt for those vain things, life and wealth, which the little old mystic, Lao-Tze, had scorned most bitterly.

A whole religion of Taoism arose. Under the in-

A "PROFESSOR OF TAOISM"

fluence of Buddhism, the Taoist hermits began to organize themselves into orders. All their lives they did everything imaginable just to acquire great monasteries in which to do nothing! . . . Temples arose, and in them priests—*Wu* they were called—offered sacrifices to idols! Even a high-priesthood arose, and to this day there lives on top of a mountain in the province of Kiang-si a pope of the Taoist Church who calls himself T'ien-shi, the "Heaven Master!"

And thus has time played scurvily with the work of Lao-Tze. He who declared that the wise man never accumulates has been made the prophet of a cult that seeks naught save accumulation. He who declared that life is the sorriest of vanities has been hailed the discoverer of magic potions to make life everlasting. Above all, he who laughed at the gods and scoffed at their worship has himself been made a god. . . . What irony! For two thousand and eighty-one years now, ever since 156 B. C., that little old nihilist, Lao-Tze, has been worshipped with sacrifices throughout the land of China! . . .

III. BUDDHISM

BUT the religion of China today is neither Confucianism alone, nor Taoism—nor even a combination of the two. A third element long ago entered into the amalgam: Buddhism. Sometime in the second century B. C., after having made its way through Afghanistan and Turkestan, Buddhism finally entered China. It did not spread at once, however. Buddhism then was not yet sufficiently bedizened with easy doctrines and lovable idols for it to have any great proselyting power. But by the second century A. D. it had become an entirely new religion, very generously salvationistic and frankly compromising; and then it spread with great rapidity.

The new Buddhism seems to have had an irresistible lure for the people of China. It had comforts to offer that their own old religions knew nothing about. For one thing, it offered them a very personal and personable god, an idolized Buddha whose serenely placid face and gracefully rotund body could be seen and kissed and kow-towed to in every temple. Confucianism allowed neither idols nor temples. Sacrifices were offered only to tablets, and on altars under the open sky. But this new religion from India brought with it a whole galaxy

A CHINESE BUDDHA

192

of attractive idols, and a whole art of temple architecture.

Then, too, Buddhism had a great deal of information to impart concerning life after death. Confucianism, for all its eagerness to obtain aid from the dead, had nothing at all to say concerning their abode. But Buddhism had a very wonderful heaven and a very terrible hell of which to tell, and made prayer for the dead a desperately important matter. After the coming of Buddhism the Chinese in their worship of the ancestors began to pray *for* the souls of the dead, as well as *to* them. At present, even in Chinese homes where Buddhism is not accepted, it is usual for masses to be recited for the peace of the dead.

A CHINESE ALTAR

But the new Buddhism's greatest attraction lay in the fact that it was so thoroughly a religion of salvation. To poor blind people groping about in the darkness of life, it offered light. It told them that they had merely to believe in the Buddha, in him who was called the "Enlightened One," and straightway all would become as day for them. Neither Confucianism nor Taoism had a tithe as much to offer. Confucianism, indeed, had nothing to say concerning salvation. It was so busy telling men *how* to live that it forgot even to ask—let alone to answer—the question *why* they should live. And Taoism, fallen till it was a mere slut in the laboratories of alchemists, was no better. Even though it did ask why men should live, it offered an answer that the masses could not possibly fathom. It assured the coolie in the rice-swamp that he lived to make it possible for the emperor and his magicians to go hunting the elixir of life—and that was far from an adequate explanation for him.

So Buddhism—or more exactly, the religion that was called Buddhism seven hundred years after Buddha died —had no very great difficulty in winning adherents in China. From the third century on it flourished openly. Temples and monasteries sprang up throughout the land, and Chinese by the myriad were converted. The governing class, it is true, did not always favor the new faith. It was something new, and from their Confucian point of view it was therefore bad. . . . In the fifth century dreadful persecutions of the Buddhists took place. Monasteries and pagodas were pillaged and burnt, and unnumbered monks and nuns were deported or put to death. But in a little while came a reaction, and at the beginning of the sixth century the very emperor himself abdicated his throne in order to become a Buddhist monk! In the following centuries the faith continued to fluctuate in public favor. Again and again the mandarins protested against it, claiming it was altogether incompatible with the authentic old Chinese spirit. They accused it also of fostering lewdness, especially in its nunneries. In 884 A. D. violent persecutions broke out again, and Buddhism then suffered a blow from which it never fully recovered. All the forty thousand Buddhist monasteries, temples, and pagodas in the land were ordered to be razed to the ground. Their bronze images, bells, and metal plates were melted down and coined into money, and their iron statues were recast into ploughshares and shovels. As for the monks and nuns—who numbered well over a quarter of a million—they were all summarily commanded to return to secular life or leave the country. And though in later years Buddhism managed to rebuild some of those monasteries and fill them with new throngs of monastics, never did it regain its pristine importance.

2

SO China today is the land of the "Three Truths": Confucianism, Taoism, and Buddhism. Confucianism is largely the religion of the learned classes, and all candidates for civil service appointments are expected to pass an examination in its nine holy books. Taoism and Buddhism are the faiths to which the masses alone render allegiance; but both are little more than a dark cloaca, swarming with spirits, devils, ghosts, vampires, werewolves, and green-eyed dragons. The mind of the Chinese peasant today is simply cluttered up with crowds of jostling demons. Throughout the land one finds the Wu, the demon-chasing priests, eking out a living by uttering spells over the diseased and the maimed. A great dread prevails everywhere of unlucky days and unlucky places. Months, even years, are spent in a terrified hunt to find a lucky plot for the burial of the family dead. (In the days of anti-Buddhist agitation, many a Buddhist monastery was spared by the rulers of the locality solely because its presence was supposed to make the surrounding soil lucky for use as a graveyard.)　There is a rooted conviction throughout the land that each place on earth has its own *feng-Shui,* its own "spirit climate."　No house, no grave, no shop can be built without first consulting the Feng-Shui magician as to whether its proposed site is lucky. . . .

And to such a sorry faith has a great old Chinese race descended.　Fear is to blame for it, of course.　It was fear that picked out China's eyes, and made her blind. And it is fear that now flaps its ghastly wings about her, and makes her clutch at every spirit.　Fear . . . fear. . . .

Book Five
What Happened
in Persia

197

BOOK FIVE

WHAT HAPPENED IN PERSIA

I. ZOROASTRIANISM

1: The animism of early Iran—did Zoroaster ever live?—the legends concerning his life 2: The gospel of Zoroaster—Good vs. Evil—the fire altars—the future life. 3: The ordeal of Zoroaster—his first converts—death. 4: The corruption of the gospel—ritual—burial customs—"defilement"—the priesthood —Mithraism. 5: The influence of Zoroastrianism on Judaism —on Christianity—on Islam—the Parsees.

BOOK FIVE

WHAT HAPPENED IN PERSIA

I. ZOROASTRIANISM

THE scene of our story shifts westward, leaving the walled cities and rice-swamps of China and going up to the wild plateau of Iran in western Asia. The first white men in Iran, the region now called Persia, were of the Aryan stock; and their religion was closely akin to that of the Aryans who invaded India and Greece. It was an animism centering in the worship of Ashura, Anahita, Mithra, Haoma, and many other spirits supposed to dwell in natural objects. Just how or where that animism had its origin, no one knows; for no one knows whence the Aryans came. Nor do we know exactly when that animism came to an end, for no authentic records exist as to the history of Iran before the seventh century B. C. All that is known is that a primitive animism arose, flourished and then disappeared—and that for its disappearance a certain man named Zarathustra—or more popularly, Zoroaster—was responsible.

But even that much is not known with indisputable certainty. Some scholars today are convinced that there never was a Zoroaster on earth. They maintain he is but another of those mythical personages conjured up by a later generation to explain some vast religious or political change in its past. Moses, Mahavira, Buddha, Lao-Tze, Krishna, and Jesus, are similarly classed by them as figures devoid of genuine historicity, as mere fictional heroes created to dramatize and personify slowly matured and impersonal movements. And it must be admitted that there is no unchallengeable evidence to prove the existence of any one of those colossal figures, no carvings in enduring stone, or contemporary records set down on still-existing scrolls. All that remains concerning them are webs of legend and gospel spun by generation after generation of zealous but imaginative disciples. Most of those legends were on the loose tongues of men for ages before they were first set down in writing. And even after that, they no doubt still came in for great change at the hands of nodding or overconfident scribes. It is far from easy to base a critical faith on their florid and purely traditional testimony.

Yet most reputable scholars, even of the most critical school, incline to agree that those webs of tradition contain at least a few threads of truth. They do so on the score that the acceptance of the historicity of Moses, Buddha, or Jesus puts less strain on our reason than the alternative of rejection. After all, wherever a new and heretical religion was founded, there must have been some outstanding individual to take the lead in founding it. It is naturally less difficult to believe that effects have adequate causes than to believe that they have not. . . .

But it is only on such a basis that one can accept

the historicity of Zoroaster. It seems less incredible that
he did exist than that he did not, for some striking
personality must have been at least in part responsible
for the tremendous religious transformation that came
over the ancient people of Iran. Proof less negative
is not at hand. The Persian scriptures, the Avesta, contain a group of hymns called the Gathas which *may*
have been the work of Zoroaster; but just how old
they are, no one knows. Tradition gives 660 B. C. as
the date of the prophet's birth; but actually it may
even have been as early as 1000 B. C. And tradition
gives the northwest of Iran as his birthplace, a place
somewhere in the neighborhood of the present Armenian
frontier; but actually it may have been at the very
other end of the land. Tradition further declares his
birth to have been the outcome of an immaculate conception. (It is appalling, how little pride men have
in their own species. Rarely can they bring themselves
to believe that supreme greatness can spring from their
own loins. No, always they must ascribe its paternity
to the gods.) An incomprehensible trinity made up
of the "Glory," the "Guardian Spirit," and the "Material Body," is reputed to have been responsible for the
appearance of Zoroaster on earth. Innumerable miracles
occurred while he still lay in the womb of his mother
to save him from destruction. Demons sought to hold
off the birth, going even to the extreme of trying to
choke the child at the very moment of its delivery. But
in vain. The prodigy was born, and with its very first
breath it uttered a mighty laugh of triumph that was
heard around all the earth.

ZOROASTER SEEKS SALVATION

Zoroaster was indeed a wonderful child—according to the legends. At a very early age he engaged the priests of the old religion in a bitter debate, and routed them. And when grown to the age of youth, he took staff in hand and went off into the world in a quest for righteousness. Sore troubled by the sight of the evil in the world, young Zoroaster could find no peace amid the comforts of his home. So he fled. For three years he tramped the desert trails in search of salvation, of a reason for life. And failing to find it, a great gloom came over him. For seven years then he remained silent, morose and silent, while he brooded over the impenetrable blackness which life had become for him. . . . And then of a sudden, light came. Of a sudden day dawned in his long-benighted soul, and once more he took up his staff and began to wander. But now he was no longer a wanderer seeking for light. No, now he was instead a bearer of light to all others who still sought for it. He went about preaching the salvation that had come to him, and telling how others, too, could attain it. Across the length and breadth of Iran he beat his way, hawking everywhere the gospel that had brought him peace.

2

THE gospel of Zoroaster was as thoroughly native to Iran as its frowning mountains and desert winds. It was stern, rigorous, demanding. There was in it neither the florid confidence revealed in the Vedas, nor the livid despair shown in the Upanishads. Rather there was in it a steel-gray valor that could know life for what it really was, and yet could continue to hope. Religions are so varied largely because the earth contains such varied lands and climates. Religion, as we have already seen, is the technique wherewith man seeks to conquer his environment; and therefore it must necessarily vary according to the locale in which it is employed. The religion of the overabundant valley of the Indus could not very well be anything but one of ease. In the intolerable furnace of the Ganges Valley, the religion could hardly be anything else than one of hopelessness. And on the stern plateau of Iran, it could not but be one of fierce courage and struggle. For Iran was a land of perpetual struggle, of perpetual warfare against wind and ice and wilderness. Overwhelming contrasts faced its inhabitants: a great salt desert prostrate with heat at the base of encircling snow-peaked mountains. And the religion there conceived and proclaimed by Zoroaster was likewise one of contrasts. According to it, all the universe was one great battle-ground on which Good and Bad struggled for mastery. On the one side was Ahura Mazda, the Wise Spirit, supported by his six vassals: Good Thought, Right Law, Noble Government, Holy Character, Health, and Immortality. Pitted against him was Angra

Mainyu, the Lie Demon, supported by most of the old gods of the popular faith. And midway between the two contending armies stood man. It was absolutely incumbent upon man to choose on which side he would battle: on the side of Good, Purity, and Light, or of Evil, Filth, and Darkness. There could be no slightest compromise or evasion. One had to enlist on one side or the other, just as the beasts, the winds, the very plants were enlisted.

And once each man had chosen his side, then his every word and deed had its effect on the fortunes of the war. It was not prayer but work that was demanded of the worshippers of Ahura Mazda. Their noblest act of devotion was the performance of a task like the irrigating of a desert patch or the bridging of a torrential stream. Ahura Mazda was in essence the spirit of civilization, and the only worship acceptable to him was the spreading of order and stability. He who declared himself on the side of Ahura Mazda was in duty bound to devote all his days to fighting the battle for Light. No mercy was to be shown by him to the enemy, be that enemy some weed or beast or savage from the Turanian wilds. Ahura Mazda was the god of justice, not of mercy, and in his warfare he neither gave nor received quarter. In his service there was no room for sentimentality; one had to be hard and unbending. The one great law of ethics was to give aid to those—and only those—who were also on the side of Good, and never to do them the slightest injury. Even beneficent animals such as those that destroyed rodents, snakes, and other evil creatures, were considered holy and deserving of aid. The penalty for killing a hedgehog was

nine lives spent in hell; for killing an otter it was—
well, to begin with—ten thousand lashes with a horse-
whip.   An inviolable sanctity was attached to the life
of all domestic animals, especially cows, dogs, and sheep.
To care for them and help multiply their number was
the devoutest act of faith. . . .

It was an extraordinary religion, this of the ancient
prophet of Iran.   It preached a technique of coping
with the evils of the universe that was totally at vari-
ance with anything ever before conceived by man.
Zoroaster had no patience with the old gods, Mithra,
Anahita, Haoma, and the rest, and denounced them
all as demons.   The very word *deva*, which had always
meant "gods," he made to connote "devils."   (Both
connotations somehow found their way into the stream
of European languages, and that is why there is still
today so close a likeness in sound between "deviltry"
and "divinity.") . . . Only one heathen rite did
Zoroaster take over, and that was the veneration of fire.
(Some say he came of a family of ancient fire-priests.)
But according to the prophet, fire was not a god to be
worshipped as it may have been worshipped by the
earliest Iranians.   No, it was a mere symbol of Ahura
Mazda.   Fire-altars were to be erected solely as a testi-
monial to the veneration in which the "Wise Spirit"
was held.   Zoroaster may himself have gone about the
land erecting such altars and reciting the hymns called
the Gathas what time he attended the holy flames.
But he made it clear that the erecting or serving of a
fire altar was not the sole or even the chief approach to
the "Wise Spirit."   The chief approach to him was
through daily toil.   "He who sows corn, sows religion."

Laziness was a thing of the Devil. Every morning the demon of laziness whispers in the ear of man: "Sleep on, poor man. It is not time yet." But he alone who arises the first, declared Zoroaster, would be the first to enter Paradise.

No one was left in doubt that there was indeed a Paradise. And there was also a Hell. The true servants of Ahura Mazda would as surely enter the one, it was believed, as the slaves of Angra Mainyu would be hurled into the other. And ultimately the two realms would meet to engage in a terrible climacteric struggle. The long protracted war between Good and Evil would come to a close in "The Affair." Then for a season thick darkness would cover the face of the earth, and the whole universe would quake with the shock of the encounter. Fire and death would swirl over all, and there would be gnashing of teeth and dreadful wailing. The terror in the world would be "like the terror of the lamb when it is devoured by the wolf." . . . But at last the fury would abate, and slowly, wearily, almost ready to perish because of the severity of the ordeal, Ahura Mazda would emerge—the victor. Then all the hills and mountains would melt and pour down over the earth, and all men would have to pass through the boiling lava. To the just and righteous, however, that lava would be as warm milk; only to the wicked would it be scalding and fatal. The just and righteous would wade through it with laughter on their lips, rejoicing over a victory so well won. And the earth thereafter would be an everlasting Paradise wherein there would be no more mountains or deserts or wild beasts or savages. The Kingdom of Ahura Mazda

would have reached its consummation, and all would
be well thenceforth forever and aye. . . .

3

SUCH, as best the scholars can make it out, was the
religion which Zoroaster sought to bring to his fellow
Iranians.   Perhaps it was not so free of heathenisms,
not merely so exalted and superbly spiritual, as the
scholars have pictured it.   Save on the basis of the
miraculous, one finds it nigh impossible to explain the
sprouting of so altogether fair a religion before the night
of barbarism had yet quite lifted in Iran.   But however
much less noble it may have been than it is now pic-

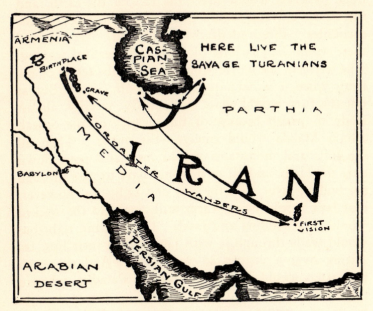

THE WANDERINGS OF ZOROASTER

tured, still it was far too noble for its time. Tradition
declares that for ten harrowing years the appeal of
Zoroaster was like a voice in the wilderness. None
would give ear to the man, or, giving ear, could make
him out. Solitary and misunderstood he went about,
harried by the heathen priests, imprisoned by heathen
princes. More than once he cried out desperately to
his God:

> To what land shall I turn,
> Or whither shall I go?
> Far am I from kinsmen,
> Distant from friends;
> Foully am I dealt with by peasants and kings.
> Unto Thee I cry, O Wise Spirit,
> Unto Thee I cry, Give me Help!

He needed help, did poor Zoroaster, for his was no
light task. It was a day when the conversion of a
people could come only as a result of converting their
prince—and princes were not willing to be converted.
After ten long years of struggle, the outcome seemed
altogether hopeless. When one winter's night he was
refused shelter even for his "two steeds shivering with
cold," a great temptation to surrender almost tore him
from his faith. The Lie Demon—so goes the legend—
took hold of Zoroaster and tried to shake him from his
devotion. "Hold!" cried the Lie Demon. "Dare not
to destroy my handiwork! Remember, thou art the
son of thy mother, and thy mother worshipped me.
Renounce the right religion of Mazda, and obtain at
last the favor of kings." Fierce then waxed the struggle
in the soul of the tired prophet; but in the end the truth

was victor. "No!" the prophet cried back to the Lie Demon. "I shall not renounce the right religion of Mazda—not though life and limb and soul be torn asunder!" . . .

And soon thereafter Zoroaster made his first convert. He was not a prince, however—merely one of his own cousins. Still, it was a start—enough of a start to keep the prophet at his task for two years more. And then at last a real prince was converted, a mighty ruler named Vishtasp who became the Constantine of the new faith. A church militant was formed, and holy wars were waged against the Turanian savages on the north. Those Turanians were wild bedouin raiders

THE TURANIANS WERE BEDOUIN RAIDERS

who made the life of the Iranian farmers a nightmare, and they seemed to Zoroaster the personification of all Ahura Mazda hated. The prophet waged war without mercy against them. "I am he that tortureth the sinners," he declared, "and he that avengeth the righteous. Though I bring bitter woe, still must I do that which Ahura Mazda declareth right." Yet for all his unsparing zeal, Zoroaster seems not to have been narrow. "If even among the Turanians there arise those who help the settlements of Piety," he declared, "behold even with them shall the Lord have his habitation." According to tradition, one of Zoroaster's most loyal and trusted followers was a Turanian named Fryana. . . .

Such was the gospel by which Zoroaster lived—and for which he died. For it may be that he did die in its ministry. Legend has it that Zoroaster was struck down while he stood ministering at an altar of fire, brought to book by one of those heathen priests whose worship he had routed. . . .

4

WE may not be quite certain as to just what was the teaching of Zoroaster himself; but there can be no doubt as to what it became at the hands of his successors. It degenerated. The faith voiced in those prophetic hymns called the Gathas was too nobly exacting, too exaltedly strenuous to last in its original purity. It was too bright for the weak eyes of ordinary men to gaze on steadily, too vast for their little hands to grasp. So very soon its brightness was dulled by the streaming breath of sedentary theologians, while its vastness was eaten

away by the attrition of greedy priests.   In the beginning, Ahura Mazda may have been but a spirit, a dream,
an ideal.   He may have been little more than the name
that stood for all that was good in the world, a conviction around which to build one's life. But a later generation made Ahura Mazda the name of a person, a super-
human being with not a few crudely human attributes.
Ormuzd, he was called. . . . And Angra Mainyu, the
Lie Demon, the name that stood for all that was evil in

the world, also became
the name of a person.
Ahriman, this p e r s o n
was later called, and he
was then thought to be
not merely the Agent of
E v i l, but its original
creator. . . . The s i x
spirits, Good Thought,
R i g h t Law, and the
others, which Zoroaster
had thought of as quali-
ties s e r v i n g Ahura
Mazda, became very per-
sonal angels, and were
increased in n u m b e r
from six to s i x t y,
seventy, a thousand, ten
thousand! And opposed
to t h e m were set up
m a n y thousands of
d e v i l s. . . . All the
winning simplicity of

THE PROPHET OF IRAN

Zoroaster's vague ideas was bit by bit destroyed by be-dizening theologians.

But this elaboration of Zoroaster's stark doctrine was not nearly so tragic as the perversion that ensued. The poetry and truth of Zoroaster became prose and error at the hands of those who came after him. If he said "be pure," meaning clean with righteousness, straight-way they imagined with their literal minds that he meant be *ritually* pure. Currency was given to the most ex-travagant notions of taboo and "defilement," and to the absurdest rules for their removal. Certain things were declared to be "holy" and certain other things "un-holy"; and ne'er the twain dared be brought together. That led of course, to all manner of complications. For instance, among the things considered "holy" were fire, water, and earth; while a corpse was thought to be dreadfully "unholy." The disposal of the dead there-fore became a serious problem. Since the corpse might not be buried or burnt, or drowned, there was nothing left but to expose it on a high "Tower of Silence," where it could be devoured by the vultures. Elaborate precautions had to be taken lest a drop of rain touch the dead body, and funerals were permitted only on dry days. Professional bearers, who took the most scrupu-lous care to guard themselves against "defilement," car-ried the corpse to the top of this tower. There it was left until the carrion birds had made an end of their ghoulish feast, and only after three days of exposure were the bleached bones cast into a pit. To this day the Parsees, the descendants of the old Zoroastrians, still dispose of their dead in that way. . . .

Not merely corpses, but all manner of other things

were considered taboo and "unclean."   So many indeed
were they, and so difficult to think of, that success in
the task of avoiding all "defilement" became practically
hopeless.   Therefore, in order to be on the safe side,
it was forbidden that any religious task be essayed unless
the celebrant first "purified" himself as though from an
actual and definitely remembered "defilement."   Cow's
urine was considered the most potent "purifier" and
those who desired to cleanse themselves ritually had to
swab themselves with the stuff six times a day every
third day, for nine days.   They had to rub down one
member after another with it, until finally the demon
of "defilement" was driven all the way from the head to
the feet.   The point of exit for the demon was always
the big toe of the left foot, and when ejected thence, it
went off with a shriek to the north where all the demons
—and once all the Turanians—dwelled.   Every time a
man touched a corpse, or a menstrual woman, or any
other tabooed thing, he had to go through that revolting
process of ritual purification all over again.   That is
still the law among orthodox Parsees. . . .

Now the growth of such a ritual law was almost
as natural and inevitable as the growth of lichens on
a rock.   Only the great souls, the sages and prophets,
have ever been able to find salvation in a religion naked
of ceremonial adornment.   Ordinary men even today
are incapable of comprehending abstract ideas.   Before
a thought can become real to them it must be concretized
and made obvious through symbols or symbolic action.
That is why the career of every prophetically founded
religion on earth has been a career of more or less pro-
gressive frustration.   What happened in Jainism,

Buddhism, and Taoism happened also in Zoroastrian- ism. The prophet was succeeded by priests, by ordinary men of more than ordinary talent who attempted to "organize" the truth their master had uttered. And tragedy was then inevitable. In the first place, those priests were incapable of really comprehending their master's truth. They were men of talent, not of genius; and talent is not enough for the full understanding of a great gospel. In the second place, even had they been

THE AHRIMAN DRAGON

able to grasp the prophet's truth, they could not possibly have organized it. For truth, by its very nature, is in- capable of being organ- ized. It belongs gene- rically to the realm of the ideal, and it can no more be regimented than the rainbow can be hung with clothes. Conse- quently there was no avoiding frustration. The priests reached out to lay hold of Zoro- aster's truth, but their blunt fingers could close only on falsehood. Eagerly they strained to light their brands at the brave little flame which he held up against the dark swirling immensities of fear; but they succeeded only in getting their brands to smoke and crackle in shamed impotence.

But though the priests failed to preserve Zoroaster's gospel they succeeded all too well in preserving themselves. Indeed, the more they failed with the one, the more they succeeded with the other. For the more they made salvation a prize that could be won only by strict observance of the ritual, the more they made themselves the donors of salvation. No doubt that was why the ritualization of the religion was carried to such inordinate lengths by the priests. It paid. It gave those priests enormous power over the populace, and enabled them to establish themselves as a permanent caste in Iran. They organized themselves into an hereditary order, and at one juncture even instituted a papacy in the land. They were called the Magi, and their fame as necromancers later spread through the world.[1] Their chief function was to officiate at the regular temple and household services. Masked with thick veils to keep their breath from polluting the holy flames, they served at the fire-altars five times each day. With like punctilio they served also at the haoma-altars which Zoroaster in his day had tried most strenuously to destroy. Haoma (called Soma in India), an intoxicating vegetable extract, was considered highly sacred among the primitive Aryans, and was used in the earliest religious rites. Evidently its hold on the masses was so firm that despite Zoroaster's reform it was able to continue as a sacramental property. In the priestly law-books we find detailed accounts of just how the haoma rites were performed after the prophet died. Twigs of the sacred plant were pounded in a mortar; the heady juice

---

[1] It is from their name, Magi (pronounced with the "g" soft and the "i" long, as in "gibe"), that we get our words magic and magician.

was mixed with milk and holy water; it was strained; and then it was swallowed by the priests. (A potent cocktail it must have made!) At one time it took eight priests to perform the rite, one to recite the Gathas, one to pound the haoma, one to mix the juice with the milk, four others to stand by and help, and one to watch over all!

But the haoma rites were not the only relics of the old heathenism that returned after Zoroaster's death. Many of the old fallen gods, too, were dragged back into fashion—Mithra and Anahita and others. The very Gathas of Zoroaster were corrupted by interpolation, or at least misinterpretation, so that they might give the impression that the prophet himself had commanded the worship of those gods. . . . Mithra especially became popular; and as we have already seen, his cult later spread beyond the borders of Persia into Babylonia, Greece, and finally into Rome itself. For at least two centuries that cult struggled with Christianity for the dominance of the Roman Empire. And when in the end it was vanquished, its place was taken almost immediately by Manichaeism, a religion founded in the third century by the Persian prophet, Mani, who was crucified by the Magian priests as a heretic. . . .

5

BUT the importance of Zoroastrianism has always been qualitative rather than quantitative. Its highest significance lies in the influence it has exercised on the development of at least three other great religions. First, it made contributions to Judaism, for between 538 B. C. (when the Persians under Cyrus captured

Babylonia and set free the Jews exiled in that land) and 330 B. C. (when the Persian Empire was destroyed by Alexander) the Jews were directly under the suzerainty of the Zoroastrians. And it was from these suzerains that the Jews first learnt to believe in an Ahriman, a personal devil, whom they called in Hebrew, Satan. Possibly from them, too, the Jews first learnt to believe in a heaven and hell, and in a Judgment Day for each individual.

Zoroastrianism had developed quite fantastic ideas about the Judgment Day which the prophet had declared to be the consummation of all things. In the first place, his professed followers had grown a little tired of waiting for this universal "Affair" that Zoroaster had prophesied. They had begun to take more stock in an "affair" for each individual, a dread day of trial that was due immediately after death. The soul of each dead person, it came to be believed, was convoyed up to a fateful bridge and then commanded to march forward. If it was the soul of a righteous man, then the bridge opened up into a broad thoroughfare over which the soul marched straight on to the Heaven of Ormuzd. But if it was the soul of a wicked man, lo, the bridge contracted till it was as narrow as the edge of a sharp scimitar, and the guilty soul was sent hurtling down into the foul Hell of Ahriman. . . . And that naive idea was taken over into Judaism, which until then had known of nothing more than a vague "pit" called *sheol,* into which all souls at death were cast indiscriminately.

And the Zoroastrian picture of the ultimate "Affair" for all the universe also left its impress on Jewish thinking. Scholars today are fairly agreed that most of the

Biblical and Apocryphal accounts of what would happen in "the end of days," all the wild apocalypses from Daniel through and beyond Revelation, were inspired at least in part by Persian eschatology.

Through Judaism, the religion of Persia left its mark also on Christianity; and not merely through Judaism, but also through Mithraism. When we come to tell the story of the rise of Christianity we shall have to refer at some length to the many compromises with Mithraism which seem to have been made by the victorious faith.

Very directly, also, Zoroastrianism influenced the religion preached by Mohammed. Many ideas set down in the Koran reveal that influence; and even more of the ideas set down in later Moslem writings. . . .

And in our very own day we find a modernized form of Zoroaster's faith being preached by Mr. H. G. Wells! . . .

Only by virtue of this pervading influence of its ideas can Zoroastrianism be called a world religion today. Its nominal confessors are few, very few, in number. They were mercilessly persecuted and almost exterminated when the Mohammedans swept into Persia in the eighth century; and they have been persistently oppressed from that day on. Only about nine thousand of their posterity are left now in all the land!

But there is a significant colony of them in India, in all about ninety thousand Zoroastrians who dwell in and around Bombay. There they seem to be a veritable leaven in the whole population, and their importance is far out of proportion to their numbers. They are known there as the Parsees (really, the Persians), and their culture, honesty, and benevolence are bywords in all India. Even their present multitudinous rules of ritual "purity" have failed to smother the fires of faith which Zoroaster lighted unnumbered centuries ago. The Parsees are still in their way servants of Ahura Mazda, warriors for Right in the battle which is life. A tiny minority, forever harassed and scorned, nevertheless they are today among the very noblest of mankind. . . .

By worldly standards, Zoroastrianism failed. It was so overwhelmed by Christianity and Mohammedanism that today it is the size of a forgotten denomination. But by truer standards, Zoroastrianism triumphed. It triumphed as have few other faiths on earth, for its fire, though often on the altars of strange gods, still illumines much of the world. . . .

BOOK SIX
WHAT HAPPENED
IN ISRAEL

BOOK SIX

WHAT HAPPENED IN ISRAEL

I. JUDAISM

1: The cradle of the Hebrew people—the lure of the Fertile Crescent—Egypt and the Exodus. 2: Moses—the covenant with Yahveh. 3: How the nature of Yahveh changed in Canaan. 4: The political history of the Hebrews. 5: The work of the prophets. 6: Amos—Hosea—Isaiah—Micah—Jeremiah—Yahveh becomes God. 7: The spiritual exaltation of Israel—the Messianic Promise—its influence during the Babylonian Exile—Deutero-Isaiah. 8: The rise of the priests—their influence—the new prophets—the Destruction of Jerusalem—the Messianic Dream again. 9: The rise of the rabbis—the Wall of Law—Judaism today—Zionism—the goy-fearing people—Messianism, the heart of Judaism.

BOOK SIX
WHAT HAPPENED IN ISRAEL

I. JUDAISM

IN EGYPT thirty-five hundred years ago there was already a great civilization, and magnificent temples were being built there to the glory of the animal-headed gods. In Babylonia there was already a knowledge of writing, and in India the Rig-Veda was already old. The Chinese by that time had so long been established in their land that they imagined they had always lived in it; and the Minoans had already profited by a full thousand years of peace. But the Hebrews, that little people destined to play so large a part in the drama of world civilization—they were still half-savages homeless in the desert.

Like the Babylonians and Phoenicians, the Hebrews were Semites, for their cradle-land was that vast wilderness we call the Arabian Desert. Thirty-five hundred years ago the Hebrews were but half-savage tribesmen who lived off the bedraggled flocks and herds which they drove from one oasis to another. And their religion, like the religion of all other primitive peoples, was a barbaric animism. They imagined that all objects

223

around them were possessed of terrible spirits, and their worship was no more than a dark magic-mongering. Fear was very mighty in the bones of those first Hebrews, for life for them was brief and brutally hard. By day their world quivered with the heat of the sun, and by night it shivered because of the cold of the wind. Perpetually their world, the desert, was parched, wind-stormy, and terrifying beyond words. . . .

There seemed but one way of escape from the evil which was their life, and that was through migration from the desert. Far to the north there was a great half-circle of verdant soil made up of the valleys of the Tigris and Euphrates, and the coast of the Mediterranean Sea. Modern historians call it the "Fertile Crescent," and it was the Eden of the desert nomads, the Paradise, the Promised Land. Generation after generation those nomads struggled their way up to its borders, and then by brute force beat their way in. The Fertile Crescent seems never to have been without inhabitants ready to fight off all newcomers. Before the dawn of history it was populated in large part by non-Semitic peoples called the Sumerians and the Hittites. But later it became a region belonging almost exclusively to Semites. Certain tribes out of the desert inundated the eastern tip of the Crescent and became the Babylonians. Others smashed their way into the middle of the Crescent, and became the Arameans. Still others conquered the coastal plain, and became the Phoenicians and Canaanites.

There is reason to believe that the Hebrews, when their turn came to invade the Crescent, tried first to use the eastern tip as the gate of entrance. Only later did they try their fortune in Canaan in the west. (The tradition that Abraham—evidently a tribal sheikh who led one of the first sorties into Canaan—came from "Ur of the Chaldees," may have that much basis in fact.) Perhaps for many centuries the Hebrews roamed about on the borders of the verdant region, awaiting their chance to break in. Time after time they may have made desperate lunges, murdering and pillaging until they were well inside the Crescent, and then recoiling beneath the b l o w s of the recovered natives. They s e e m to h a v e gone through s u c h experiences first in Babylonia, then in Haran, later in Canaan, and finally in E g y p t. But out of Egypt they were never ejected; they fled! For when they broke their way into Egypt, they

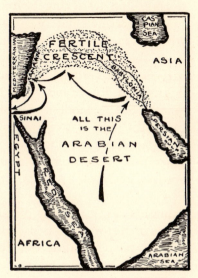

HERE GO THE HEBREWS

got more than they bargained for. They had entered the land in search for food—but instead they got slavery. From loose-footed bedouins they had been violently changed there into sweating laborers who in chain gangs were forced to build pyramids for the mummified bodies of dead emperors. It was only by taking advantage of a moment when Egypt was desperately trying to fight off hordes of savage invaders from Libya and pirates from the Aegean Islands, that the Hebrews managed to escape. They fled into the wilderness, roamed there as in olden days, and finally made still another lunge at the Fertile Crescent. And that time they managed not merely to squeeze into the coveted region, but also to stay on in it.

2

IT was out of crisis of the flight from Egypt that the beginnings of a distinctive Hebrew religion arose. Before that time the faith of the Hebrews must have been quite like that of most other Semite bedouins prowling in the desert. It must have been a vague and inconstant animism in which the spirits of various mountains and heavenly bodies and oases were placated with sacrifices and spells. Not until the Exodus did it become a definite and differentiated cult.

The leader in that Exodus was a man named Moses, one of the most fascinating and bewildering of the great men of antiquity. Tradition has woven so many threadbare legends around his name that many scholars today are moved to doubt his very existence. But, as in the case of Zoroaster and Jesus and the other ancient prophets, it seems sounder to accept the historicity of Moses than to reject it. Not the historicity of the rock-splitting, Pentateuch-writing, priest-loving Moses of tradition, of course. That is quite obviously a piece of propagandist fiction concocted by the priesthood of a far later day. No, the historicity only of some daring primitive Hebrew who managed to prod his brethren into rebellion against the Egyptians, to appoint himself their chieftain, to weld them into a unit by giving them

a god, and finally to get them ready for another
desperate effort to enter the Fertile Crescent.   Whether
he was ever found amid bulrushes by an Egyptian
princess, or saw bushes burn unconsumed, or actually
turned rods into serpents, rivers to blood, dust to lice,

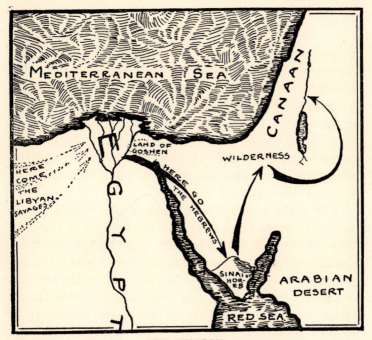

THE EXODUS

and seas to dry lands—all that is irrelevant.   What
alone is relevant is the elemental task which Moses
accomplished: the giving to the Hebrews of a god.   For
thereby he founded what was destined to become one
of the most exalted and influential of the religions of
all mankind.   Over eight hundred millions of people—

WHAT THE HEBREWS BUILT IN EGYPT

full half the population of this believing world—claim
to cherish a religion that in definite respects grew out of
the religion proclaimed by Moses!

It was far from a perfect faith—this cult instituted
by Moses. One must remember that it was founded
over thirty-two hundred years ago, by the chieftain of
a horde of marauding desperadoes just come up out of
bondage. It was just as crude and savage as were the
Hebrews themselves. At its root lay the idea that there
was but one god—for the Hebrews. For other tribes
there might be other gods, but for the Hebrews there
was only Yahveh. This Yahveh (or Jehovah, as his
name is usually mispronounced) was probably the
spirit dwelling in a certain desert volcano called Sinai
or Horeb; and from time immemorial he had been worshipped by a bedouin tribe called the Kenites. Now
Moses, according to tradition, had once dwelt among
the Kenites, and had married the daughter of their chief
priest. When it became necessary for his band of run-
away Hebrews to be provided with a god, it was therefore only natural for Moses to choose Yahveh. He
took his forlorn followers to the very foot of the Holy
Mountain of Yahveh located somewhere in the desert,
and solemnly committed them there to this god. A
covenant was entered into; a holy contract binding the
Hebrews to worship Yahveh, and Yahveh to favor the
Hebrews. Ten commandments were given as the basis
of the worship of the deity; and it was understood that
so long as they were observed, the Hebrews could be
assured of his divine protection. An "ark" was built
as a haven for the roving spirit of Yahveh—it probably
was a sort of tribal fetish—and the Hebrews carried it

at the head of their columns in every sortie. It cleaved
the fear that walled their way, and opened wide a path
to triumph. With this "ark" bearing the spirit of

IN THE WILDERNESS

Yahveh in their van, the Hebrews beat their way back
into the Crescent. When at last they managed to cross
the Jordan and wrest from the Canaanites the little
land "flowing with milk and honey," Yahveh, the
spirit of a desert volcano, was still their chief deity.

3

BUT in Canaan the nature of Yahveh was subjected
to a great change—for a great change came over his
followers. The nomad Hebrews became farmers; from
tending sheep they turned to ploughing fields. And
since a god is worshipped only because he helps make
life less troublous and insecure, because with his aid men
believe they can more successfully fight off fear and

death, therefore he must change with every change in their life and needs. Yahveh, who had been chosen originally because he seemed able to help men wrestle with the terrors of the desert, was forced to reveal new abilities once his followers settled in a fertile land. He had to do that, or die.

Almost he did die. Throughout the books of Judges, Samuel, and Kings, we see signs of the fierce war of the gods that ensued. Hebrew conquered Canaanite far more easily than Yahveh conquered Baal. Indeed, though Yahveh did triumph in the end, still he never quite crushed his old enemy. The Bible declares: "And they served idols whereof Yahveh had said to them: 'Ye shall not do this thing.'" Long centuries after the first settlement in Palestine, we still find Hebrew peasants worshipping the Baalim on the "high places," and Hebrew kings passing their children "through the fire" to Moloch. The licentious festivals of the Canaanitish cults were made part and parcel of the cult of Yahveh, and these agricultural rites became dominant in what had once been altogether a bedouin religion.

It is now well established that the so-called "Five Books of Moses" are a compilation of different documents belonging to many different centuries. When these various documents are separated and chronologically rearranged, we can see in them quite clearly how gradual and tortuous was the development of Israel's religion. The final idea of Yahveh accepted by the Hebrews was not the product of a sudden revelation but of a gradual evolution. Moses did no more (but it was enough!) than preach one great basic doctrine:

that Israel belonged to Yahveh. His Yahveh was, of course, far from a gentle, loving, merciful deity. Had he been that sort, he would have been utterly useless to the straggling band of fugitives and desperadoes whom Moses was leading through the wilderness. Yahveh had to be bloody, hard, vindictive in character—even as was the life of his worshippers. He had to be a Lord of Hosts, a god of battle, or else he could be of no value to the embattled hosts of Israel. Only later was Yahveh thought of as a god of mercy and love. Only through the preaching of a long line of mighty prophets did this Thunderer out of the desert, this ruthless Yahveh of a nation of ruthless marauders, become *God*. . . .

4

IT is not easy to tell in measured and dispassionate terms of the transformation wrought by those prophets. Above the ruck of fussy priests and slavish worshippers those pioneers of ethical thought stand out so majestic, so tremendous, that it is hard to speak of them save in hyperbole. Had it not been for those few prophets, Israel would today be no more a name than Idumea or Philistia. Had it not been for their insight and courageous labor, Yahveh would have been no more to civilization than Baal-Melkart or Dagon. Sons in blood to Moses, brethren in spirit to Ikhnaton, Zoroaster, Buddha, and Lao-Tze, they loom up in the story of religion as veritable supermen.

The history of Israel as a political unit was like the history of most of the other little peoples of antiquity. In brief it was this: Under the leadership of tribal priests and sheikhs—"judges" they are called in the

Bible—the Hebrews first clawed their way into Canaan, and then settled there.   The exigencies of defense against their enemies compelled the tribes to unite under a king.   For a while they were highly successful together in warfare, and under David they actually carved out what was almost an empire.   But the waste and extravagance of Solomon, who seemed bent on imitating the ostentatious despots of Egypt and Babylonia, brought swift ruin.   A revolution ensued, and its close saw the land divided into two kingdoms: Israel and Judah.   Israel was situated in the north, and Judah in the south—and in the years that followed, these two tiny kingdoms simply bled themselves to death in incessant warfare.   Canaan, their land, lay on the highroad between the empires of the East and West, and invasions by world-conquerors and trading kings were a never-ending source of misfortune.   The Hebrews, thus harassed from without as well as within, could not hold out for long.   First the northern kingdom, Israel, went down to defeat, and its population was taken captive and deported to Assyria and Media.   (That was in 722 B. C., the year from which we date the "loss" of the Ten Tribes.)   Then, in 586 B. C., it was the turn of the Kingdom of Judah; its population, too, was taken captive and scattered to the far ends of the Orient. And with that debacle the whole story of the Hebrews came to an end—almost.

5

BUT then something happened, something extraordinary, almost miraculous.   The surrender and annihilation of little kingdoms was a common incident

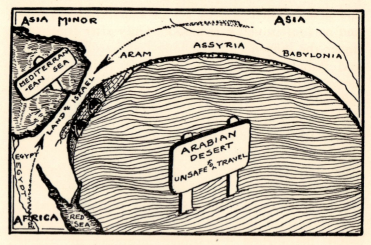

THE BRIDGE BETWEEN THE EMPIRES

in the ancient world. The Philistines and the Phoenicians and the rest of Judah's small neighbors were all of them sooner or later drowned in that vortex which was—and is—the Orient. But miraculously, Judah cheated that fate. It was harried and butchered, conquered and deported—but of all ancient peoples it alone was never destroyed. Even though one can explain that phenomenon, it still remains a miracle, for the explanation itself can hardly be explained. Even though one can glibly say that Judah's survival was due entirely to the might of her faith, and that the might of her faith was due entirely to her prophets, yet how is one to account for her prophets? . . .

The religion of Israel, as we have already said, was a result not of a sudden revelation, but of a gradual evolution. In the beginning it was crude and simple, a mere cajoling of a desert spirit with sacrifices of blood

and flesh.   There was as yet no established sanctuary
and no professional priesthood.   Only after Israel came
under the influence of the long-"civilized" Canaanites
and Babylonians, did an elaborate ritual arise and
along with it a powerful hierarchy.   And that foreign
influence did not reach its ascendency until *after* the
Babylonian Exile.   So that the saving power of the religion—that power which made it at all possible for the
Jews to survive the Exile—could not have proceeded
from its priestly side.   No, the sacrificial cult in Israel
was not the cause, but rather one inevitable accom-
paniment of Israel's survival.   The real cause was the
prophetic spirit that had been breathed into the people.

Of the earliest Palestinian prophets, of Samuel,
Nathan, Adonijah, Elijah, and the rest, we have little
record left save legends.   They seem to have been wild
evangelists who went up and down the land exhorting
the people to remain true to Yahveh.   (The Hebrew
word *nevi-im*, "prophets," may originally have meant
"shouters.")   They were the "troublers in Israel" who
were forever denouncing the kings for their wickedness,
the priests for their venality, and the people for their
transgression of the ancient covenant with Yahveh.
Again and again they were imprisoned and put to death;
but nevertheless they kept right on.   In the trying days
when the Hebrews were being made over from shepherds into farmers, from tent-dwellers into town-folk,
it was those prophets alone who kept the people from
being utterly demoralized in the process.   We have
already referred to the devastating effect of agricultural
"civilization" when it first is taken up by erstwhile
nomads.   If that effect worked extraordinarily small

havoc among the Hebrews, it was solely because of the
vigilance and zeal of their early *nevi-im*.   Those
prophets were the old desert conscience incarnate.   They
stood unfalteringly against the Canaanite goddesses
with their obscenities and lustful rites; they showed no
tolerance to the similar cults of Phoenicia, Assyria,
and Babylonia.   They were Yahveh's invincible
champions in his hard fight to hold the Hebrews from
worshipping Baal, Moloch, Ashtoreth, and all the
other gods and goddesses of Asia Minor.

6

BUT although the prophets labored so intensely to
keep the old Yahveh on his throne, they did more to
destroy him than even the priests of the rival deities.
When they were done keeping him on the throne, he
was no longer the same Yahveh at all.   Although the
prophets set out only to revive the ancient faith,
actually they did not revive it so much as totally reform
it.   They reformed Yahvism from end to end, so that
when they were done it was no longer Yahvism at all—
it was Judaism!   They transformed a jealous demon
who roared and belched fire from the crater of a volcano, into a transcendant spirit of Love.   They took
a bloody and remorseless protector of a desert people,
and without realizing it, changed him into the merciful Father of all mankind.   In fine, they destroyed Yahveh and created God!

Read intelligently—that is, critically—the Bible
makes that course of evolution strikingly clear.   The
Hebrews settled in Canaan in about the twelfth century
B. C.   By the eighth century the simple nomadic re-

ligion they had brought with them had been almost entirely superseded by an agricultural cult. Especially was this true in the northern kingdom, Israel, where "civilization" was further advanced. There morality had been completely ritualized by the priests, and it had come to be firmly believed that animal sacrifices to the deity could atone for the most heinous crimes against man. What had happened in E g y p t, Babylonia, India, and almost everywhere e l s e, had happened also in Israel; the deep-seated tendency of human nature to rely on religious rites as the source of safety and security had led once more to the triumph of the p r i e s t. Corruption was regnant, and tyranny seemed to be right beyond challenge.

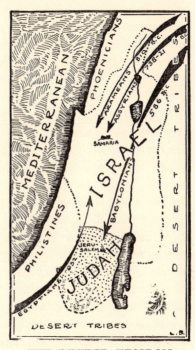

THE DIVIDED KINGDOM

And in a land where such a religion went unquestioned, there suddenly appeared a strange man named Amos. He was an unknown sheep-herder from the hills in the south, and at one autumn festival he arose in a temple where the nobles and priests of Israel were revelling in sacred license, and cried:

Hear this, you who trample upon the needy,
and oppress the poor of the earth. . . . The
Lord Yahveh hath sworn by his holiness:
'Behold, days are coming upon you when
you shall be dragged away with hooks, even
the last of you with fish-hooks!'

He cried out much more in that same strain. He
whipped the drunken worshippers with his scorn, and
terrified them out of their sordid smugness with his
prophecies of an inevitable doom. What they did to
him for his daring, no one knows. Perhaps they put
him to death; or perhaps they let him preach on, thinking him but a noisy dervish. For so soon as the passion
that went into their utterance was spent, those words
must have seemed to the Israelites no more than the
ravings of sheer lunacy. No one until then had ever
dared to declare that Yahveh himself might punish his
own folk. The belief was rooted that, so long as
Yahveh was fed with enough sacrifices, there was no
possible chance of his failing to protect his people. He
would fight their battles for them, water their lands,
fecundate their cattle, and prosper their deals. The
novel idea that the god was revolted by such things as
social crimes, by the perverting of justice or the exploit-
ing of the poor, or by wine-bibbing or harlot-chasing
must have been totally incomprehensible to the gentle
folk of Israel twenty-eight hundred years ago!
    Yet that was just the idea that Amos, a simple peasant
from the hills of Judah, dared to cry out in the temple
at Beth-El. He declared it was all wrong to believe that
Yahveh was a mere tribal possession, a monoply of

Israel. If Yahveh had brought the Hebrews up out of
Egypt, behold he had also brought the Philistines from
Caphtor, and the Arameans from Kir. Indeed, the
Hebrews, Amos declared, had no more chance of curry-
ing undue favor with Yahveh than the black-skinned
Ethiopians! . . . So all hope for special indulgence
was vain. Yahveh was remorselessly a god of Justice,
and if Israel continued to rely on ritual rather than
righteousness, then he would destroy the nation root
and branch for its sin! . . .

And thus was attained the first rung in the ladder
which brought Yahveh up to the Throne of God.
Yahveh was now no more a mere glutton for sacrifices;
he was the inflexible Commander of Justice. . . .

The ascension of the second rung must be credited
to another prophet, Hosea. He appeared shortly after
Amos, and in that same northern kingdom. He, too,
was well acquainted with the wickedness that prevailed
in Israel, and he, too, was convinced of the impending
doom. But he, unlike Amos, saw a chance, a belated
yet nevertheless certain chance, for Israel to be saved.
For Yahveh, who to Amos had been wholly an inexorable Commander of Justice, was to Hosea also a Father
of Love. Yahveh was merciful as well as just, and knew
how to forgive. Therefore, said Hosea, if only Israel
would repent, of a surety Yahveh would spare the
land. . . .

But Israel did not repent, and within a generation
the kingdom met its end. The doom came, and the ten
tribes of the North were hounded out of the land of
their fathers into the oblivion of endless exile. After
722 B. C. only Judah was left, and the rest of the ascent

of Yahveh to the altitude of God over all the earth was
achieved in and around the city of Jerusalem.   Quick
and dramatic became that ascent, as prophet swiftly
followed prophet.   First Isaiah appeared, and through
his preaching the majesty and omnipotence of Yahveh
became established.   The natural tendency of the priests
to make their rites superior to the gods was by him
effectively frustrated in Judah.   In India, Babylonia,
Egypt, and wherever else the power of the priests was
allowed to grow unchecked, the gods were almost unfailingly debased and made as slaves.   But in Judah that
evil was averted through the labor of prophets like
Isaiah.   They made it glaringly plain to the people that
not all the sacrifices on earth, nor all the magic spells,
could exercise the slightest coercive power over Yahveh.
As Micah, another prophet, put it tersely:

> What doth Yahveh require of thee?
> Save to do justice, to love mercy,
> And to walk humbly with thy God.[1]

But the process did not end even there.   There was
yet to come a prophet greater than all who had gone before him.   In the most trying years of Judah's history,
when the little land was making its last mad and futile
stand against Babylonia, there came that mighty prophet
named Jeremiah.   And he dared to exhort his people
to put down their arms and submit.   Vain was it for
them to resist, he declared, for Yahveh was not on their

---

[1] That oft-quoted verse from Micah is profoundly significant.   It
epitomizes the contributions of Amos, the prophet of justice, and Hosea,
the prophet of mercy, and Isaiah, the prophet of heavenly majesty.   In
a score of simple words it tells the whole story of the exaltation of
Yahveh and the moralizing of Yahvism.

side. On the contrary, He was on the side of the enemy, and Nebuchadnezzar of Babylonia was but His instrument. For Yahveh was not the mere godling of the Hebrews; He was God of all the earth! He could do as He willed not merely with one nation, but with all. Indeed, He was the Founder of *all* nations, the Creator of *all* the earth! . . . Amos had not been able to get nearly so far as that; neither had Hosea nor even Isaiah.

Only with Jeremiah was the claim clearly made that there were no other gods save God. There was no Asshur for the Assyrians, Dagon for the Philistines, Bel for the Babylonians, or Osiris for the Egyptians; there could not possibly be any local deities with fortunes inextricably bound up with the fortunes of their own nations. There was only —God!

JEREMIAH

And thus at last, toward the end of the seventh century B. C., Israel's religion became truly a monotheism. Thus at last Yahveh really became God! . . .

7

BUT side by side with this exaltation of Yahveh came also the self-exaltation of Israel. It was inevitable. Having declared their Yahveh to be the Supreme Ruler in heaven, it was logically necessary for the Israelites to

declare themselves to be the chief nation on earth. And
they did just that. Despite recurrent defeat and hu-
miliation and exile, the Jews persisted in thinking themselves the Chosen of God. Of course, the prophets,
every one of them, encouraged that thought. Even
though they denounced their fellow Hebrews and heaped
scorn on them for imagining they could curry favor
with Yahveh, those prophets themselves never ceased
to declare that the Hebrews were still the Chosen of
Yahveh. Only they insisted that the Hebrews were
chosen not for special indulgence but solely for the task
of bringing the knowledge of this Yahveh to all the
world. They promised that if the people would but accomplish that task, then lo, they would indeed be the
first nation on earth! Their truth would conquer all
mankind, and the whole earth would be a Paradise in
which their own Messiah, their "Anointed One," would
reign as "Prince of Peace!" . . .

It proved an astoundingly potent force, that promise.
It became the very heart of Israel's religion, giving it
color and warmth and life. It accomplished the one
fundamental purpose at the root of every great religion,
for it offered its followers a reason for remaining alive.
The Jews believed in that Messianic promise implicitly
and unhesitatingly; and believing in it, they were saved
by it. In the dread days of exile, when they sat by
the waters of Babylon and wept, that promise was the
one thing that kept them alive. For its sake they braced
up and preserved themselves as a people, cherishing the
memories of their past, and incessantly planning for
their future. All during those slow bitter days in Babylon their leaders seem to have busied themselves with

preparations for the great triumph to come.   They made
collections of the legends recounting the exploits of their
ancient patriarchs and prophets and kings, writing
down on scrolls the countless glowing tales that had
been handed down by word of mouth for twenty generations or more.   They also gathered together all their
old laws, and elaborated
them so that they might
fit new needs.   Modern
scholars a r e convinced
that much of the mate-
rial in the "Five Books
of Moses" was written,
and all of it was first
edited, not before, but
during and immediately
a f t e r, the Babylonian
Exile.   No doubt that is
why we find in the Pen-
tateuch so many myths
and taboos and priestly
laws that strikingly re-
semble t h o s e of the
Babylonians.   It must
have been impossible for
the Jews to resist the in-

BY THE WATERS OF BABYLON

fluence of their environment.   Seeing priestliness ram-
pant on every side in prosperous Babylonia, the exiles
naturally breathed a measure of it into the books they
were preparing for their own soon-to-be-prosperous
Zion.

    But this law-code, despite its dominantly priestly

character, depended for its conception and birth on the prophetic urge. (That was why, for all its similarity, it yet managed to differ so fundamentally from the Babylonian code from which it had been derived.) This Jewish law-code was prepared solely in anticipation of the day when the old Messianic promise would be fulfilled. No one seemed to know just when that day would come; but all expected it in the near, the very near, future. And the greatest prophet of the exile, that unnamed genius whom we call Deutero (the Second) Isaiah, pictured the glory of that day in words that the Jews never forgot. He brought the self-exaltation of Israel to its climax, investing the future of the people with a dignity and a significance such as no earlier prophet had dreamed of. According to this unnamed prophet, the whole people of Israel was the Messiah, the "Anointed One." All Israel was the "Suffering Servant of the Lord," the "light unto the Gentiles, that the Lord's salvation may be unto the end of the earth."

In this character Israel was destined to be utterly triumphant, promised the prophet. What other nations without number had tried and failed to accomplish with the sword, Israel would succeed in doing merely with the Word of God. And thus the Jews would ultimately be victorious over all the earth: *their* spirit, *their* ideals, *their* God, would reign supreme. Jerusalem in that perfect day would be the center of the world, and its Temple would become a house of prayer for all nations. They, the despised Jews, now scattered and broken and regarded with contempt—they in the end would be the mightiest conquerors of all! . . .

Such was the gospel of that unnamed Jew whose words are recorded in Chapters 40 to 55 of the Book of Isaiah. By contrast that gospel appears almost incredibly high and hopeful. In that same century, six thousand miles away in China, Confucius was plodding from village to village in futile search for a prince who would bring back the past. All that was glorious seemed to him to have already been, and all that was right seemed to belong only to yesterday. . . . In India, almost three thousand miles away, Mahavira the Jina, and Gautama the Buddha, were groping in jungle fastnesses, seeking not a prince to bring back the past, but a principle of circumvention that might aid them to elude the future. All the past seemed to them to have been as bad as the present, and the future looked to be no whit better than the past. The whole cycle of life seemed one long-drawn-out weariness to the flesh, an abomination to be destroyed at any price. . . . But there in Babylonia stood this homeless Jew, he who had every right to mourn for the past and tremble for the future, he who should have been the most dejected and despondent of souls—there he stood, happy, exultant! There was no trace of despair in his soul. On the contrary, he was full of hope, of mad, ecstatic hope for the Great Release to come. Not release *from* life, but *for* life; release for life nobler, richer, more abundant than it had ever been before. "Comfort ye, comfort ye, my people!" he cried. "Fear not, thou worm Jacob. I shall help thee, saith the Lord. Behold, thou shalt yet thresh the mountains, and beat them small; yea, thou shalt make the very hills as chaff!"

So cried this Unknown Prophet of the Exile. . . .

8

AND then, almost immediately, came the release—
or at least its beginning. In 538 B. C. Cyrus of Persia
conquered Babylonia and set the exiles free. The Jews
were free then to conquer the world—with the word of
the Lord.

But the glorious conquest began most ingloriously.
When the Jews returned to their own little land, they
took back with them the law-code which their scribes
had prepared for them in exile. And, as we have already
said, it was in effect a priestly code. From then on,
therefore, the voice of the prophets grew fainter and
fainter, and the chanting of the priests grew ever more
strident. What happened in India, China, Persia, and
every other "civilized" land, happened also in Judea.
Instead of seeking to win God's favor and save themselves by doing justice and loving mercy, the Jews tried
to accomplish those ends by offering sacrifices and mumbling prayers. (It was much less difficult a technique
to try.) And thus the priests were brought into power.
The priests were the chief sponsors for the easier technique, and therefore they were vastly enriched by its
popularity. The more the people sought to bribe their
way to God by means of priestly ritual, the more the
priests rose in might. There was no escaping that sorry
development, for the masses were not yet ready to follow
the high commands of the prophets. They were ready
only for the little laws of the priests, for the petty rules
made by those men of petty spirit who imagined they
could *organize* morality.

It is quite possible that in the beginning those priests

were most sincere in their labors. Perhaps they believed
they were being utterly true to the prophets when they
sought to organize prophetic truth. But in a little while
they became so involved in the process of organization that they began to lose all sight of the truth. The
means became more important than the end; the *how*
overwhelmed the *why*. The labor of the prophets,
that fury of preaching that had somehow dragged the
cult of a marauding desert-folk up hill until it became
the superlative ethical faith of the ancient world, was
now bit by bit undone. For almost six hundred years
after the return from Babylonia, the priests let the religion of Israel degenerate into an ever more ritualized
morality. Indeed, if during those six hundred years
the religion did not degenerate entirely, it could have
been only because prophetic protest, though intermit-
tently choked, was still never quite strangled. Ever and
again isolated prophets arose to decry the sacerdotalism
and corruption of the priests and people. Some of them
were beheaded, like John the Baptist; and some were
crucified, like Jesus of Nazareth. But they came nevertheless, an unbroken succession of heroic and godly
protestants. It was the old promise of the Messiah
that spurred them on. Despite all the agonies and hu-
miliations they endured in those years, despite all the
outrages visited by Persian, Greek, Syrian, and Roman
overlords, some Jews still believed that they must be
triumphant in the end. Always a remnant of the tiny
folk looked forward to the immediate coming of the
"Anointed One," to the speedy coming of the Kingdom
of God. Indeed, the more dreadful and crushing their
plight, the more frenziedly this saving remnant looked

forward to that advent. Throughout the land there went strange men as its spokesmen, crying to the people: "Repent ye, for the Kingdom of Heaven is at hand!"

But though it seemed ever at hand, it never came. Darker and darker grew the world of the Jews as the vast black wings of Rome closed down over it. Israel writhed in the bloody talons of the Empire for more than a century. And then, goaded almost into insanity, Israel rebelled. Tired of waiting for the Messiah, the Jews tried to *force* the day of His coming. The whole country flared up in rebellion, and Israel made its climacteric effort to preserve itself as a nation. Two of Rome's greatest generals were sent down to quell the uprising, and for four years every wady in the land ran red with the blood of the slain. For many months the holy city of Jerusalem was besieged; and when finally in the summer of 70 A. D. it was captured and destroyed, the Jewish nation was destroyed too. The dread Diaspora, the "Scattering," began in earnest then. The Jews either fled or were hounded to the uttermost ends of the earth, and the glory which was Zion was ended, it seemed, forever.

But it was not ended. Not at all. On the contrary, it but began then anew. Though the Temple was destroyed, and the whole sacrificial cult had become a thing of the past, Israel still continued to live. For the one great promise of the prophets was still effective, even though the little laws of the priests were now null and void. Even after the Dispersion the Jews continued to cherish their dream of the Messiah. It may have been an irrational dream, ridiculous, altogether mad—but it persisted. And so long as it persisted, the Jews per-

sisted. Even to this day it persists. It has been denounced and betrayed, attacked and violated—but it
has never been quite forgotten.

9

THIS is not the place for a detailed account of the
history of the Jews during the last nineteen centuries.
One wishes it were, for that history is like none other
in all the saga of religion. The story of the Parsees,
those exiled descendants of the ancient Zoroastrians,
comes perhaps closest to it; for that people, too, persisted
because it cherished a hope. But save for the little group
of Persians still awaiting the triumph of Ormuzd, none
other is to be likened to the Jews. The Jews stand
out among the races of the world, a strange, an inexplicable folk, with a history far stranger than fiction.

But at least a hint as to that history must be given
here. When the Temple was destroyed and the old
priestly cult was ended, the whole technique of the religion had to be radically altered. The priestly organization was no more, and a new organization had to be
created. So the rabbinical cult resulted. A gigantic
legal literature called the Talmud was developed in the
first five centuries after the Destruction, and later an
even more gigantic literature of Talmudic commentaries
and super-commentaries. It is not difficult to explain
why the development took such a form. The prophets
had for all time answered the *why* of life for the Jew.
They had said that for a while he must live and suffer
so that ultimately he might triumph, so that ultimately
he might bring on the Kingdom of God. But those
prophets had been far from explicit as to the more im-

mediate matter of the *how*. Granted there was a purpose in life, yet *how* could the Jew keep alive long enough to realize it? He saw himself to be quite helpless in that whirlpool of races and creeds which is the world. He had no home, no might, no prestige—nothing save an ineluctable belief in his own importance to mankind. And that by itself was far from enough to keep him afloat in the whirlpool. So he began to tremble for his very existence. Fear took hold of him almost as acutely as once it had taken hold of his savage ancestor in the wilderness. But whereas fear drove the savage to have recourse to fetishes, it impelled this remote descendant to take to laws. The savage had tried to save himself from drowning in fear by conjuring up reeds of magic to which he could cling. For exactly the same reason the Jew built up a dyke of law behind which he could hide.

It was that Wall of Law that saved the Jew from destruction after his own home was destroyed. It kept him apart from the Gentiles, regulating his prayer, his food, his very raiment, so that he could never for a moment forget his identity. The dream of the prophets made life reasonable for the Jew, but only the law-code of the rabbis made it possible. And so long as the Gentile world kept fear palpitating in the heart of the Jew, so long that wall stood firm and unbroken. If it is crumbling visibly in our day, it is largely because the world is growing less intolerant, and the fear in the heart of the Jew is being dispelled. If the old Orthodox Judaism is disintegrating in our day, and "Reform" or "Liberal" Judaism is growing, it is because the wind of emancipation is sweeping the soul of Israel free of dread.

But there is no certain assurance that that process is going on with any rapidity. Of the sixteen or seventeen million Jews in the world today it is doubtful whether even two million of them are unhindered by orthodox taboos and scruples. Intense fear of the *goy*, the Gentile, still lingers in the soul of the Jew, be he a dweller in Washington or in Warsaw. A terror pounded into him incessantly for twenty or thirty centuries can hardly be dispelled in a generation. No, fear is still tormenting the Jew, and as fast as the Law is crumbling, he is building a new wall—or rebuilding an old one—of nationalism. In spirit, if not often in body, he is now returning to old Palestine. At least, his young men and maidens are returning there, to tread once more the soil of Amos and Jeremiah. And thus through a re-created nationalism is the contemporary Jew seeking to save himself from extinction.

So it is on the now familiar *motif* of fear that we must close this book, too. The Jew clings to his ritual law largely because he senses subconsiously that otherwise he will lose his identity among the non-Jews. In other words, he is God-fearing largely because he is Goy-fearing. But it should be noticed that this fear at the heart of Judaism is generically different from the kind that nourishes most other religions. It is fear not for the destinies of the individual, but of the group. Until the Jews were brought into contact with the Zoroastrians, they seem to have had no notion of individual immortality. Until then, the hunger of the Jews seems to have been only for national immortality. And even though the idea of a personal after-life has since struck deep root in Judaism, the earlier idea still remains the

more important.   The Jews still seem far more concerned about their future as a group than as individuals.
No doubt that is why they have been so willing all these
centuries to suffer persecution and death rather than
forswear their faith.   Their religion has taught them
that as individuals they do not count; that only as
members of the Jewish group do they possess any dignity or significance.   And accepting that teaching implicitly, the Jews have managed to survive twenty centuries of the bitterest oppression ever visited on any folk
on earth.   Not merely have they survived; in a measure
they have even flourished.   They have so grown in numbers and advanced in power that they are to be found
in conspicuous positions almost everywhere in the world.
And wherever they dwell they are as a leaven in society,
stimulating an incessant ferment of prophetic protest
and rebelliousness.   Oppression, far from weakening
them, has only tempered their spirit.   Like a sword the
Jew has been stretched out on the anvil of history and
with every blow has grown only more resilient and
durable.
     And it is the Jew's religion, his certainty of an ulti-
mate deliverance from the Gentiles, his faith in a Messianic future for his people, that has made the miracle of
his survival possible.   The Jew seems almost organically
incapable of forgetting that high-born promise made to
him by his prophets twenty-five centuries ago.   He still
believes, albeit unconsciously, that it is his duty to keep
alive because he has a mission to fulfil.   His Bible, his
daily prayers, even his folk-songs and fairy-tales, all
beat into his soul one obsessive belief: that he is pre-
eminently the sword of the spirit that shall yet clear

the way for the coming of the Kingdom of God!   That
may very well be a foolish, an irrational, a presumptuous belief—but so is every other in all this believing
world of ours.   All religions are built on one utterly
undemonstrable and apparently irrational dogma: that
somehow and somewhere some human beings may yet
be able to cope with the universe.   Therefore Judaism
cannot be said to be more presumptuous than any other
religion in its basic conviction.   It can only be said that
the Jews seem more closely bound and more firmly sustained by their conviction than the adherents of most
other religions.   But that, far from revealing a defect in
the Jew's religion, proclaims what is probably its chiefest
virtue: Judaism works. . . .

book seven:
what happened
in europe

BOOK SEVEN

WHAT HAPPENED IN EUROPE

I. JESUS

1: Palestine in the first century—the Zealots and saints.   2: The childhood of Jesus—youth.   3: John the Baptist—Jesus begins to preach.   4: His heresies—his tone of authority—did Jesus think himself the Messiah?   5: Jesus goes to Jerusalem— falls out of favor—is arrested, tried, and crucified.   6: The "resurrection"—the disciples begin to preach.   7: The religion of the Nazarenes—the growing saga about Jesus.

II. CHRIST

1: The mysteries in the Roman Empire—the philosophies.   2: The story of Saul of Tarsus.   3: The work of Paul.   4: Jesus becomes the Christ—the compromises with paganism—the superiority of Christianity—the writing of the Gospels—persecution by Rome.   5: Constantine and the triumph of Christianity.   6: The cost of success—the schisms.   7: The spread of Christianity—the ethical element in Christianity— how it sobered Europe.   8: The development of the Church— Protestantism—why Christianity has succeeded.

BOOK SEVEN
WHAT HAPPENED IN EUROPE
I. JESUS

SORE was the travail in Israel because of the oppression of the Romans. Armies thundered up and down the countryside, ploughing a bloody furrow wherever they went; and spies slunk about in the alley-ways of the towns, carrying slander and dealing death as they moved. Rome, the mighty power that could conquer whole continents, could not possibly keep tiny Palestine in check. Rome could not fathom the Jews, could not understand their maddening obstinacy and rebelliousness. She could not understand why the Jews went mad at the thought of worshipping the images of emperors, or why they deafened the world with lamentations when their Temple money was used for building aqueducts. And naturally, therefore, Rome lost all patience. At the least remonstrance she hacked at the Jews mercilessly, not reckoning what whirlwind might rise from the enforced order she sowed. . . .

And the Jews, racked with pain beyond bearing, weak from loss of blood, went almost mad. They had

257

come to an impasse in which they knew not what to do. They dared not surrender, for they still cherished their ancient Messianic hope. Despite all the terror that had been their lot almost from the day of their creation, the Jews still believed that their Anointed One, their Messiah, would come, and that with Him would be ushered in the Kingdom of God on earth. On this score there seems to have been no division among the Jews. Only as to the means of bringing on the Great Day, was there any division. As to that, some of the Jews counseled war, and others counseled prayer. They who were strong of body and fiery of temper could look forward to no salvation save one wrested by the sword. These were called Zealots, and they went up and down the land attacking lone Roman garrisons, murdering Roman sympathizers, plotting, protesting, fighting, dying, all to bring on by brute force the Reign of Peace. . . . And what they brought on in the end was only a bloody debacle, a final conflict that simply wiped out the Jewish nation and scattered its hapless survivors to the four corners of the earth. . . .

But those who were strong of soul rather than body sought to win salvation by quite other means. To them it seemed that the Reign of Peace would be brought on only by ways of peace, and they therefore cried to the people to rebel against their own doings rather than the doings of Rome. They begged the people to purge their own souls of sin, to crush their own lust for power and vengeance, to be humble and meek of spirit, to be loving and forgiving, to return good for evil, and thus quietly, prayerfully, to await the wondrous day of

reward to come. . . . And in the end those preachers
of peace somehow helped give rise to a new religion,
a great faith which, though it never brought release to
Israel, did bring salvation to half the rest of the
world. . . .

2

THE prologue of the story of that new religion opens
in Galilee. Almost two thousand years ago there was
born in the Galilean village of Nazareth, a Jewish child
to whom was given the name of Joshua, or Jesus. We
do not know for certain how the early years of this
child were spent. The Gospels recount many legends
concerning his conception, birth, and youth, but they
are no more to be relied on than the suspiciously similar
legends told many centuries earlier about Zoroaster. In
his youth Jesus seems to have followed the calling of
his father, and was a carpenter. His schooling had
probably been slight, for his people were humble
villagers, and in all Galilee there was notoriously little
learning in those days. He cherished many of the
primitive notions of the simple folk to whom he belonged, believing that disease and sometimes even death
were caused by the presence of foul demons, and could
be removed by prayer. He knew little if any Greek,
and could never have even heard of Greek science or
philosophy. All he knew was the Bible, and probably
the text of that had been taught him only by rote. Like
every other Jewish lad, he had been made to memorize
the ancient prophecies in the Bible, and to keep the
Biblical and Rabbinical laws of his time. Above all he
must have been taught to prize as dearer than life the

old obsession of his people that some day they would be miraculously freed by the Messiah. Indeed, so well was that last drilled into him that, as he matured, the hunger for the realization of the hope became his all-consuming passion. It seems to have given him no rest in that sheltered little village where he plied his craft.

THE MAN FROM GALILEE

He could not sit by and patiently wait. He had to take staff in hand, and go out and do what he could to *hasten* the coming of the Great Day!

There was nothing extraordinary in such conduct. As we have already seen, Palestine then swarmed with young Jews bent on a similar mission. Most of them, of course, joined the Zealots, and went around fomenting war against Rome. There were others, however, who counselled only peace with God, and it was to them that the simple Galilean carpenter joined himself. It must have been a queer company that he fell into. Most of those preachers of peace were burning evangelists who, in imitation of the ancient prophets, had clad themselves in camel hair and leather girdles. Some were obviously mad: wild-eyed, tousle-haired, frothy-lipped epileptics who rushed about screaming meaningless chatter in the ears of all who would listen. Others, however, were just as obviously of that type which throughout history has given us our prophets and geniuses: that madly sane type whose members so often are stoned while alive and enthroned when dead. . . . But insane and sane alike, they were all in a white heat to get the people prepared for the swift coming of the Messiah.   Up and down the land they went, crying: "Repent ye, for the Kingdom of Heaven is at hand." And they stood on the banks of the Jordan and immersed the repentant in its holy waters.   It was terribly important, according to these evangelists, that one should be thus baptized in the Jordan, for thus alone could one be proved worthy of inheriting the Kingdom of God on earth.   They declared that all who were caught unbaptized—that is, uncleansed of evil spirits— when the Messiah came, could never, never know the joys of the Millennium. . . .

3

NOW at this time there was in the land an evangelist so successful in drawing the people to the Jordan that he had come to be called John the Baptizer.   He was a rough, ascetic person who lived on locusts and wild honey, and who clothed himself in animal skins: a veritable re-creation of the ancient prophet Elijah.   To him it seemed that yet another day, another hour, and behold, the Kingdom of Heaven would be here! . . .

It was to this John the Baptizer that Jesus came when he left his home in Nazareth.   For a time he was a follower of John, one of a multitude of young Jews and Jewesses who believed in the mission of the wild prophet and tried to aid him in his work of saving souls. But when a little while thereafter John was imprisoned for his denunciation of the reigning tetrarch, Herod Antipas, Jesus went back to Galilee and began to preach by himself. His gospel was much like that of his teacher. "The time is fulfilled," he cried, "and the Kingdom of God is at hand. Repent ye!" So did he cry wherever he could find ears to hearken. He went to the beach of the Sea of Galilee, where the fishermen could be found at their labor; he went into the synagogues in the villages, where the pious and the proper folk could be found at their worship; he even went into the houses of shame, where he could reach the publicans and sinners. And wherever he went, few could resist his eloquence. There must have been some quality in his bearing, something in the intensity of his spirit and the earnestness of his preaching, that simply compelled the harried Galileans to give ear. And giving ear, drinking in the words of comfort which he uttered, they could not help but believe. And believing, accepting wholeheartedly the promise which he made, they could not help but feel saved.

When the stories of that young preacher's wanderings were gathered together in later years and set down in writing, it was said that he performed all manner of miracles as he went about the land. Perhaps there is a fragment of truth in that tradition, for if people will only believe with sufficient faith, miracles become not at all impossible. The blind—if their eyes have not been taken right out—will be able to see, and the halt—if their limbs have not been torn away—will be able to walk. The working of such wonders has been ascribed to almost every great prophet and saint in history, and even allowing for the inevitable exaggeration brought on by enthusiasm and time, there is still left a core of truth that cannot be discounted. Implicit faith, which on ten thousand and one occasions has made even a medicine-man's dance effective as a medium of cure, could not but make effective a prophet's hand. . . .

And Jesus could quite command implicit faith. He himself believed; with all his heart and soul he believed that soon would come the Great Release. So the poor Jews and Jewesses of Galilee, the simple fishermen and farmers' wives, the blear-eyed publicans and low women of shame, were compelled to believe with him. They could not possibly resist. For this young man brought them in their distress their only ray of hope. Without that promise which he held out, their life was left one hellish gloom. There they were, starved, sweated, diseased, and full of fear. Wretched peasants and slum-dwellers that they were, they had nothing whatsoever to live for, *nothing*—save that promise which Jesus proclaimed.

So they hearkened and believed and were saved. By the score, by the hundred, they flocked to hear him, plodding many a weary mile through the dust of the hilly roads to stand at last before him and hear his words. He spoke without the slightest flourish, using plain words and homely parables. He indulged in no philosophy or theology, for, after all, he was an untutored toiler who knew nothing of such vanities. Nor, seemingly, did he preach any inordinate heresies. Unlike Buddha, to whom he is often compared, he did not preach a radically new gospel. "Think not that I am come to destroy the law or the prophets," he declared. "I am not come to destroy but to fulfil." His prayers were made up of verses which the Pharisee rabbis were wont to recite in the synagogues, and which are to be found even today in the orthodox Jewish book of prayer. His garb, even to the wearing of the fringed hem, was the garb of an observant Jew. He actually went out of his way to pay the Temple tax to the priests, and saw no absolute wrong in offering sacrifices. No, he was not a heretic in the sense that Ikhnaton or Zoroaster or Buddha were heretics. Outwardly he was distinctly a conforming Jew.

4

YET for all his conformity in these and other respects, Jesus was definitely a rebel. Like most of the great prophets who had preceded him in Israel, he scorned the rich and the proud, the priests in the Temple and the rabbis in the synagogues. His heart went out only to the downtrodden, to those sorry wretches who could win their way to God neither with costly sacrifices nor erudite learning. His whole gospel was intended but to comfort the disinherited, for it declared that no matter how unlettered they might be they could nevertheless be taken into the Kingdom of God when it came. For it was repentance alone, according to Jesus, that could make one eligible for entrance into that Kingdom. Indeed, wealth and pedantic learning, he declared, were hindrances; only purity of heart was of any worth.

Now such a gospel was literally saturated with heresy. Because it denounced the rich and commanded them to divest themselves of all their possessions, it attacked the whole sacrificial cult. For that cult, with its priests and levites, its elaborate Temple and costly parade, depended entirely upon wealth for its existence. A people without possessions could never possibly afford fat bullocks to burn or skins of oil to pour away. Besides, if purity of heart was the sole credential of any avail, what sense was there in offering *any* sacrifices? . . . Moreover, because this gospel minimized the importance of learning, and commanded men to keep merely the spirit of the law, it attacked the whole Rabbinical cult. For that cult, created by the Scribes and Pharisees, depended on scholarly knowledge of the letter of the law for its importance. The "Wall of Law" of the rabbis had been built out of the involved interpretations and re-interpretations of every word in the Pentateuch; indeed, of every letter and of every illumination around each letter in it. And it seemed to many of the rabbis that only one who knew that Pentateuch word for word, and all the innumerable interpretations thereof, could possibly be a righteous soul. Many of those rabbis despised the "man of the earth," the peasant, saying that his ignorance of the minutiæ of the law was a mill-stone that dragged him down to the level of the heathen. Obviously, therefore, this gospel of Jesus declaring that the "man of the earth" could be the very salt of the earth, was charged with quite devastating heresy.

But the heresies of Jesus were not at all without precedent in Israel. Innumerable prophets had arisen before his time to attack the greedy priests; and the very rabbis themselves reviled in their Talmud the hypocritical and bigoted in their midst, calling them "the Pharisaic plague." What really marked Jesus as one unlike any preacher that had come before him was not so much what he said, as the authority on which he said it. His tone was altogether novel in Jewish experience. Every other prophet had uttered his heresies in the name of God. "Thus saith the Lord," had preceded their every declaration. But this carpenter from Nazareth, for all his meekness and humility, spoke only in his own name. "Take *my* yoke upon ye," he said. . . . "Whosoever shall lose his life for *my* sake," . . . "ye have heard that it was said of old time . . . but *I* say unto you . . ." So did he speak, not as the mouthpiece of God, but as one vested with an almost divine authority of his own.

It was that tone which in the end cost Jesus his life. The priests and scholars must have been incensed by it beyond bearing. Such a tone would have sounded blasphemous to them even in a prince or a learned man. In an untutored laborer, in a peasant from benighted Galilee, it must have seemed the most outrageous impudence. . . . But it was that tone, after all, that endowed Jesus with his striking magnetism. It created and sustained the impression that he was a transcendent person, and bestowed on him the power to take cringing serfs and make them over into towering men. Only because he believed in himself so firmly, only because he was so superbly confident, could he make others accept his words. His tone was not that of a mere prophet, but almost that of God Himself. And that was why men began to say he was more than a man, that he was the Messiah! It was not merely that he could perform what were thought to be miracles, casting out demons and

raising the dead—though such reputed powers must
have furnished the most convincing proof to the majority of his peasant followers. It was more that he
could carry himself with the divine assurance of an
"Anointed One," casting out fear and inspiring the
living.

Whether Jesus himself was convinced he was the
Messiah is a problem still unsolved. His refusal to make
the claim in public, the almost too astute way in which
he avoided a direct answer whenever the question was
put to him, presents to this day a dilemma to the faithful. But it is certain that many of those who followed
Jesus believed him to be the Messiah. The sight of that
ragged young Jew hurrying beneath the hot sun of
Galilee, poor, unlearned, yet able to breathe a perfect
frenzy of hope and cheer into vast throngs of forlorn
derelicts, must have seemed proof indisputable that he
was indeed the "Anointed One." There was a wondrous love in his preaching and, coupled with it, an air
of certainty, of authority. For five hundred years some
Messiah had been awaited, and more than once it had
been men of the basest stuff that had been mistaken for
Him. Charlatans and madmen, arrant knaves and
driveling fools, had time and again been hailed by the
hysterical mob as the Awaited One. Is it any wonder,
therefore, that an exalted person like this young carpenter, Jesus, should have been hailed likewise? . . .

5

THAT Jesus was indeed an exalted person is hardly to
be doubted. Even when one has discounted all the

legends, all the stupid and silly and gross extravagances, all the pious embellishments and patent falsehoods that clog and confuse the Gospel accounts, one still is left with an extraordinary personality to explain. It must be remembered that Jesus was not the only preacher of kindness or worker of mircles that ever had been known among the Jews. Many such men had preceded him; many there were in his own day; and many more came after him. But none other succeeded in so impressing his character on his followers. It took only a little while for his fame to spread throughout Galilee, and soon great crowds came out to see and hear him wherever he went. He was often heckled by the elders in the synagogues, and more than once he was slandered and persecuted. But that only increased his following. We are told that once when he began to preach by the Sea of Galilee, the surging throng on the beach became so heavy that he had to get into a boat and speak from the water! . . .

But it was only in Galilee that he was then famous, and Galilee was simply a remote and unimportant section of the country. It is probable that in Jerusalem, the capital, not even a rumor of his appearance was yet known. So there came at last the day when Jesus determined to go out from Galilee, and carry his gospel to the rest of his people. He determined to go even as far as Jerusalem and attempt to utter his word in the very stronghold of the priests and rabbis. The time chosen was just before the Passover, for Jesus knew the capital would then be thronged with Jews come from every corner of the land to celebrate the feast in the Temple. So with his twelve chief followers, his dis-

ciples, and a little group of women devotees, he courage-
ously set out southward. . . .

But then came swift tragedy.   By the time Jesus
reached the capital, his fame had already preceded him.
A great mob rushed out to meet him, wildly throwing
their cloaks to the ground beneath the feet of the colt on
which he rode.   They
hailed him as their Mes-
siah, as the long-awaited
Son of D a v i d who
w o u l d deliver them
from their t r a v a i l.
"Hosanna," they cried
ecstatically. "Blessed be
he that cometh in the
n a m e of the Lord!
Hosanna!" . . . One
wonders whether those
poor wretches out of the
alleyways and dunghills
of old Jerusalem under-
stood w h o the m a n
Jesus really was. (One
wonders whether even
his own disciples under-
stood—or whether even

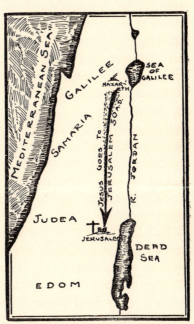

THE PATH OF JESUS

his most pious devotees today understand.)   To that
frantic mob, at least, he was simply an arch-Zealot, a
martial hero who had come to lead them in bloody rebellion against Rome.   And when, after three days of
teaching in the Temple courts, they discovered that he
was nothing of the sort, when they began to see that he

wanted them to make peace with God, not war against Rome, they deserted him as quickly as they had flocked to his support. Poor desperate wretches, they were in no mood to seek peace or return good for evil, or turn the other cheek. They did not want to render unto Caesar that which was Caesar's. They wanted to kill. They wanted to make a holocaust of the whole Roman army, and to become once more a free and prideful nation! . . .

And the moment the populace turned against him, Jesus had no chance. The priests at once began plotting decisive measures against him, for they hated him no less than men of similar kidney had hated every other prophet in Israel. He had scorned them and attacked the whole basis of their cult. Besides, he had publicly flaunted them, storming into the Temple courts one day, and hurling their money-changers out into the street. They dared not let him go on. . . . And although the rabbis despised the priests no less than did Jesus, yet they could not rally to his defense. He had scorned them, too, flaying them for their love of the letter and neglect of the spirit of the Holy Law. He had dared call them hypocrites and whited sepulchres. And, above all, he had outraged them with his unwonted tone of authority. So they, too, were against him.

At the last moment Jesus seems to have realized how reckless he had been in daring to come to Jerusalem. His disciples had warned him against it when they were still safe in Galilee; but young Jesus, in his ardor, had paid no attention. And now he knew himself lost. Belatedly he tried to escape with them, but he was pursued, betrayed, and taken prisoner in a wooded place outside the city walls. He was hurriedly tried by a Jewish court which seems to have been made up largely of priests. Then summarily he was adjudged guilty. From the haste with which the whole trial was conducted, one can judge how terrified were the priests. They seem not to have cared in the least what it was they condemned him for. They were afraid of Jesus, afraid not merely because his heresies endangered their own position, but even more because the excitement which he had aroused among the masses might endanger the peace of the whole land. Rome, the overlord, was wont to put down every sort of public turmoil with scant mercy or patience. So in a panic the elders of the Jews took this young preacher and turned him over to the Roman governor.

And by that governor he was sentenced to die.

There was no justice in it all. How could one expect justice in times so tense and a land so mad? The governor, Pontius Pilate, could have had no understanding of what that young carpenter had done or had dreamed of doing. This Pilate probably thought him but another mad young Zealot, a rebel against Rome, a pretender to the throne of Judea.

And the very next day the life of that young Galilean was snuffed out. The Roman soldiers took him to the top of a hill nearby, scourged him with rods, crowned him in derision with a wreath of thorns, and nailed him to a cross. They nailed him to a cross between two thieves, and over his head they carved the mocking words, "King of the Jews." And there in mortal anguish he hung for hours. Had he been stronger of body, perhaps life would have lingered in him for days. But had he been stronger in body, no doubt he would never have joined the school of John the Baptist and become a saver of souls. Instead, he would have joined the Zealots, fighting with the sword against Rome, and coming to his end not on a cross but behind some blood-soaked rampart. No, from the beginning his strength must have been not the strength of body but of soul; and toward the end even that strength must have ebbed low in him. For as he hung there on the cross of shame, he was alone, deserted. Gone were the huzzahing crowds; gone even were his own trusted disciples. Only a little knot of desolated women stood by to watch him breathe his last. In the city he was already forgotten. The members of that mob which had so ecstatically received him a few days earlier were now busily preparing for the Passover feast. And his disciples were hiding in the fields, too terrified to confess that they had even known the martyr. So deserted he hung there on that lone hill.

The sun began to set, and the wild violet glow in the west crept up till it lost itself in the blue of the evening sky. The prophet Jesus, his poor body sagging from the bloody spikes that tore his hands and feet, could endure the pangs no longer. He began to moan. Brokenly he moaned as the throes of death came over him. "My God, my God, why hast Thou forsaken me?" he begged.

And then he died.

6

BUT he died only to come to life again, to come to a life more enduring, more wondrously potent than had ever been vouchsafed to him in the days before his shameful death.   Indeed, he *literally* came to life again —according to those who had most earnestly followed him.   For ere a week had passed, a revulsion had come over those terrified disciples.   In the dread hour of the trial they had fled from their Master; and now their mortification knew no bounds.   They trembled at the thought of returning home to Galilee to face the bitter contempt, or worse still, the deathly dejection of their comrades there.   Even more, they trembled at the thought of living out the rest of their lives without their Jesus to believe in.   That young preacher, with his supernal magnetism, had come to mean too much to them.   Without their faith in him and his Messiahship, their own lives became empty, meaningless.   Skulking there amid the rock-strewn hills outside Jerusalem, they realized as never before that they still had to believe in him—or die. . . . And, because believing in a corpse was too difficult, they began to believe that Jesus was still alive.   They began to say that three days after his burial he had miraculously arisen from the dead.   They even declared they had actually seen him in the act of rising from the sepulcher, had seen him as he was taken up to Heaven, right up to the throne of glory.   They began to tell how his spirit had actually walked and talked with them, had even broken bread with them! . . . It was not a desire to deceive that impelled those disciples to tell such stories.   They sincerely believed the stories themselves.   They were overwhelmingly convinced that Jesus had really come to life again, and was now in Heaven waiting to return once more.

And with this new conviction grown strong in their

hearts, the eleven disciples emerged from their hiding-places and began to preach again. It was not at all a new religion that they began to preach, however. They were still Jews, and they continued to be faithful to the established synagogue and Temple worship. They differed from their fellow Jews only in that they believed that the Messiah had already come, and that He had come in the person of Jesus of Nazareth. They were for that reason called Nazarenes, and probably they formed but one more of many such Messianic sects already in existence. There were the Johannites, who believed John the Baptist had been the Messiah, and who persisted in the belief for yet many generations. There were also the Theudasians, who believed a certain mad preacher named Theudas was the Awaited One, and who clung to the belief until the Romans cut off Theudas's head. The whole land swarmed with such little sects, for the hunger for salvation in Israel was then as agonizing, and as unsatisfied by the established religion, as it had been, for instance, in India in the day of Buddha and Mahavira.

7

OF the life of the first Nazarenes we know exceedingly little. It would seem that they dwelt together in little communist colonies, loving each other and sharing each other's joys and sorrows. They ate at a common table and had no private property. With the noblest ardor they set out to live as their Master had commanded them. . . . And continually, unflaggingly, they sought new members. They went throughout the land, even as far as Damascus, trying to win converts to their little movement.

But it must have been slow and discouraging labor, for the Messiahship of Jesus was far from easy to prove. Even when the shamefulness of his death could be explained away by a miraculous resurrection, there was still the obscurity of his life to be justified. The Jews had been taught to expect that the Anointed One would be no less than a scion of the royal dynasty of David, an heroic and magnificent prince who would destroy all Israel's enemies with a mere wave of the hand, and would ascend a throne of gold and ivory and precious stones, to rule then over all the world as the Prince of Peace. It was just the sort of grand and gaudy dream one might expect of a people with a tremendous will-to-live cramped in a frail and tortured body. And a village carpenter from half-heathen Galilee, an obscure evangelist who had tramped through the dust to Jerusalem with a tiny following of ragged peasants and reformed sinners, only to be summarily snuffed out by Rome—such a sorry figure hardly measured up to the requirements set down for the hero in that dream. The contrast between the actual Jesus and the imagined Messiah had not been so patent when the preacher had still been alive. The magnitude of his spirit and the fervor of his preaching had been so absorbing as to make men forget altogether whence he had come and how raggedly he was clad. They had been swept away by his simple stirring eloquence, and men had then been quite ready to hail him as the Son of David. . . . But now that Jesus was no longer physically present on earth, all this was changed. To those Jews who had not known him, who had never heard him preach or seen him cast demons out of the mad and the palsied,

it was enormously difficult to prove that he had really
been the Promised One.

No doubt that was why the disciples began to piece
together the genealogies we find in the Gospels. No
doubt that, too, was why those extravagant legends concerning the conception, birth, childhood, and ministry
of Jesus began to be devised. Uncharitable critics may
say the disciples resorted to fraud in these matters—but
it was all intensely pious and well-intentioned fraud.
Before the ordinary Jew could be made to accept Jesus
as the Messiah, Jesus simply *had* to be proved a descendant of David, whose whole life had been a literal ful-
filment of the ancient prophecies. The disciples may
not have been even remotely conscious that they were
departing from the truth when they solemnly repeated
those genealogies and stories. Overzealous disciples
never are. . . .

But even with all those new proofs and appealing
legends to convince them, the Jewish people as a whole
still refused to accept the Messiahship of Jesus. They
obstinately kept on awaiting the first coming of the
Anointed One, praying for his advent day and night.
And the Nazarenes remained obscure, and few in
number.

II.   CHRIST

AND then something happened. Of a sudden—at
least, so it seemed to those who had not marked the
mounting of its steady ground swell—that little Nazarene sect, so long but an eddy unfelt even in tiny Judea,
became a high sea that broke and rolled across the whole
Roman Empire. A veritable tidal wave it became,

sweeping over one land after another until finally it had inundated the whole face of the West and half the face of the East.   To explain how that could have happened, one must remember what was going on just then in the Roman Empire.   A great hunger was gnawing at its vitals, a desperate hunger for salvation.   The whole Roman world seemed to be writhing in the throes of death, and fear of that death drove it to a frantic and panicky clutching after any and every chance of life.   As a result, the mysteries, those secret cults which whipped men into mad orgies of hopefulness, flourished everywhere.

We have already dealt at some length in this volume with those mysteries of Greece and Rome.   In origin they were largely Oriental, and in essence they grew out of the belief that by certain magic rites a man could take on the nature of an immortal god.   In most instances that god was portrayed as a young hero who had been murdered treacherously and then miraculously brought to life again.   That same legend was told—with variations, of course—concerning Dionysus, Osiris, Orpheus, Attis, Adonis, and heaven knows how many other such gods.   Arising out of the common desire for an explanation of the annual death and rebirth of vegetation, that legend was common to many parts of the world, and was believed during unnumbered centuries.   It became the basis of a dozen different religions, providing all of them with the root-dogma that by means of sacrifices, spells, prayers, trances, or other such devices, mortal man could become immortal.   By the first century of this era, the legend had spread to every civilized province in the Roman Empire—save, of course, that stub-

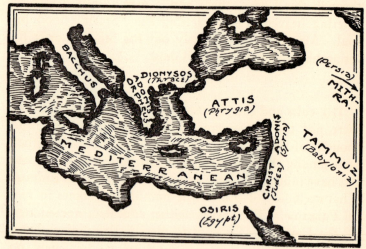

THE SAVIOR-GODS

bornly resisting little province of Judea—and had everywhere made the people drunk with the heady liquor of its mystery salvation.

And side by side with these religious cults flourishing among the lower elements in the population of the Empire, different schools of philosophic thought flourished among the more learned folk. One of these was the philosophy developed in the city of Alexandria by an Egyptian Jew named Philo. According to this philosophy, God, the Father of All, was too vast to have direct contact with the earth, and therefore manifested himself only through an intermediary called the *Logos*, the "Word." This Logos, which was sometimes called the "Son of God" or the "Holy Ghost," had created the earth, and was the sole mediator between it and heaven. Man's only approach to the Father, therefore, was through this Logos, this "Son"; man's only chance of entering heaven was by letting the "Spirit" flood his soul. Man could find a way out for himself, only by losing himself in the "Holy Ghost." . . .

2

THE cults and the philosophies we have just described were not the only elements in the religious life and thought of the Empire. Not even remotely. But they were among the dominant elements, and they could not but have influenced every educated citizen of the Empire. That excluded, of course, the humble Nazarenes in far-off Palestine. They were neither educated, nor citizens of the Empire. They were merely Palestinian Jews, poor artisans and peasants most of whom knew no tongue save the Aramaic dialect used in their homes and synagogues. And if in later years the Nazarene faith began to take on the color and shape of those heathen cults and strange philosophies, these Palestinian Nazarenes were not in the least responsible. It was one from outside the original brotherhood, a Jew from beyond the borders of Palestine, who was responsible. It was Saul of Tarsus who brought on that change.

Saul was both a Jew and a citizen of the Empire. He was born in Tarsus in Asia Minor, a city of some consequence as a trading center and a seat of learning; and while still a boy he seems to have distinguished himself as a student. A Pharisee, and the descendant of Pharisees, his chief training was in Rabbinic law; but he also knew Greek, and must have had rather more than a passing acquaintance with Greek and Alexandrian philosophy. Most important of all, he must very early

have learnt from slaves in the household, or from Gentile
playmates, of the mystery cults which were prevalent in
his native city, and of the savior-gods in whom the
masses put their impassioned trust. . . . Despite these
early heathen influences, however, Saul remained a Jew.
When grown to young manhood he even went down

SAUL OF TARSUS

from Tarsus to Jeru-
salem so that he might
complete h i s religious
studies under the great
Rabbi Gamaliel there.
(It seems not to have
been uncommon for the
sons of wealthy Jews
living outside the home-
land to come to Jeru-
salem to finish their edu-
cation.)   And there in
Jerusalem Saul for the
first time came in con-
tact with the Nazarenes.
. . . Now Saul was a
person of very violent
likes and dislikes, and
when he h e a r d what
those Nazarenes w e r e
preaching, he was convulsed with anger. He is said to
have been an epileptic, and certainly he was a man of
strange temperament. Whatever he did, he did with an
intensity and an extravagance that were distinctly ab-
normal. So that when he took his initial dislike to the
Nazarenes, he could not merely shrug his shoulders in

disapproval and let them be. He had to persecute them. Nor was he content with persecuting them merely in Jerusalem. On hearing that their movement was growing virulently in Damascus, he actually dropped his studies and set out to run them down there as well.

But on the way to Damascus a queer thing happened to him. He was suddenly overcome by a seizure of some sort, and in a trance a vision came to him of the resurrected Jesus. A "light from heaven" shone round about him, and a voice cried out: "Saul, Saul, why dost thou persecute me?" And when, trembling and astonished, Saul came to himself, behold he was a changed man!

When he got to Damascus he arose in the synagogue, and instead of persecuting the Nazarenes, he began actually to praise them. He had become a complete convert to their cause, believing in the Messiahship of Jesus and in his resurrection with an unshakable conviction.

Saul had never seen Jesus in the flesh or come under the spell of his loving gospel. But that made no difference to him. Actually he was but little interested in the gospel of the man Jesus; he was interested only in the death and rebirth of the savior-god, Christ. *Christos* is the Greek word for "Anointed One," and Saul, whose mother tongue was Greek, built his whole personal faith around that word. He became the great preacher of "Christ crucified," journeying about all over the Empire, to Cilicia, Galatia, Macedonia, the islands of the Mediterranean, and even Rome, in a great passion to have the world share with him his belief. . . .

3

AND thus at last Christianity as a world religion was really founded. Jesus had not founded what the world calls Christianity, for Jesus had lived and died a Jew within the fold of Judaism. Jesus had lived and labored merely to guide his fellow Jews to those elements in their own Jewish religion which might make their sorry

THE WANDERINGS OF PAUL

lives glorious. He had tried but to lead them to salvation through distinctly Jewish channels, and he had on occasion even turned away heathens who had come to him for help. He was not the founder of Christianity, but its foundling. . . .

Nor had his immediate disciples created the new faith. They had remained conforming Jews, and the Messiah put forward by them had all along been the *Jewish*

Messiah.   The Kingdom of Heaven they had dreamed of inheriting was a kingdom reserved primarily for Jews.

Nor was it Saul, the studious young Pharisee, who founded the new faith, but his other self, Paul, the citizen of Rome.   (He changed his name sometime after the conversion.)   There are two hostile selves, the Saul and the Paul, in almost every sensitive Jew who has ever lived in the Gentile world.   The one tries to hold him fast within the small and limiting circle of his own people; the other tries to draw him out into the wide, free circle of the world.   And because in this instance the man was of so intense a nature, the conflict was all the more marked.   What-time the Saul in him was triumphant, this man was ready actually to murder every Jew in whom the Paul so much as lifted its head.   And when the Paul in him got the upper hand, he was all for putting an end to the Sauls.   He openly proclaimed that all the laws which kept Jew apart from Gentile were now no longer of any worth.   With the coming of the Christ there had come a new dispensation, he believed.   Circumcized and uncircumcized were now alike, and he that ate "defilement" was no less in the sight of Christ than he that scrupulously kept all the Mosaic laws.   For the Christ was not the Messiah merely of the Jews; he was the Savior of *all* mankind.   The shedding of his blood had washed away the sin of *all* men, and now one need but believe in him to be saved.   No more than that was demanded: believe in Christ, and one was redeemed!

And it was due to this breaking down of the "Wall of Law" that the Nazarene faith, so long obscure and unnoticed in tiny Judea, flooded out and inundated the world.

It is unfair to compare Paul to Jesus, for the two belonged spiritually and intellectually to entirely different orders of men. The one was a prophet and a dreamer of dreams; the other was an organizer and a builder of churches. In his own class Paul was one of the stupendously great men of the earth. If at moments he could be violent and ungracious, he was nevertheless a superb statesman. And he was possessed of an energy, a courage, and an indomitable will, the like of which have rarely been known in all the history of great men. Again and again he was scourged and imprisoned by the outraged elders of the synagogues in which he tried to preach. (Paul usually tried to obtain a hearing in the local synagogue whenever he arrived in a strange city.) Mobs were set on him; more than once he had to flee for his life. The orthodox Jews looked on him as an apostate, and some even of his own fellow Nazarenes fought to depose him from leadership. All the years of his ministry he was plagued by Jews who hated him, Nazarenes who distrusted him, and Gentiles who could hardly make out what he was talking about. And yet he persisted, never resting from his grueling labor of carrying his Christ to the Gentiles, incessantly running to and fro, incessantly preaching, writing, arguing, and comforting, until at last, a tired and broken man, he died a martyr's death in the city of Rome. . . .

4

IT was in the year 67, according to tradition, that Paul was beheaded by the Romans. He had spent per-

haps thirty years in the labor of spreading the idea of
Christ, and by the time of his death that idea had already
struck root far and wide in the Empire.   It had divorced
itself from Judaism, taking over the Sunday of the
Mithraists in place of the Jewish Sabbath, and substitut-
ing Mithraist ritual for Temple sacrifice.   In most of
the cities there were already thriving Christian brotherhoods, little secret societies much like those of the mysteries, but with greater proselyting passion.   While the
leaders were still for the most part converted Jews, the
membership was largely of pagan origin.   And as, with
the passing of the years, the pagan element grew ever
more preponderant, pagan ideas came more and more to
dominate the religion.   The life-story of Jesus was em-
bellished with a whole new array of marvels and miracles, and the man himself was made over into a veritable
mystery savior-god.   His character and nature fell into
the maw of an alien philosophy, and then came drooling
out in sodden and swollen distortion.   He became the
Lamb whose blood washed away all sin.[1]   He became
the Son of God supernaturally conceived by the Virgin
Mary when the Holy Ghost of God the Father entered
into her womb.   He became the Logos and the Avatar
and the Savior.   And throughout the Empire little
churches were to be found in which his pictures (extra-

---

[1] Those who remember the description of the pagan Tauroboleum
given in the chapter on Rome will find this good Christian hymn profoundly suggestive:

> "There is a fountain filled with blood
>   Drawn from Emmanuel's veins;
> And sinners plunged beneath that flood
>   Lose all their guilty stains."

ordinarily like those of Horus) were worshipped, and in which his "flesh and blood" (amazingly like the symbols used in the magical rites of Mithras) were taken in communion.

That is why this section is entitled "What Happened in Europe." Although the religion of Jesus and of the first disciples was distinctly Oriental, although the whole Messiah idea was markedly a thing out of the East, the religion about a Savior Christ was largely European. And it was no less far a cry from the one to the other than was the distance from Nazareth to Rome. Indeed, one gravely doubts whether Jesus, the simple peasant teacher in hilly Galilee, would have known who in the world that Savior Christ was! . . .

But it was inevitable for that change to come about. Christianity in those years was gaining too many converts too rapidly. It would not have been so bad had they been converts from a world of ignorance—that is, converts who had naught to forget when they came over to the new faith. But they were converts instead from a world of what we would call stupidity. Their minds were crowded with fears and superstitions and magic rites and extravagant dogmas which they were supposed to forget when they became Christians—*but they never succeeded in forgetting them.* So it was inevitable, we repeat, that this new faith, oversuccessful as it was in hurriedly displacing the old, should in the end become very like unto the old.

But for all that growing likeness, a significant element of disparity always remained. There was a zeal, a missionary ardor, in the early church that was largely unknown in the older cults. There was a constant run-

CHRISTIANITY IN 110 A. D.

ning to and fro of prophets and deacons from one center to another, and a diligent spreading of tracts and epistles among all who could read. There were, for instance, the letters of Paul giving advice on matters of administration, and explaining matters of doctrine to various of the little churches he had founded. And later there were the Gospels. The Gospels, as we now have them, could not have been written by the disciples whose names they bear, for they are written in Greek, and the native language of most of those disciples was Aramaic. Nor do they seem to have been direct translations from Aramaic accounts. Scholars today are agreed that the earliest of them is the one entitled "The Gospel according to Mark," and they date it about the year 65 —that is, thirty-five years after the crucifixion. The latest of the Gospels, that of John, with its unconscious effort to make Jesus fit the Logos, could not have been written (according to many of the scholars) until well after the year 100. Such writings must have been circulated freely by the missionaries wherever they ventured, and it is evident that they were distinctly effective. No such testaments could be offered by the priests of Mithras, Cybele, or Attis, for their deities were after all mythical. Only the Christians had a real man to worship: a unique and divine man, it is true, but nevertheless a person who had known human woe and pain, who had suffered, and who had for at least three days been dead. That element of naturalism, of closeness to human reality, must have made Christianity a faith of extraordinary attractiveness.

And being so attractive, it rapidly began to eat into the ranks of the other mysteries. It won away their followers at such a rate that it began at last to present a distinct menace to the Roman governors. Spread everywhere, from the Thames to the Euphrates, its half-secret brotherhoods formed what amounted to an empire within the Empire. Its initiates fanatically refused to conduct themselves like Roman gentlemen. They opposed the basic institutions of the Roman social system, and they hated the theater and the gladiatorial shows, the chief amusements of the time. Worse still, they refused absolutely to worship the Emperor as god, thus openly inviting the suspicion of disloyalty to Rome. So attempts at suppression were in the nature of things almost unavoidable.

At first the Christians were persecuted only to gratify the lusts of the Roman mob; but later more systematic efforts had to be made. After the year 303 the imperial government realized that its very existence was in danger so long as Christianity was allowed to flourish, and it therefore made one supreme attempt utterly to annihilate the revolutionary cult.   The churches were burnt down, all copies of the Gospels and Epistles were destroyed, and the Christians themselves were martyred by the score.   The government seemed determined to stamp out Christianity, as modern governments seek to stamp out Communism or Pacifism or Anarchism. (Early Christianity, according to Prof. Gilbert Murray, might indeed have seemed to the Romans what "a blend of pacifist international socialist with some mystical Indian sect, drawing its supporters mainly from an oppressed and ill-liked foreign proletariat, such as the 'hunkey' population of some big American towns, full of the noblest moral professions but at the same time aliens," would seem to modern men of affairs.)   There were tortures and executions beyond number, and the jails were filled with Christian devotees.

But nevertheless the movement grew.   There was a wondrous comfort in that religion, a mighty zeal that made it possible for the martyrs to go to their death actually with a smile on their lips.   It took vile slaves out of the slums where they rotted, and somehow breathed supernal heroism into them.   It told them that sacrifice was at the very core of righteousness, that death for the truth could mean only life everlasting.   Had not the Savior himself died for the truth?   Of a surety, therefore, he would not desert those who died likewise. He would take up their tortured souls in his comforting arms, and heal them in Heaven where he reigned.   Death could have no sting for them, nor the grave any victory, for the Crucified Christ would be with them and bring them through to blessedness eternal! . . .

So no matter how madly Rome hounded the Christians, Christianity could not be crushed.

5

AND then came Constantine and, in the year 313, an end to the persecutions. Constantine was born out in

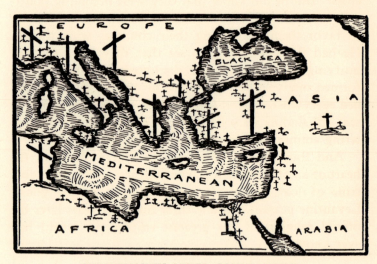

CHRISTIANITY AFTER CONSTANTINE

Servia, and is reported to have been the illegitimate son of a Roman general and a village barmaid. He was inordinately ambitious, and by dint of much energy, intrigue, and not a little use of murder, he managed to raise himself actually to the imperial throne. But his position was challenged by a rival emperor, and in his dire need of help from any and every quarter, Constantine suddenly turned to the Christians. With characteristic shrewdness he realized that those fanatical Christ-worshippers were a power to be reckoned with. Here they were, established everywhere, and possessed of an insuperable will-to-live. Constantine probably had no clear idea as to what it was they really believed. He may have thought them Mithraists who for some queer reason, best known to themselves, worshipped a cross. But he did know that they were becoming politically of superlative importance. So he began officially to favor them, showering their churches with wealth. He had the intelligence to see that they were the sole unifying force left in the disrupted empire. They formed one vast and powerful brotherhood that ramified everywhere. And Constantine, whose chief concern was the finding of some way of bolstering up the tottering empire, felt forced to resort to them for help.

And thus it came about that a fervent hope in the heart of an obscure little Levantine race, and a sweet doctrine of love and peace preached by a simple young Levantine peasant, became three hundred years later the official religion of the greatest empire the world had ever known! . . .

6

BUT it was a costly triumph for Christianity, as every other such triumph has been in all history. What happened to Buddhism when it set out to conquer the Far East, now happened also to Christianity in the West. It became an official and successful institution—and so degenerated. A faith cannot be institutionalized, for it is a thing of the spirit. Even dogmas or rites, which are things almost of the flesh, cannot be organized beyond certain bounds. So that even after Christianity became primarily a thing of dogmas and rites, it nevertheless began to crack and crumble. All sorts of schisms occurred. In the process of organizing the idea of the Christ, a myriad differences arose. Paul had used his theological terms rather loosely, and had spoken of God, the Son of God, and the Spirit of God. Now, were these three the names of one Person or three? Was the Son of God actually God Himself, or merely similar to God? Was the Spirit of God a part of or separate from God? . . . Paul had spoken of a Divine Christ and a human Jesus. Well, then, were these two beings one, or really two? And if they were one, when had they coalesced? Had Jesus never been a human being, but the Christ from the very beginning of creation? Or had he become united with the Christ at the moment of his conception or birth? Or had the Christ descended upon him when at the age of thirty he was baptized by John? . . . Paul had spoken of Jesus as a Savior. He had said that God, the loving Father, had sacrificed His only-begotten Son to redeem the world. But why should God have found it necessary to make any such sacrifice? To whom could He, the All-powerful, be beholden? For that matter, if He was indeed the God of forgiveness, why had He not forgiven without ever bringing the agony of the crucifixion to His beloved Son? Could it be that there were really two Gods: the unforgiving God of the Old Testament, and the forgiving God of the New? . . .

Scores of such questions arose to perplex and divide the organizers of the religion. Jesus had not been conscious of even the most ponderous of such questions.

That dear, fervent young preacher, who had lived and died in the sublimity of a simple faith, could never possibly have been conscious of them.   Had he heard them posed, he would probably have shaken his head in mute bewilderment. . . . But in Europe three centuries later, such abstruse metaphysical enigmas were considered the very bone and sinew of the religion.   The early church fathers disputed over them with a heat and rancor that sometimes did not stop even at murder.   When one puts beside the Gospel accounts of the preachings of Jesus, the official records of the wranglings and bickerings of those church fathers, one feels that here is to be found the most tragic and sordid epic of frustration that the whole history of mankind can tell. . . .

7

BUT the rest of the chapters of that epic cannot be told here.   In all fairness no more may be done here for Christianity than has been done for the other great religions of the world, and having told of the founding of the church, and of its original faith, room remains for no more than a broad hint as to its later development.

More than sixteen hundred years have passed since Christianity was made the state religion in the decadent Roman Empire.   Throughout all those years it has been extending its borders, winning new converts in every pagan land on earth.   It is estimated that at the present time about one-third of the entire population of the world is Christian—approximately five hundred and sixty-five million souls.   There is hardly a region on earth where there is not a church bearing its name or, in default of that, some zealous missionary trying his utmost to erect a church.   And of course, it is to the spirit of Paul regnant in Christendom that one must credit that enormous expansion.   It is because countless monks and healers and warriors and saints have felt Paul's call to go out and win the heathen to Christ, that today more souls are turned to Christ than to any other deity on earth.

But as we have already pointed out, these wholesale increases in numbers were not made save at a high price. Grave compromises had to be made everywhere with the defeated cults.   Just as Buddha had to be idolized before he could conquer the East, so Jesus had to be idolized to gain his victory over the West.   His mother had to be idolized, too, for pagan Europe loved its goddesses too intensely to consent to forswear them entirely.   Indeed, during the medieval centuries Mary seems to have been revered, in practice if not in dogma, even more than her son.   Much of the old love for Isis, and especially for Cybele, the great Mother of the Gods, was taken over into the church and translated into the worship of Mary, the Mother of Christ. . . . Similarly the worship of the old local deities was made a part of Christianity.   The pagan gods and goddesses were discreetly made over into Christian saints, as is instanced by the case of St. Bridget.   Their "relics" were sold far and wide in Christendom as fetishes guaranteed to ward off evil; and their ancient festive days were made part of the Christian calendar.   The Roman Parilia in April became the Festival of St. George, and the pagan midsummer orgy in June was converted into the Festival of St. John; the holy day of Diana in August became the Festival of the Assumption of The

A PRIESTESS OF BRIDGET

Virgin; and the Celtic feast of the dead in November was changed into the Festival of All Souls. The twenty-fifth of December—the winter solstice according to ancient reckoning—celebrated as the birthday of the sun-god of Mithraism, was accepted as the birthday of Christ, and the spring rites in connection with the death and rebirth of the mystery gods were converted into the Easter rites of the Crucifixion and Resurrection. . . .

Yet despite all these compromises, the new religion remained always heavens above the old. By assimilating pagan rites and myths and even god-names, Christianity became at last almost completely pagan in semblance; but it never became quite pagan in character. The Old Testament puritanism which had so marked the life of Jesus was never routed. It remained like a moral emetic in the faith, forcing it to throw up the lust and license in the pagan rites it assimilated. If the spirit of Paul insisted that Cybele be taken over as the Mother of Christ, the spirit of Jesus insisted that her wild Corybantes with their lustful rites, and her holy eunuchs with their revolting perversions, be left severely behind. If the spirit of Paul demanded that the wild Celtic goddess named Bridget be accepted into Christianity, the spirit of Jesus demanded that first she be made lily-white and a saint. For the spirit of Jesus was innately Jewish and puritanical. It set its face hard against sacred prostitution and against all those other loosenesses and obscenities which arose out of the pagan's free attitude toward sex. It hated license and beast passion in any form, whether it showed itself in feast, tourney, or battle. Inexorably it insisted on moral decency and restraint.

For that reason Christianity never became quite pagan in spirit. It remained too profoundly concerned with ethics. The old mysteries had been largely devoid of any distinct ethical emphasis. Most of them had promised immortality to their initiates as a reward for the mere mechanical performance of certain prescribed rites. Few of them had pried into the private life of an initiate to discover whether he was good or bad in his daily conduct. Few of them had been in the least interested in daily conduct. Morality had become completely religionized with most of them. They had maintained that to be saved one need be merely ritually proper, not ethically clean.

That was just where Christianity differed most radically from even the highest of the old mystery cults.

The spirit of Jesus flickering in Christianity made it at least nominally a religion of ethics. For Jesus, one must remember, had not been in the least concerned with ritual. Like every other great Jewish prophet, he had preached only ethics. And despite all the compromises of the world-conquering Pauls, that ethical emphasis in the teaching of Jesus persisted as a mighty leaven in the church. It gave to the early Christians that gentle nobility which history tells us graced their lives, and that heroic stubbornness which certainly marked their faith. It took hold of wild berserker races and somehow frowned them to order. It took hold of a savage Europe and somehow subdued it, civilized it. Not altogether, of course. The history of Europe, with all its wars and recurrent brutalities, can hardly be called the history of a civilized continent. Even the church itself, with its foul record of crusades and inquisitions and pogroms, cannot be said to have ever been really civilized. But that admission does not at all discredit the potency of the spirit of Jesus. It merely reveals how tremendous were the odds against it, how brutal was the world it sought to make divine. True, there were indeed Dark Ages in Europe when the power of the Church was at its height. But who knows how far darker they might have been, and how much longer they might have endured, had the Church not existed? True, there were indeed religious wars early and late in Christendom, but who knows how much bitterer and more devastating they might have been had they been tribal or racial wars. For wars were inevitable. A world with too little food and too much spleen simply *had* to fight.   If religious differences had not been at hand, other excuses would have been found for warring.   And because those other excuses would have been deeper-rooted and more primitive, they would no doubt have brought on infinitely more dreadful desolations.   Wars for Christ, after all, could never be fought with a blood-lust utterly free and untrammeled.   Their virulence was always partially sapped by the innate irony of their pretensions.   The insistent pacifism of him in whose name those wars were fought could not but have had some tempering influence.   None can doubt that the adoration of a Prince of Peace, the worship of a Good Shepherd, even though drugged almost dead with ritual, must have had a profound effect on the people.   None can doubt that the veneration of a gentle, loving, helpless youth as the very incarnation of perfection must have been as ice to the hot blood of the race. . . .

One must remember that Christianity came into a world that was sinking—sinking momentarily into an abyss of savagery.   And it was almost the only force that sought to stay that debacle.   It alone sought to keep civilization going.   It failed.   It could not keep from failing.   But be it said to its glory that at least it tried. . . .

8

HOWEVER, the glory of trying to save the world from bestiality belongs primarily to but one element alone in Christianity: the original Nazarene element.   And that element, one must remember, was never dominant in the faith save during those years before it was really Christian.   Once Paul came on the scene, the light of

the religion *of Jesus* began to fade, and the glare of the
religion *about Christ* blazed over all.   Yet though the
light from Galilee faded, though for a while it died
down into no more than a mere lingering spark, it never
was quite snuffed out.   For long centuries it smouldered
there, barely living, barely keeping aglow.   The compromising, theologizing, church-organizing religion
about Christ blazed away unchallenged.   In the West
it gave rise to the Holy Roman Empire, that pathetic
travesty which was never holy or Roman or imperial.
In the East it created a farrago of sects arising from
fatuous differences as to the metaphysical nature of
Christ. . . . And then slowly that forgotten spark
began to brighten once more.   A devastating incursion
of Huns and Saracens blew the spark to a flame.   As
never before in full six hundred years, the Christians
began to think again of their suffering Savior.   And like
a mad fire the hope spread over Europe that the year
1000 would see the return of the Redeemer.

The year 1000 passed and no Redeemer came—but
Europe was a little redeemed nevertheless.   Its spirit was
sobered and its life deepened.   The hunger for salvation
became too strong and acute to be allayed with mere
ritual any longer.   Men turned from what the Church of
Christ insisted on offering them, and instead began to
grope after the gospel of Jesus for themselves.   They
took to reading the Scriptures in their original tongues,
and reading them they began to see at last how far the
Church had wandered from the pristine truth.   They
discovered at last how shamelessly the priests had sub-
stituted rite for right, how flagrantly they had ritualized
all morality.   Heretical sects arose everywhere, and the

clerical authorities took alarm. Despotically they issued
proclamations prohibiting the laity from even glancing
at the Bible, and the priesthood from interpreting it save
in accordance with the tradition of the Church. Then
they instituted the Inquisition to see that the prohibition
was observed.

But the Bible was read nevertheless. Inquisitions and
crusades and massacres proved of no avail. The flame
of heresy burned on, and not even a sea of blood was
enough to quench it. In the fourteenth century, Wycliffe did godly mischief in England; in the fifteenth,
John Huss carried on in Bohemia; in the sixteenth,
Luther, Zwingli, and Calvin led the protestant revolt
throughout northern Europe. And thenceforth the
Catholic Church ceased to be catholic any more even in
the West. Land after land went over to the heretics,
and European Christianity was cleft in two.

But one must not imagine that Protestantism was
ever purely Nazarene in spirit—any more than Catholicism was ever unrelievedly Pauline. (Bishop Laud in
the seventeenth century was a Protestant, while St.
Francis of Assisi in the thirteenth century was a Catholic. . . .) Protestantism includes every type of religious thought and organization from "high church"
Anglicanism to high-principled Quakerism, from ecstatic Methodism to relentlessly intellectual Unitarianism.
Only slowly, and with many pangs, is even Protestantism shaking off the religion about Christ. Only
slowly, very slowly, is it beating its way back to the
religion of Jesus. . . .   .

And with that word we must leave the tale of what
happened in Europe. The story of Christianity is long

and bewildering, for it stretches through twenty centuries and is written in a hundred tongues.   In part it is a story of almost incredible rapacity and bitterness, of incessant war and intrigue, and low, greedy self-seeking.   But in far larger part it is a story of wondrous kindness and saving grace.   Though the Church of Christ may stand guilty of untold and untellable evil, the religion of Jesus, which is the little light glimmering behind that ecclesiastical bushel, has accomplished good sufficient to outweigh that evil tenfold.   For it has made life livable for countless millions of harried souls. It has taken rich and poor, learned and ignorant, white, red, yellow, and black—it has taken them all and tried to show them a way to salvation.   To all in pain it has held out a balm; to all in distress it has offered peace. To every man without distinction it has said: Jesus died for *you!*   To every human creature on earth it has said: *You too* can be saved!   And therein lies Christianity's highest virtue.   It has helped make the weak strong and the dejected happy.   It has stilled the fear that howls in man's breast, and crushed the unrest that gnaws at his soul.   In a word, it has worked—in a measure. . . .

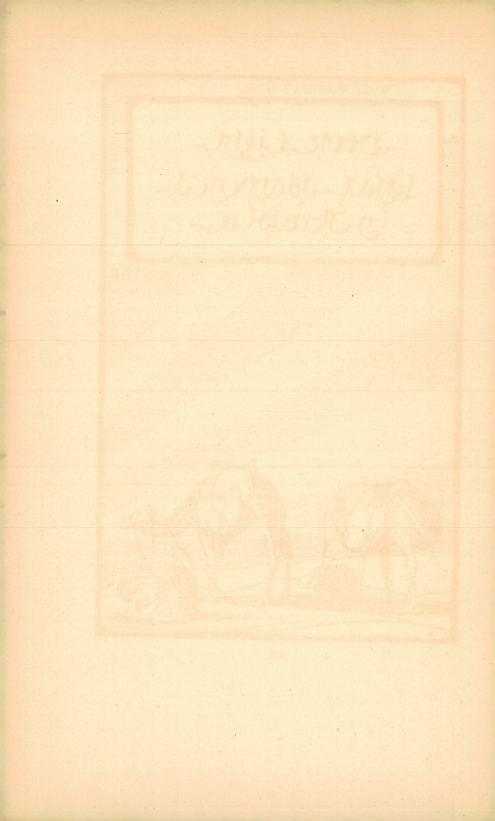

Book Eight
What Happened
in Arabia

303

BOOK EIGHT

WHAT HAPPENED IN ARRABIA

I. MOHAMMEDANISM

1: The idolatrous religion of primitive Arabia—Mecca and the Kaaba. 2: The story of Mohammed—his gospel. 3: The preaching of the gospel to the Meccans. 4: The preaching to the pilgrims. 5: The flight to Medina. 6: The Jews refuse to be converted—conflict with Mecca. 7: The military character of Islam—the Holy War. 8: The character of Mohammed—his compromises—the pagan elements in Islam. 9: The qualities in the religion.

304

BOOK EIGHT
WHAT HAPPENED IN ARABIA
I. MOHAMMEDANISM

AND now we are come to the founding of the latest—perhaps the last—of the great world religions: Islam. For the third time the Arabian Desert plays a major part in the history of our believing world. In that region's giant womb there had already been conceived the Babylonian worship of Ishtar and the Hebrew worship of Yahveh. Now, more than two thousand years after the birth of that second child, the desert conceived and brought forth yet a third: the Mohammedan worship of Allah.

The religion of the Arabian Desert in the sixth century A. D. was much what it had been a thousand or even two thousand years earlier. Changes come rarely in the desert, for rarely are its denizens able to remain in any one place long enough to advance or even decay. Therefore, long centuries after the East had gone Buddhist and the West had gone Christian, Arabia, that vast wasteland pinched between East and West, still remained crudely animist. Each bedouin tribe worshipped its own tribal fetishes, rocks and trees and stars; and the only approximation to a national cult among them was a general awe of a particular fetish resting in the city of Mecca. This fetish, a black rock enshrined in a small square temple called the Kaaba, was thought to be possessed of dreadful potency. An energetic priesthood arose in Mecca, and perhaps it was largely responsible for the national reputation enjoyed by that fetish. Perhaps, too, that priesthood was largely responsible for the national custom of making pilgrimages to Mecca. From every end of the desert the tribesmen were wont to straggle down to Mecca during one season of the year, in order to prostrate themselves before the Kaaba. And just as the merchants of a modern city arrange for minimum exactions by the railway men for all those coming to a convention in their midst, so the priests of ancient Mecca arranged for minimum hazards from highwaymen for all those on pilgrimage to the Kaaba. Somehow they forced the whole land to recognize and respect a solemn taboo against waylaying pilgrims. During four months in the year the open desert, where every shepherd clan was also a robber band, became as safe as a walled city to all who were on their way to Mecca. And as a result, Mecca became not merely the religious center, but also the great market-place of Arabia. In a land where wealth was almost nonexistent, and authority seemed scattered beyond hope of concentration, Mecca somehow managed to become rich and unchallengeably powerful.

2

NOW in about the year 570 A. D. there was born in this city a child to whom was given the name Ubu'l-Kassim. In later years he came to be called Mohammed,

the "Praised One," just as Gautama came to be called
Buddha, the "Enlightened One," and Jesus came to be
called Christ, the "Anointed One."   But to Ubu'l-
Kassim in his early years was accorded very little praise.
Although he was of the priestly caste, he belonged—like
Jeremiah in Israel, and perhaps Zoroaster in Iran—to a
branch of the caste that had been crowded and elbowed
out of power.   (Cynical historians find in that cir-
cumstance the major reason why Jeremiah and Zoroaster and Mohammed ever attacked the ruling priest-
hoods in their lands.)   The lad was orphaned while
still young, and because his immediate relatives were for
the most part poor, he soon had to shift for himself.   He
became a camel-driver, and went off with trading caravans as far as Syria and perhaps even to Egypt.   He was
grossly untutored, of course, and probably could neither
read nor write.   But he was quick-witted and had an
insatiably inquisitive mind.   Unlike the other Arab
camel-boys, his eyes were wide open to the wonders of
the strange lands he visited, and his ears were pricked
up to catch all that was being said in the foreign market-
places.   Especially was he inquisitive on the subject of
the religions in those far away places, for he seems to
have been innately of a religious temperament.   We are
told he was given to spells of melancholy and to occa-
sional fits of what may have been epilepsy.   (So many
of the greatest religious leaders in history are said to
have been epileptics or otherwise neurotic, that psychologists are inclined to believe religious genius is somehow
a result of a disease of the mind.   But that is no reflec-
tion on religion, for every other form of genius seems

MOHAMMED WAS A LOWLY CAMEL BOY

also a product of a disease of the mind—as the pearl is a product of a disease in the oyster. . . .)

We have no undisputable data concerning the early life of Mohammed. All we know with any certainty is that, after years of travel with the caravans, he managed to better his lot by finding favor in the eyes of his employer. She was a rich widow named Khadija, and the good-looking young man with the large head and beautiful black beard so attracted her that finally she

decided to marry him. She was already forty, and he
only twenty-five; but he appears to have acquiesced with
alacrity. Khadija was a woman of high character and
understanding, and quite probably Mohammed loved
her. (He remained true to her until the day of her
death.) And certainly he must have been grateful to
her, for in a day she lifted him from the low station of
a camel-boy to high place as a rich and respected
Meccan trader.

Relieved of the necessity of earning his livelihood,
Mohammed now began to indulge his contemplative
nature. We are told that he went off into the desert
again and again to commune there with his soul. The
humdrum life of a rich fruit-and-produce merchant
did not satisfy him. It was comfortable and yet not
comforting; it could keep him occupied, but not satisfied.
Like every other great soul, he was not content with the
knowledge merely of *how* to keep alive: he wanted to
know *why*. And seeking that higher knowledge, groping in a great fury and pain for that ultimate blessedness
which is called salvation, he finally fought his way
through to the idea of Islam. It came to him with overwhelming conviction that there could be but one way
out of the confusion which was life: through submission
to God. Not to any little venomous god pent up in a
rock or a tree; not to any one of those low djinns or
spirits which his fear-harried brethren tried to bribe with
blood and frenzied praise. No, to the One Great God
who must be in and over all the earth!

The patron deity of his own particular tribe was
known as Allah, and, for want of a better name, Mohammed instinctively gave that one to his new God of

the Universe.   But he was not blind to the fact that other peoples knew Him by other names.   He realized that this Allah whom he had just come to know had been known to the rest of the world for centuries.   Great prophets as ancient as Abraham and as recent as Jesus had proclaimed this God to the peoples beyond the desert.   Indeed, every great city had had its prophet of this One God—every great city save Mecca. Mecca alone was still foul with idol-worship; Mecca alone knew not the One Allah.   And as Mohammed wandered there in the loneliness of the desert, brooding over that evil, it seemed to him that at last it must come even Mecca's turn to be saved.   Even more: the conviction took hold of him that *he* must be its savior.   He, Ubu'l-Kassim of the tribe of Koreish, he who had risen from squalor to be spouse of the wealthiest woman in Mecca, he must be Allah's Apostle to Mecca.   Many prophets had come before him, and right nobly had they sought to bring a measure of the knowledge of Allah to the world.   But only with *him* could there come to mankind the final knowledge of the One God.   For he, Ubu'l-Kassim, was none other than the "seal of the prophets!"

Such was the conviction that somehow began to take hold of that queer and moody fruit-and-produce merchant of Mecca.   When he came to tell of it in later years, he declared the conviction had come to him in a sudden revelation.   He insisted that it had come to him miraculously in a vision.   Perhaps that was true. Being one of that strange band of great religionists— the band that includes Buddha, Zoroaster, Jesus, and almost every other great prophet of history—he was subject to those psychic storms that do yield "visions."

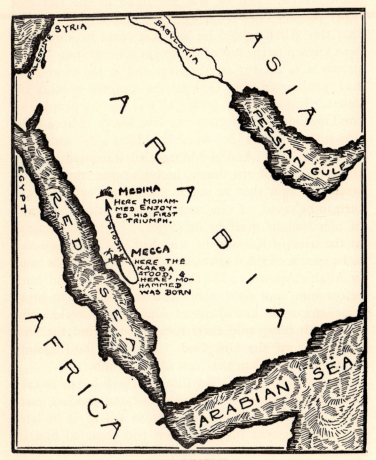

THE DESERT

But one cannot doubt that the sudden revelation came to him, as it did to every one of the others, only after a long evolution of inward disturbance and uncertainty. One can see quite clearly in Mohammed's conviction the result of much pondering on the religious notions of the Jews and Christians and Zoroastrians he had met in the market-places of Syria. In the hidden recesses of Mohammed's being, the idea of Allah, the One God, must have been welling up for years before at last it flooded over the threshold and so imperiously revealed itself to his conscious mind.

3

BUT from that day forth, Ubu'l-Kassim, the indolent, dreamy husband of the rich Khadija, showed himself to all the world a changed man. No longer did he seem melancholy and lost. He had found himself. He had a purpose now: to win idolatrous Mecca to the worship of the Omnipotent Allah.

But he was no reckless fool. He realized that to announce himself at once to the whole city as its savior would bring him only jeers or worse. So he confided his secret first to his wife, and she, perhaps to his amazement, neither laughed nor scolded. On the contrary, she firmly believed him when he said he had been visited by Allah in a splendid vision and had been appointed the Prophet of Mecca. And fortified by her confidence, he then whispered his tale to others. He still acted discreetly, however, and approached only his closest friends and relatives. And somehow they, too, were impressed. They accepted his amazing tale as true, and secretly convinced others of it, who in turn convinced still others. And thus the movement began to spread throughout the town. Everything was done with the greatest secrecy, for it was realized that if the rulers of the city discovered what was on foot, little mercy would be shown to

Mohammed. He would be regarded as the ringleader in a political conspiracy, as one who sought to overthrow the priests of the Kaaba and rule in their stead; and he would be treated accordingly. So the process of winning converts had at first to be carried on with the sharpest caution.

But a day came at last when Mohammed's following seemed strong enough for him to dare take his life in his hands and announce himself. Immediately there ensued a tumult in the city, and a great fury of debating and strife. The ruling oligarchy was thrown almost into a panic, for when at last Mohammed announced himself as the prophet, his following was already too large to be crushed out summarily. Diplomatic overtures were made to the pretender (for so he was considered by the rulers); but he refused to bargain. And then less conciliatory means were resorted to.

Unhappily for the rulers, they could not resort to the assassination of Mohammed as a means of putting a swift end to the insurrection. Mecca was a holy city, and there was a dread taboo against the shedding of any blood within its precincts. The person of Mohammed could therefore not be touched, and the only possible way left of stamping out his rebel movement seemed to be by a systematic boycott of his followers. This was soon begun, and it brought bitter suffering to the poorer of Mohammed's supporters. But it utterly failed to check the movement. It only aroused an enthusiasm and a fervor in those devotees of Mohammed that seemed able to withstand any privations. Finally, therefore, the frustrated rulers were driven to a declaration of open war. They drove Mohammed and his abettors into one quarter of the city and blockaded them there. (The taboo against shedding blood did not prohibit the slaughter of people by starvation.)   For months the Mohammedans were held prisoners in their houses, until finally, starved to despair, they surrendered.   Moham- med, who throughout the siege had been having new revelations from Allah, now suddenly announced that the One God had assured him it was no sin to worship the Meccan djinns and spirits.   And with that capitula- tion to the idolatry fostered by the priestly oligarchy, the blockade was raised and the erstwhile rebels were allowed to go free.

But almost immediately Mohammed repented.   Re- morse overcame him at his cowardly defection, and he cried out that he had sinned.   He declared a new revela- tion had come to him and made it plain that the previous one had been a whisper from the devil.   (Mohammed had taken over as part of his religion the Persian belief in a wicked Ahriman.)   There was, after all, to be no worship of the Meccan goddesses and spirits, for Allah forbade it.   In the camp of His true followers there was room for the worship only of Allah! . . .

And then persecution began anew.

4

BUT this time Mohammed did not remain in the city and try to hold out against his enemies.   He knew he was not equal to it.   His first and dearest believer, his wife Khadija, had just died; and he was left a dejected and broken man.   He could not possibly continue facing the unrelenting persecution by his enemies—so he fled. He stole off to the neighboring oasis of Taif, and tried to gather new converts there.   But he failed dismally, and finally he was reduced to entering a plea for permission to come back to Mecca.   The rulers were willing to grant it, but on condition that Mohammed altogether refrain from ever again stirring up dissension among the Meccans.   And only on his acceptance of that humiliating condition was the hapless prophet allowed to drag his way back to Mecca.

But though fallen so low, the prophet soon began to try to rise again.   Almost from the moment he returned, Mohammed began once more to preach his iconoclastic doctrine.   He was careful, however, to keep the letter of the agreement which bound him scrupulously to avoid preaching to the Meccans themselves. Only the strangers in the city, the traders and pilgrims and bedouins encamped for the night, did Mohammed approach with his gospel.   And not infrequently these strangers would hearken to him eagerly, for many were the Arabs who were ready for his ideas.   For centuries there had been many tribes of Jews living in the desert. For centuries, too, there had been strings of Christian traders wandering along all the caravan routes.   And from these Jews and Christians the whole land of Arabia had heard tell of the One God.   So when Mohammed sat there cross-legged in the bazaars of Mecca, and held forth to the strangers gathered in a silent circle about him, he uttered religious sentiments for which they were already well prepared.

One pictures him there, that good-looking Arab prophet, amid all the traffic and din and stench of that Oriental market-place, seated in the half-light of a shadowed court and talking, talking, talking of his

Allah. He talked well; his speech was rich with that glowing imagery so dear to the heart of the Oriental. He told many tales which he said had been revealed to him by Allah, but which actually were only garbled versions of the Biblical stories he had heard from the lips of Jews and Christians in his youth. He told of Ibrahim, the first of the prophets, and of Ishmael his son, the founder of Mecca. He discoursed also on Suleiman, the

MOHAMMED SAT IN THE BAZAARS AND PREACHED

great king, and on Jesus, who had been born in a manger. And the eyes of his auditors twinkled with delight in the dimness of the courtyard. . . . Or he told of the paradise which all true believers would inherit, and the eyes of the listeners gleamed with eagerness; or of the devil's hell, and their eyes fairly popped with fright. . . .

At death, said this prophet, the soul of the believer

was lifted gently out of the body, and was convoyed up
above by "a driver and a witness."   To it was shown a
ledger of reckoning wherein two angels had set down all
its deeds on earth.   Even though the fate of each man
hung around his neck from the beginning, still was each
man's soul held to a reckoning after death.   He who
had been pious on earth was translated to a garden of
bliss after death; and there, clad in robes of shimmering
green silk, he lolled forever on green-cushioned divans.
(How like a desert Arab, to paint paradise a place that
is green!)   Fruit and forgiveness did the pious man enjoy in Paradise, gorging himself on ripe bananas that
ne'er caused aching belly, and quaffing whole flagons of
wine that ne'er caused aching head.   Maidens of surpassing beauty, large-eyed and well-rounded of hip—
but modest withal, and "restraining their looks"—
served him there and brought him comfort.   And thus
did the pious man delight in his reward, living in Paradise without labor or care, without want or fear of
want, throughout all the endless ages! . . .

But he who was a sinner, he who "believed not in
Allah nor fed the poor"—he fared far otherwise.   On
his death his soul was torn violently from his body.
Down into Hell that soul was hurled, there to wear a
cloak of fire and drink scalding water and pus.   With
maces was the sinner beaten in Hell, until he begged
piteously for release.   But there was no release for him.
No mercy could be shown him, nor could his torture
cease, until at last the final Judgment Day arrived.   But
when that day did come, lo, he would be annihilated
utterly!   Not even his soul would remain existent.   And
the pious in Paradise would then be brought back to

earth, and on a paradisiac earth they would revel in bliss forevermore! . . .

Thus would the prophet talk on with solemn mien to those who sat about him. And when one of them, shaking off the spell of the speaker's words, would ask in a scoffing tone: "Huh! Shall I, though reduced to dry bones, become alive again?"—then would the prophet give answer with a grim smile: "If thou dost doubt it, wait till the Judgment Day comes, and then thou wilt find out!"

So would Mohammed labor with the strangers from far away places. And when those strangers went back to their homes, glowing reports of the strange prophet would go back with them. The fame of Ubu'l-Kassim spread. Throughout the length and breadth of the desert, people began to talk wonderingly of the Prophet of Allah who dwelt in Mecca.

5

NOW on the main caravan route north from Mecca there was a settlement called Yathrib which from of old had been a rival of the capital. And the elders of Yathrib, hearing of Mohammed and of his persecution at the hands of the elders of Mecca, sent secret emissaries to him, entreating him to take refuge in their midst. They even offered to make him the ruling sheikh of their city if he would come. And Mohammed did not reject their overtures. Perhaps he had begun to despair of ever attaining his end by "boring from within" the city of Mecca. He may have begun to wonder whether he could not accomplish more by "kicking from without." So he sent his own emissaries back to Yathrib with word that he would come—on condition, however, that the men of Yathrib were willing to join him in a holy war to make Allah the god of all Arabia.

But before the negotiations could be finally concluded, a rumor of what was on foot reached the ears of the rulers of Mecca. They saw immediately that it would not do to temporize any longer. Mohammed was too dangerous a man to allow around, and, taboo or no taboo, he had to be destroyed. But, in order to distribute the guilt, the ruling clans agreed to share equally in the crime. Each appointed one of its members to serve on an assassination committee, and on the night of the sixteenth of July, in the year 622, the committee broke into Mohammed's sleeping chamber to strike him dead. But when they rushed at the couch, behold, Mohammed was not there! His cousin Ali was lying in his place, and the prophet was nowhere in sight. Apprised of the plot, he had already escaped from the city long hours before the assassins set out for his house. And although the Meccans sent their fleetest camel-men to pursue after him on the road to Yathrib, they could not overtake him. Mohammed had guessed they would pursue him on the road north, and had gone south instead. With only Abu Bekr, his most trusted disciple, he stole away and hid in a cave far south in the desert. And there he lurked in trepidation many days. Abu Bekr was frankly terrified. "Behold, we are but two against a whole multitude," he complained. But straightway Mahomet answered, "Nay, not two, but three—for Allah is with us!"

But for all that he was so sure that Allah was with him, Mohammed took no chances. Only after weeks of hiding did he and his friend venture out into the open and begin to make their way north. For weeks they crawled furtively through the desert, until finally on Friday, the twentieth of September, they reached their goal. At last they were safe in Yathrib.

6

WITH that flight, the *hejira* as it is called in Arabic, the Mohammedan era begins. (To this day the Moslems date all records from the time of that Hejira, as all Christians date them from the supposed time of the birth of Jesus—and all chroniclers of the village of Hamlin date them from the supposed time of the coming of the Pied Piper.) Once in Yathrib, the prophet immediately set out to convert all who were in sight; and to a degree he was successful. But there was one element in the population that stubbornly refused to be won over. There were in Yathrib several tribes of Jews that had lived in that region almost from the time when the Romans drove them out of their own home in Judea. They were by now hard to distinguish from the Arab tribes, differing from them, indeed, only in religion. Despite more than five centuries of life in pagan Arabia, these Jews still worshipped their One God and prayed for their Messiah to come. When rumor first reached them of a prophet who was being hounded out of Mecca for preaching the idea of a One God, they of course were interested. In a moment of wild hopefulness they even wondered if that prophet might not really be their long-awaited Messiah. And when Mohammed arrived in Yathrib he made every effort to encourage that impression. Revelations of a pro-Jewish nature now came to him thick and fast. He commanded his followers to turn as did the Jews toward Jerusalem when they prayed. He forbade them to eat pork or the meat of any animal that had not been ritually slaughtered; and he appointed the Jewish Day of Atonement the great holy day of the year. He even changed the name of his One God from Allah to Rachman—the "Merciful." Out of all his following he chose a Jew to be his scribe to set down his revelations in the book that later came to be called the Koran. . . . But despite all these concessions, the Jews as a body refused to come over into his camp. The moment they discovered his ignorance of the Holy Law and the Prophets, and his by now notorious weakness for women, they began to scoff at his pretensions. Their poets wrote satirical ballads against him, and their elders refused to take him seriously.

And thereupon Mohammed made a complete about-face. Realizing with chagrin that there was nothing to be hoped for from the Jews, he brought all his proselyting energies once more to bear on his own people. Fresh revelations now came to him reversing the earlier ones, and declaring that the true direction of the worshipper in prayer was toward Mecca, not Jerusalem, and that the great annual holy season was the old Arab Festival of Ramadhan, not the Jewish Day of Atonement. And with such concessions to the ancient paganism, the winning of converts from among the Arabs in and around Yathrib increased rapidly.

But material problems began to trouble the prophet. His property in Mecca had been confiscated after his flight, and what wealth he had brought with him had dwindled away in Yathrib because of bad investments. To add to his difficulties, scores of believers who had fled after him from Mecca were now wandering about in Yathrib without employment. It was clear, therefore, that some means of providing for himself and his followers had to be found, and found immediately. So Mohammed gathered his followers together and sent them out to waylay caravans from Mecca. For almost a year he sent them out on such expeditions, until finally he saw that even highway robbery, when practiced according to the rules, was unprofitable. He was then forced, therefore, to practice the profession with no respect for the rules. The Meccan caravans were too well armed during most of the year to be held up successfully. Only during the pilgrim season, when they were protected by that ancient inviolate taboo, did the caravans dare to sally forth unarmed. So now, in desperation, Mohammed actually decided to stage attacks on them during that season.

Such tactics amounted to an almost unprecedented outrage, and only by a stratagem could the prophet manage to inveigle his followers into committing the first treacherous holdup. But once the deed was done, and the reward seemed to be not death but enormous booty, his followers—and most of the other Yathribites too— were quite willing to repeat the outrage. The Meccans leapt to arms immediately, however, for they realized that this thing put into jeopardy their whole future as the masters of Arabia's commerce. They sent out a whole army, and fierce battle was joined with the Yathribites. Mohammed did not fight in person in the battle. He seems to have been physically a rather weak

man; even the sight of blood made him sick.   Tradition
declares that he hid afar off, and kept his swiftest camels
in readiness lest his men be defeated and flight become
necessary.   Even then he fainted soon after the battle
began. . . . But when the battle was over, and the
Yathribites emerged the victors, Mohammed came riding
back into the city like a conquering hero.   Substantially
he was indeed the hero, for it was because of his astute-
ness as a tactician in planning the battle that his
army won.

Mohammed was now the unchallenged master of the
town, and its name was changed appropriately enough
from Yathrib to Medina, "The City (of the Prophet)."
He no longer troubled to try to win the unconverted by
suasion.   Instead he ruthlessly put them to the sword.
Gone was the gentleness that had marked his preaching
in the former days.   Gone was his old confidence in
the power of abstract truth.   In Mecca he had declared,
"We hurl the truth against the falsehood, and truth
crashes into it so that falsehood vanishes."   But now he
hurled armies instead.   "When ye meet those who mis-
believe," he now declared, "strike off their heads or
hold them for ransom!" . . .

7

THE war with Mecca continued to rage, but in the
end the Meccans were compelled to cry quits.   Mohammed obtained consent to return as the virtual dictator
of the city where but a few years earlier he had been
a hunted criminal.   And then he entered on a great
holy war to win all Arabia to his cause.   Armies were

MOHAMMED RETURNS TO MECCA

sent north and others south to convert or slay in the name of Allah. And because the Byzantines and the Persians owned vast tracts of the desert in the north, Mohammed finally felt compelled to pit himself against them too. Nor did his ventures turn out unsuccessful even against such hosts. Somehow he could whip his followers into a frenzy of courage and recklessness. The Arabs had always loved violence, and he made violence holy for them. Mohammed assured them that to die fighting for Allah meant certain and immediate translation to Allah's Paradise. There was but one way to prove complete faithfulness, he declared, and that was by complete resignation to the will of Allah. Islam, which may be translated "submission," he made the watchword and the name of his faith.

Mohammed's whole movement thus took on the character of a religious militarism. Islam was the army of Allah, and prayer was made a discipline quite like drill-duty in a modern army. To this day a bystander thinks of a sentry sounding the alarm when he hears the muezzin uttering the call to prayer from his lofty minaret. An observer thinks of soldiers "forming fours" and "presenting arms," when he sees the Moslems drawn up in ranks in their mosques and praying and prostrating themselves with almost mechanical precision. Actually the Moslems do form a religious army to this day. Mohammed welded them into such a body almost twelve hundred years ago. "If you help Allah, lo, Allah will surely help you!" he cried to his followers. And because the help Allah seemed to exact was just the sort the warlike Arabs had ever loved to give, they helped with irrepressible zest. In the name of Allah and His Prophet, the army of Islam began to wage a Holy War that almost conquered the world! . . .

Mohammed only lived to see that war begin. In the year 632, just ten years after the Hejira, the prophet died. But he had lived long enough to set a movement on foot that has not halted to this day. Within twenty-five years after his death, his followers had already become masters not alone of Arabia, but also of Egypt, Palestine, Syria, Babylonia, and Persia. Within seventy-five years they had conquered all the northern coast of Africa and almost all of Spain. Another decade, and they were marching up into the interior of France. And today, twelve hundred years afterward, Islam, the religion founded by that amazing fruit-and-produce merchant who saw visions in Mecca, stands next to Christianity as the most flourishing religion in the world. In twenty years, and without royal patronage, there was created in the heart of darkest Arabia a religion which today numbers well over two hundred million adherents! . . .

8

TO follow the Arabs on their great invasions and trace the tremendous influence exerted by them in Europe, Asia, and Africa, would lead us far from the main purpose of this book. Europe owed to those invasions its awakening from that stupor which was the Dark Ages; and even Persia and India, along with Africa, were vitalized and advanced by them, too. It was the last (or was it only the latest?) plunge of the desert-folk out into the Fertile Crescent; and though it drowned the Crescent and half the rest of the world in blood, it also brought forth a blossoming of civilization almost unprecedented in history.

Islam, one must remember, is a great and wondrous religion. Even in Mohammed's day it was, relatively at least, a high and noble faith. Few non-Moslems seem to realize this. They remember only the petty vices and crimes of the prophet of Mecca, and forget entirely his indubitable religious genius. They remember only the flagrant compromises, the arrant opportunism, the almost blatant charlatanry, that marked his career after the Hejira. And, especially if they are Christians, they love to mull over reports of the inordinate interest Mohammed evinced in women in his later years. Christianity has always looked on sex as in some way indecent and sinful; and for that reason most Christians cannot possibly associate a truly religious nature with an unsuppressed libido. But that is no more than a prejudice.

Mohammed, despite his fondness for his harem, might have remained to his dying day a man of the noblest prophetic character.

He did not remain that, of course. It cannot be gainsaid that, after the Hejira and his first taste of triumph, the exalted prophet in Mohammed gave way to the greedy, ambitious, unscrupulous priest. The "organizer" in him triumphed. From then on he was no longer the daring iconoclast, the receiver of "revelations" which, even if not miraculously inspired, seemed at least spontaneous and sincere. After the Hejira the "revelations" are quite blatantly premeditated forgeries. They are long editorials circulated in the name of Allah to save the seamy face of the prophet. In the days when Mohammed was suffered to talk only to strangers as he wandered about in the bazaars of Mecca his doctrine had been superbly ethical in character. "Blessed are they," he then declared, "who are blameless as respects women, who are charitable, who talk not vainly, who are humble, who observe their pledges and covenants, and who guard their prayers; for they shall inherit Paradise." The liquor of triumph had not yet gone to his head; it had not yet even touched his lips. And he had been still a kindly, earnest teacher of love. "Paradise," he had then declared, "is prepared for those who expend in alms, who repress their rage, and pardon men. For Allah loves the kind." "To endure and to pardon is the wisdom of life." Or again: "Let no man treat his neighbor as he himself would dislike to be treated." Or still again: "Let us be like trees that yield their fruit to those who throw stones at them."

Nor was there aught of the ritualist in Mohammed

then. When a man came and said to the prophet: "Behold, my mother has died; what shall I do for the good of her soul?"—Mohammed answered: "Dig a well, that the thirsty may have water to drink! . . . The exigencies of empire-building had not yet arisen to demand a vast army bound by a rigid discipline of prayer and alms-giving. "One hour of justice," he had then said, "is worth more than seventy years of prayer." And: "Every good act is charity: bringing water to the thirsty, removing stones and thorns from the road, even smiling in thy brother's face."

Nor, finally, had there been anything of the doc-trinaire in him then. When confronted by those who told him to his face that they did not believe his words, his only response had been the challenge: "Bring ye then a better revelation, and I shall follow it."

But once success began to come to him, the worst in his nature revealed itself. His personal life became sor-did, and his spiritual integrity was sapped. His craving for increase of dominion led him to reduce his standards until the mere recital of a formula—*La illah il'allah, Muhammad rasoul allahi,* "There is no God but Allah, and Mohammed is the Prophet of Allah"— that and the paying of a tax, were enough to make one a convert. Later even the formula was overlooked, and only the tax was insisted upon. On occasion Mohammed even resorted to *buying* converts!

As a result, the very paganism which Islam had set out to destroy began to destroy Islam. The idolatrous practice of the *hajj,* the pilgrimage to the Kaaba, was made one of the dominant elements in the religion. To this day it is counted of major importance. Even now

ON THE WAY TO MECCA

the Moslem pilgrims from every end of the earth can be seen dragging their way on foot or by camel to Mecca. Two hundred thousand of them brave the dangers of the desert each year in order to come to the holy city. At five miles distance from it they halt, wash, pray, put on clean seamless gowns, and then proceed bare-headed and barefoot to the holy shrine. They reverently kiss the black stone, solemnly go around the Kaaba three times running and four times walking, run to a neighboring holy hill seven times, run to a second holy hill, and then stop to catch their breath while they listen to a sermon. Finally they spend the night on the holy Mount Muzdalifa nearby, and after throwing missiles at three unholy rocks in the valley below, they go back to their homes in far Tunis or Bombay or perhaps Samarkand, and are at peace. They have performed the *hajj,* the pilgrimage, the holy act that earns them the right to wear verdant sashes around their fezzes, in token of the verdant Paradise they will surely inherit when they die. . . .

But the old idolatry against which Mohammed inveighed in his early ministry has returned in more than the hajj. Just as Mohammed himself accepted the Kaaba, so his followers accepted the lesser idolatrous shrines scattered throughout the desert. Of course the surrender was not made openly. Exactly as in Catholic Christendom, the local djinns and goddesses were made over into Mohammedan saints. To this day throughout the Moslem lands those little shrines can be seen nestling amid the hills or in the oases. Nominally they are memorials to old holy men; but actually they are often memorials to far older djinns.

THE SHRINE OF A DESERT SAINT

The inundation of Islam by these returning tides of paganism began long before Mohammed died, and the further Islam's shores extended, the more sweeping became that flood. In India the Moslem faith took over many of the characteristics of Hinduism. It became mystical and ascetic, inducing thousands of souls to retire and seek communion with Allah in the depths of the Indian jungles. It also took over many of the Hindu superstitions. The rosary, for instance, which was an emblem of the Indian god, Shiva, was made a ceremonial object in Islam. Ninety-nine beads were strung on a cord, and each bead was made to represent one of the ninety-nine names of Allah. (It was not long before the Moslem theologians had succeeded in inventing ninety-nine names for the Unnamable.) To this day the pious Moslem tells his beads each day, "keeping his tongue moist"—and his fingers nimble—in the remembrance of Allah.

Islam, like every other healthy religion, has been in a state of incessant flux. Long centuries ago it grew to be as unlike the simple and homogeneous creed of Mohammed as Christianity became unlike the creed of Paul. In many lands it contrived to advance, became richer in emotion, deeper in intelligence, and nobler in spirit. In certain other lands it decayed and degenerated, becoming crude and animistic. Like Christianity, Islam was from the first an elastic faith, accommodating itself generously to the culture of each land which it sought to conquer. Necessarily, therefore, it was many times rent by schisms, and today there are some seventy-two sects in it. The largest of the unorthodox groups, the Shiite sect in Persia, broke away in defense of the issue that Mohammed's son-in-law, Ali, was a veritable Imam, or divine incarnation almost like the Prophet himself. Out of the Shiite came in turn the Sufi sect, which maintained that Ali was only the first of a long line of such Imams, and that even ordinary men could become almost divine by a process of asceticism and mysticism. But most of the other sects are small and obscure, and arose out of piddling metaphysical or political differences. And between many of these sects there has been a rivalry and an animosity almost—but never quite—as bitter as that between the sects in Christianity.

9

YET, for all the paganism and bigotry that still loom large in the religion of Islam, it remains nevertheless a great and wondrous faith. It has been one of the most effective civilizing forces in the history of Africa and Asia, and in a measure also in that of Europe. In Arabia itself it accomplished a social revolution. It condemned the common practice of infanticide in the case of girls, restricted the dealing in slaves, opposed gambling and drunkenness, and almost put an end to the devastating tribal feuds. And, incredible as it may sound, it also brought about a marked improvement in the condition of the desert women. Limitless polygamy had been the unquestioned law in Arabia from the time the pre-historic and perhaps mythical matriarchate came to an end. Not until Mohammed came was that practice restricted so that a man might have no more than four wives at a time. . . .

But these social ameliorations were after all the lesser gifts of Islam. They were precious to those who profited by them, but hardly of any considerable world-significance. The supreme gift of Islam was the ideal of unity which it somehow drilled into the heads of a hundred races—not merely the unity of God, but even more the unity of mankind. And preaching that ideal, commanding submission to the Oneness of the Universe as the highest of all virtues, it revolutionized life for millions of fearful souls. It robbed them of the terror which aloneness had previously brought to them. It gave them strength and a feeling of security, telling them they were each a part of a vast and invincible whole.   Every true believer was a soldier in an army, an international—and some day, pray Allah, universal —army that could not possibly fail to be victorious in the end.   So what was there to fear?   Life?   It was fixed and settled for the true believer.   All he had to do was live according to that manual-at-arms which is the Koran.   He had merely to pray punctiliously, eat ritually, provide alms regularly, and give himself to the spreading of the name of Allah—and his reward was certain.   The way of life for him was fixed, and its reason and justification, too.   He had but to submit and accept his *kismet,* his fate, lashing his body and soul to that Rock of Ages which is Allah—and Paradise was certain. . . .

Every other great religion taught more or less the same doctrine, but none with such fierceness and unrestraint.   Islam excluded no man from the army of Allah, magnifying the requirements until they could attract even the most advanced of civilized men, and minifying them so that they could appeal even to the most degraded of savages.   And that is why to this day Islam can still win converts with twice the ease of any other religion.   That is why to this day Islam is one of the mightiest institutions on earth for the ordering and beautifying of life in at least the "backward" lands. . . .

SELECTED BIBLIOGRAPHY

COMPARATIVE RELIGIONS

Encyclopedias and Source-Books

Canney, M. A., An Encyclopedia of Religions. 1 v. (N. Y., 1921).

Hastings, J., editor, Encyclopedia of Religion and Ethics. 12 v. (N. Y., 1913-1922).

Müller, Max, editor, Sacred Books of the East. 50 v. (Oxford, 1879-1910).

Textbooks

Barton, G. A., The Religions of the World. (Chicago, 1919).

Hopkins, E. W., The History of Religions. (N. Y., 1918).

Hume, R. E., The World's Living Religions. (N. Y., 1925).

Jastrow, Morris, Jr., The Study of Religion. (N. Y., 1901).

Jevons, F. B., Comparative Religion. (Cambridge, 1913).

Martin, A. W., Great Religious Teachers of the East. (N. Y., 1911); The World's Great Semitic Religions. (N. Y., 1921).

Montgomery, J. A., editor, Religions Past and Present. (Phila., 1918).

Moore, G. F., History of Religions. 2 v. (N. Y., 1919-1920)

PRIMITIVE RELIGION

Frazer, J. G., The Golden Bough. 1 v. (N. Y., 1922); Adonis, Attis, and Osiris. (N. Y., 1914); Totemism and Exogamy. (London, 1910).

Jevons, F. B., Introduction of History of Religion, (London, 1896).

Lang, Andrew, The Making of Religion. (N. Y., 1900).
Marett, R. R., The Threshold of Religion. (London, 1914).
Moore, G. F., Birth and Growth of Religion. (N. Y., 1923).

THE CELTS

Anwyl, Edward, Celtic Religion in Prehistoric Times. (London, 1906).
MacCulloch, J. A., Religion of the Ancient Celts. (London, 1911).
Rhys, J., Celtic Heathendom. (London, 1888).

THE BABYLONIANS

Jastrow, Morris, Jr., Religion of Babylonia and Assyria. (N. Y., 1898); Hebrew and Babylonian Traditions. (N. Y., 1908).
King, L. W., Babylonian Religion and Mythology. (London, 1899).
Rogers, R. W., The Religion of the Babylonians and Assyrians. (N. Y., 1908).

THE EGYPTIANS

Breasted, J. H., Development of Religion and Thought in Ancient Egypt. (N. Y., 1905).
Erman, A., Handbook of Egyptian Religion. (London, 1907).
Mackenzie, D. A., The Myths of Egypt. (London, 1914).
Petrie, W. M. Flinders, Religion and Conscience in Ancient Egypt. (N. Y., 1898).

THE GREEKS

Fairbanks, A., Handbook of Greek Religion. (N. Y., 1910).
Farnell, L. R., The Cults of the Greek States. 5 v. (Oxford, 1896-1909).
Harrison, Jane E., Themis, a Study of the Social Origins of Greek Religion. (Cambridge, 1912).

Murray, Gilbert, Four Stages of Greek Religion. (N. Y., 1912).

THE ROMANS

Carter, Jesse B., The Religious Life of Ancient Rome. (Boston, 1911).

Cumont, F., The Oriental Religions in Roman Paganism. (Chicago, 1911); The Mysteries of Mithra. (Chicago, 1903).

Fowler, W. W., Roman Ideas of Deity in Last Century before Christian Era. (London, 1914).

Glover, T. R., The Conflict of Religions in the Early Roman Empire. (London, 1909).

THE RELIGIONS OF INDIA

Brahmanism and Hinduism

Barnet, L. D., Antiquities of India. (London, 1914).

Bloomfield, M., The Religion of the Veda. (N. Y., 1908).

Farquhar, J. N., A Primer of Hinduism. (Oxford, 1912).

Hopkins, E. W., The Religions of India. (N. Y., 1898).

Pratt, J. B., India and Its Faiths. (Boston, 1915).

Jainism

Jaini, J., Outlines of Jainism. (Cambridge, 1916).

Stevenson, Mrs. S., The Heart of Jainism. (Oxford, 1915); Notes on Modern Jainism. (Oxford, 1910).

Buddhism

Carpenter, J. E., Buddhism and Christianity. (N. Y., 1923).

Davids, T. W. Rhys, Buddhism. (London, 1914).

Davids, Mrs. T. W. Rhys, Buddhism. (Home University Library).

Saunders, K. J., Story of Buddhism. (Oxford 1916); Buddhism and Buddhists of Southern Asia. (N. Y., 1923).

The Religions of China

Douglass, R. K., Confucianism and Taoism. (London, 1900).

Giles, H. A., Confucianism and its Rivals. (N. Y., 1915); China and the Chinese. (N. Y., 1902).

Legge, James, The Religions of China. (N. Y., 1881); The Chinese Classics. 8 v. (Oxford, 1861-85).

Soothill, W. E., Three Religions of China. (London, 1913).

Zoroastrianism

Jackson, A. V. W., Zoroaster, the Prophet of Ancient Iran. (N. Y., 1901).

Moulton, J. H., Early Zoroastrianism. (London, 1913); The Treasure of the Magi, a study of Modern Zoroastrianism. (Oxford, 1918).

Judaism

Abrahams, I., Jewish Life in the Middle Ages. (Phila., 1906).

Bailey and Kent, History of the Hebrew Commonwealth. (N. Y., 1920).

Barton, G. A., Religion of Israel. (N. Y., 1918).

Browne, Lewis, Stranger Than Fiction: a Short History of the Jews. (N. Y., 1925).

Graetz, H., History of the Jews. 6 v. (Phila., 1891).

Jewish Encyclopedia, 12 v. (N. Y., 1905).

Christianity

Outline of Christianity. 5 v. (N. Y., 1926).

Case, S. J., The Evolution of Christianity. (Chicago, 1914).

Clemen, Carl, Primitive Christianity and its Non-Jewish Sources. (Edin., 1912).

Hartt, R. L., The Man Himself. (N. Y., 1923).

Jackson, F. J. F., Introduction to Church History, Life of St. Paul. (N. Y., 1926).

Klausner, J., Jesus of Nazareth. (N. Y., 1926).

Montefiore, C. J., Judaism and Saint Paul. (London, 1900).

Renan, Ernest, Life of Jesus.

Smith, G. B., editor, A Guide to the Study of Christian Religion. (Chicago, 1916).

ISLAM

Ameer, Ali, The Spirit of Islam. (London, 1922).

Goldziher, I., Mohammed and Islam. (New Haven, 1917).

Houtsma, N. T., editor, Encyclopedia of Islam. 25 parts. London, 1923).

Hughes, T. P., Dictionary of Islam. (London, 1885).

Margoliouth, D. S., Mohammedanism. (Home University Library).

Muir, Sir William, Mahomet and Islam. (London, 1895).

INDEX

A

Abraham, 225, 310
Abydos, 84
Achilles, 98
Adonijah, 235
Adonis, 106, 277
Aegean, 89
Aegean Islands, 226
Afghanistan, 191
Agni, 120
Agriculture, 43
Ahriman, 211, 217, 314
Ahura Mazda, 203
Akhetaton, 79
Akirvati, 140
Allah, 20, 305, 309
Alexander, 217
Ali, 332
All Saints' Day, 64
All Souls, Festival of, 295
American Indians, 76
Amon, 76, 78
Amos, 237, 240
Anahita, 199, 205, 216
Anarchism, 288
Anaxagoras, 94
Ancestor worship in China, 169
Anglicanism, 300
Angra Mainyu, 203
Animism, 32
Anu, 68
Aphrodite, 69
Apollo, 91
Arabia, 305

Arabian Desert, 223, 305
Aramaic, 287
Arameans, 224
Aristotle, 91, 94
Ark, 49, 229
Armenian, 201
Aryan, 60, 90, 119, 199
Ashtoreth, 69, 236
Ashura, 199
Asoka, 146
Asshur, 241
Assumption of the Virgin, 294
Assyria, 233
Astarte, 68
Astrology, 70
Asura, 120
Athena, 90
Athens, 174
Atman, 32
Aton, 78
Attis, 99, 106, **277**
Augustus, 107
Avatar, 153, 285
Avesta, 201

B

Baal, 231, 236
Babel, Tower of, 71
Babylonia, 325
Babylonian Exile, 235
Babylonians, 65, 223, 235
Bacchus, 106
Banyan Tree, 138
Baptism, 99

Bel, 68, 241
Bellona, 106
Bel-Marduk, 68
Beltane, 63
Benares, 143, 164
Beni Hasan, 85
Beth El, 238
Bhagavad-Gita, 153
Bible, 154
Black Friday, 106
Bodhisattvas, 146
Bohemia, 300
Bombay, 218
Book of the Dead, 88
Brahma, 125, 136, 152, 153, 156, 160
Brahmanas, 124
Brahmanism, 119
Brahmins, 122
Bridget, 61, 70, 294, 296
Buddha, 134, 143, 160, 175, 184, 191, 193, 200, 232, 245, 264
Buddhism, 134, 190, 191
Burmah, 149

C

Caesar, Julius, 63
Calvin, 300
Canaan, 225
Canaanites, 224, 235
Caste, 122, 140, 150
Catholicism, 293, 300
Celts, 60
Ceylon, 147, 149
Chandraguptra, 146
China, 148
Chinese, 223
Chou, 184
Christ, 148, 154, 276, 281 (see Jesus)
Christianity, 110, 218, 257, 290

Christians, 156
Christmas, 295
Chungtu, 176
Church, 39
Cilicia, 281
Circumcision, 48
Communism, 288
Confucianism, 169, 193
Confucius, 175, 184, 188, 245
Constantine, 290
Corybantes, 296
Crete, 89
Crosses, 37
Crusades, 156
Cybele, 69, 104, 294, 296
Cynics, 108
Cyrus, 216, 246

D

Dagon, 232, 241
Dalai Lama, 148
Damascus, 274, 281
Daniel, 218
Dark Ages, 326
David, 233
Day of Atonement, 321
Dead, Book of, 88
Deutero-Isaiah, 244
Deva, 205
Deviltry, 205
Diana, 102
Diaspora, 248
Dionysus, 97, 106, 277
Divinity, 205
Druids, 61, 70
Dyansh Pitar, 120

E

Ea, 68
Eden, 224
Egypt, 44, 171, 225, 325

Egyptians, 75
Eightfold Noble Path, 139
Eleusinian mysteries, 99
Elijah, 235
Elysian Fields, 98
Empedocles, 94
England, 300
Epilepsy, 307
Epistles, 288
Ethiopians, 239
Etruscans, 102
Euphrates, 224
Euripides, 94
Exodus, 226
Ezekiel, 175

F

Feng-Shui, 196
Fertile Crescent, 224, 326
Festivals, 46
Fetishism, 36
Fire-altars, 205
Five Books of Moses, 231, 243
Flood, 73
Four Truths, 139
Francis, St., of Assisi, 300
Fraser, James G., 35, 62
Free-Will, 156
Fryana, 210

G

Galatia, 281
Galilee, 259
Ganges, 121, 134, 164
Ganges Valley, 130
Gathas, 201, 210
Gaul, 174
Gautama, 245
Gautama, Siddharta, 134
Genius, 100, 108
Gentiles, 250

George, St., Festival of, 294
Golden Bough, 35, 62
Gospels, 259, 276, 288
Greece, 171
Greeks, 89

H

Hades, 90, 98
Hajj, 328, 330
Hallowe'en, 64
Hamlin, 320
Haoma, 199, 205, 215
Haram, 225
Hariti, 148
Heaven, 169
Hebrews, 49, 103, 230
Hera, 90
Heraclitus, 94
Himayana, 145, 147
Hinduism, 150, 331
Hittites, 224
Holy Ghost, 278
Holy Roman Empire, 299
Horeb, 229
Horseshoes, 37
Horus, 83, 148, 286
Hosea, 239
Huns, 299
Huss, John, 300

I

Ibrahim, 316
Idol, 38
Ikhnaton, 78, 87, 88, 232, 264
India, 331
Indian Metaphysics, 159
Inquisition, 300
Indra, 120
Indus, 121
Iran, 199
Isaiah, 240

Ishtar, 67, 68, 89, 104, 305
Isis, 69, 83, 106, 148, 294
Islam, 149, 324
Ishmael, 316
Israel, 233

J

Jainism, 129
Janus, 101
Japan, 148
Jehovah, (see Yahveh) 49, 229
Jeremiah, 175, 241, 307
Jerusalem, 19, 321, 240
Jesus, 84, 184, 200, 226, 247, 257, 267, 310, 316, 320
Jews, 315, 320
Jina, 130
John, 287
John the Baptizer, 261, 247, 274
John, St., Festival of, 294
Judah, 233
Judaism, 151, 216, 223
Judaism, Orthodox, 250
Judaism, Reform, 250
Judges, 232
Juno, 100
Jupiter, 101, 120

K

Kaaba, 306, 330
Kaaba Stone, 38
Karma, Law of, 142
Kashmir, 147
Kenites, 229
Kenosis, 189
Khadija, 309
Kiang-si, 190
King, 178
Kismet, 334
Koran, 218, 321

Krishna, 153, 158, 200
Krishto, 154
Kung-fu-tze (see Confucius), 175

L

Lagash, 67
Lao-Tze, 184, 200, 232
Lares, 101
Laud, Bishop, 300
Lhassa, 148
Libya, 225
Logos, 278, 285
Lucky Stones, 36
Lugnasad, 64
Lupercalia, 101
Luther, 300

M

Ma, 106
Macedonia, 281
Magi, 215
Mahabharta, 153, 158
Mahavira, 129, 137, 141, 160, 175, 200, 245
Mahayana, 145, 147
Malay Archipelago, 40
Mani, 216
Manichaeism, 216
Manu, Code of, 151
Maponus, 61
Marduk, 68
Mark, 287
Marriage, 48
Mars, 101
Mary, 148, 285, 294
Mayday, 63
Maypole Dances, 64
Mecca, 38, 306
Medicine-Man, 34, 224, 233, 318, 323

Memphis, 76
Mencius, 182
Mesopotamia, 65
Messiah, 242, 258, 320
Methodism, 300
Mezuzoth, 37
Micah, 240
Middle Path, 139
Midsummer Night, 64
Minerva, 102
Minoans, 89
Mithraism, 218, 285
Mithraists, 291
Mithras, 109, 120, 199, 205, 216
Mohammed, 184, 218, 306, 314, 321
Moslems, 156
Moloch, 231, 236
Moore, George Foot, 28
Moses, 184, 200, 226, 229, 232
Mother of the Gods, Great (see Cybele), 104
Mt. Sinai, 49
Murray, Prof. Gilbert, 288
Muzdalifa, Mount, 330
Mysteries, 96, 104, 277
Mysticism, 161

N

Nabu, 68
Nathan, 235
Nazarenes, 274
Nazareth, 259
Nebuchadnezzar, 241
Nestorians, 148
Nevi-im, 235
New Thought, 159
Ni, 182
Ningirsu, 67, 68
Nirvana, 127, 139, 164
Noble Eightfold Path, 144

O

Oberammergau, 84
Odysseus, 98
Ogmius, 61
Olympus, 91
Ombus, 76
Ormuzd, 211, 249
Orpheus, 97, 106, 277
Orphic Mysteries, 99
Osiris, 82, 99, 106, 241, 277

P

Pacifism, 288
Palestine, 325
Parilia, 294
Parsees, 218, 249
Parvata the Terrible, 157
Passover, 272
Pater-familias, 101
Paul (see Saul of Tarsus) 283, 294, 298
Peking, 170, 176
Penates, 101
Pentateuch, 265
Persia, 325, 332
Peter's, St., 104
Pharisaic Plague, 265
Philo, 278
Philistines, 234
Phoenicians, 223, 224, 234
Pied Piper, 320
Pilate, 271
Plato, 94
Polygamy, 333
Pontifex, Maximus, 102
Pork, 40
Poseidon, 90
Prayer, 39
Predestination, 156
Promised Land, 224

Prostitution, holy, 69
Protagoras, 95
Protestants, 148, 151
Protestantism, 300
Ptah, 76
Pyramids, 85, 171, 225
Pythagoras, 94

Q

Quakerism, 300

R

Rabbis, 265
Rachman, 321
Rama, 155
Ramadhan, 321
Ramayana, 153, 155
Re, 80
Resurrection, 273
Revelation, 218
Rhea, 90
Rig Veda, 121
Ritual, 54
Romans, 100
Rome, 174, 248, 257
Rosary, 156, 331

S

Sabbath, 74, 285
Sacraments, 47
Sacrifices, 39, 54
Samhain, 64
Samuel, 235
Sangha, 133
Saracens, 299
Satans, 217
Saturnalia, 102
Saul of Tarsus, 279, 281, 283
Semites, 66, 223
Servia, 290

Set, 76, 83
Sex, 46
Sex in Hinduism, 157
Sex in Mysticism, 161
Shabatum, 74
Shaman, 34
Shamanism, 36
Shamash, 68
Sheol, 217
Shiite sect, 332
Shinto, 148
Shiva, 152, 156, 331
Shu, 178
Siam, 149
Sin, 53, 68
Sinai, 229
Socrates, 94, 95
Solomon, 233
Solon, 171
Soma, 120, 215
Sphinx, 76
St. John's Day, 64
Stoics, 94
Stonehenge, 61
Sufi sect, 332
Suleiman, 316
Sumerians, 224
Sun Day, 110
Sunday, 285
Swami, 159
Syria, 325

T

Taboo, 40
Taif, 314
Talmud, 151, 249
Tammuz, 67, 106
Tantra, 157
Tao, 186
Taoism, 148, 183, 193
Tao-Teh-king, 185

Tauroboleum, 105
Teh, 186
Ten Commandments, 229
Ten Tribes, 233
Thales, 94
Thebes, 76
Theosophical Societies, 159
Theudas, 274
Thibet, 148
Three Jewels, 133, 186
Three Truths, 195
Thugs, 157
Tigris, 224
Tower of Silence, 212
Transmigration, 126
T'ueb-shi, 190
Turanians, 204, 209
Turkestan, 191
Tutenkhamen, 80

U

Ubu'l-Kassim, 306
Unitarianism, 300
Untouchables, 165
Upanishads, 125, 203
Ur of the Chaldees, 225
Urkagina, King, 71

V

Varnu, 122
Vatican Hill, 104
Vedas, 121, 130, 150, 203
Venus, 68, 69

Vesta, 101
Vishnu, 152, 156

W

Wall of Law, 265
Wells, H. G., 5, 218
Wind-ball, 32
Wu, 190
Wu Wei, 186
Wycliffe, 300

X

Xenophanes, 94

Y

Yahveh, 229, 239, 305
Yathrib (see Medina), 318
Yogi, 159, 160
Young Men's Buddhist Association, 148

Z

Zabazins, 97
Zagreus, 97
Zarathustra, 199
Zealots, 258, 260
Zeus Pater, 90, 101, 120
Zionism, 251
Zoroaster, 109, 175, 199, 205, 226, 232, 264, 307
Zoroastrianism, 199, 216, 218
Zoroastrians, 249, 251
Zwingli, 300